CHILDREN'S
RIGHTS

A Reference Handbook

Other Titles in ABC-CLIO's

CONTEMPORARY WORLD ISSUES

Series

Abortion, 2d ed.	Marie Costa
American Homelessness, 2d ed.	Mary Ellen Hombs
America's International Trade	E. Willard Miller and Ruby M. Miller
Animal Rights	Clifford J. Sherry
Childhood Sexual Abuse	Karen L. Kinnear
Children's Rights	Beverly C. Edmonds and William R. Fernekes
Domestic Violence	Margi Laird McCue
Gangs	Karen L. Kinnear
Gay and Lesbian Rights	David E. Newton
Global Development	William Savitt and Paula Bottorf
Gun Control	Earl R. Kruschke
Legalized Gambling	William N. Thompson
Organized Crime	Patrick J. Ryan
The Ozone Dilemma	David E. Newton
Rape in America	Rob Hall
The Religious Right	Glenn H. Utter and John W. Storey
Sports Ethics	Lawrence H. Berlow
United States Immigration	E. Willard Miller and Ruby M. Miller
Violent Children	Karen L. Kinnear
Wilderness Preservation	Kenneth A. Rosenberg

Books in the Contemporary World Issues series address vital issues in today's society such as terrorism, sexual harassment, homelessness, AIDS, gambling, animal rights, and air pollution. Written by professional writers, scholars, and nonacademic experts, these books are authoritative, clearly written, up-to-date, and objective. They provide a good starting point for research by high school and college students, scholars, and general readers, as well as by legislators, businesspeople, activists, and others.

Each book, carefully organized and easy to use, contains an overview of the subject; a detailed chronology; biographical sketches; facts and data and/or documents and other primary-source material; a directory of organizations and agencies; annotated lists of print and nonprint resources; a glossary; and an index.

Readers of books in the Contemporary World Issues series will find the information they need in order to understand better the social, political, environmental, and economic issues facing the world today.

CHILDREN'S RIGHTS

A Reference Handbook

Beverly C. Edmonds
William R. Fernekes

CONTEMPORARY WORLD ISSUES

ABC-CLIO

Santa Barbara, California
Denver, Colorado
Oxford, England

Library of Congress Cataloging-in-Publication Data

Edmonds, Beverly C.
Children's rights : a reference handbook / Beverly C. Edmonds, William R. Fernekes.
p. cm. — (Contemporary world issues)
Includes bibliographical references and index.
Summary: A reference handbook on the current status of children's rights throughout the world, containing an overview of the topic, a chronology, biographical sketches, a directory of organizations and agencies, annotated lists of print and nonprint resources, a glossary, and an index.
1. Children's rights—Juvenile literature. 2. Children's rights—United States—Juvenile literature. [1. Children's rights.]
I. Fernekes, William R. II. Title. III. Series.
HQ789.E35 1996 305.23—dc20 96-43167

ISBN 0-87436-764-6 (alk. paper)

02 01 00 99 98 97 96 95 10 9 8 7 6 5 4 3 2 1

ABC-CLIO, Inc.
130 Cremona Drive, P.O. Box 1911
Santa Barbara, California 93116-1911

This book is printed on acid-free paper ∞.

Manufactured in the United States of America

Beverly Edmonds dedicates this book to Jennie, Robb, Matt, and the Geneva interns whose voices were heard at the Palais des Nations.

Bill Fernekes dedicates this book to all the students he's taught who have inspired him to remain a committed activist on behalf of human rights, notably those of children.

Contents

Preface

This book provides the reader with a comprehensive introduction and reference source on children's rights. The text emphasizes children's rights issues in the United States defined within an international context. This approach recognizes the interdependent nature of children's rights activities in the contemporary world, whether the issue be sex tourism, child labor, children and violence, children and armed conflict, or the many others discussed in the text.

Chapter 1 offers a historic overview of the development of children's rights, along with capsule summaries of critical children's rights issues requiring attention today. Chapter 2 is a comprehensive chronology of international children's rights events, activities, and trends in the twentieth century, while chapter 3 contains biographical entries on eighteen key figures and one group who have significantly influenced the development of children's rights since the late nineteenth century. Chapters 4 through 6 contain key documents, excerpts from print sources, and statistics from the U.S. government and intergovernmental organizations on children's rights and the contemporary global status of children that amplify and substantiate the argument put forth in chapter 1. Chapter 7 lists organizations that currently address children's rights issues, both in the United States and internationally, while chapters 8 and 9 offer comprehensive listings of resources for further study and inquiry about children's rights, again on the international scale. A glossary provides definitions of terms employed throughout the text, particularly in the documents located in Chapters 4 through 6.

The authors are hopeful that the reader will respond to *Children's Rights: A Reference Handbook* by examining children's rights concerns in depth and pursuing further study, particularly given the compelling need for child advocacy in today's world.

Acknowledgments

This book could not have been completed without the contributions of many individuals and organizations. In particular, we acknowledge the assistance of the following: Kathryn Burke, whose knowledge of international law caught technical errors; Wiltrud Harms of the United Nations Collection, Library of Boalt Hall School of Law, University of California–Berkeley; the late Frank Newman, Justice (ret.) of the California Supreme Court and Professor Emeritus at the Boalt Hall School of Law, University of California–Berkeley; students Robb LeMasters, Jackie Levin, and Jennie Wilke, who conducted research and interviews for the book; Matthew Werdegar, the 16-year-old student who urged nongovernmental organizations (NGOs) to include the detained child's right to parental contact in the UN Convention on the Rights of the Child and thus began the negotiations to put that particular right into the treaty; Margie Beguin-Nuveen of Geneva, Switzerland, for her enthusiasm and generosity; Geraldine Van Bueren of the Centre for International Children's Rights, Queen Mary and Westfield College, University of London, for her expertise in international children's rights law and her undying support; also to Thomas Nazario, Professor of Law, University of San Francisco; John Kortum, Esq.; Mark Stephens and the staff of Borders Books, Emeryville, California; Jo Ann Garfinkel, Assistant Head, and the History Department of the Branson School for their support and the extra hours caused by the Geneva Intern Program; Mary Fetzer, Government Documents Librarian at the Alexander Library, Rutgers University–New Brunswick; Professors Ronald T. Hyman and Jack L. Nelson of the Rutgers University–New Brunswick Graduate School of Education; the staff of the Instructional Materials Center–Zuegner Memorial Library, Hunterdon Central Regional HS, Flemington, New Jersey; Pat Dietrich of Time To Read Books, Flemington, New Jersey; the United Nations Publications Board; the International Labour Office, Geneva, Switzerland; Amnesty International USA; the many publishers and organizations who graciously granted permissions to reprint selected documents and excerpts from published works; and the intergovernmental and nongovernmental organizations that provided information and resources concerning their work related to children's rights worldwide.

Most importantly, we acknowledge the invaluable assistance of Sheila Fernekes, whose patience, love, and technical expertise made completion of this project possible.

1 An Introduction to Children's Rights

Two recent reports on the status of children reveal some sobering statistics.

- In the 1980s and 1990s, "approximately two million children have died in wars, between four and five million have been physically disabled, more than five million forced into refugee camps, and more than twelve millions have been left homeless" (Grant, 1995, 2).
- In 1994, over 22 percent of all U.S. children lived in poverty, the highest child poverty rate since 1964 (Children's Defense Fund, 1995b, 101).

If children's rights are integral aspects of commonly accepted universal human rights of the late twentieth century, then why are the United States and other countries unsuccessful in guaranteeing all children their rights? This book seeks to explain how children's rights originated, what they are, and what steps can be taken to implement them as our world moves into the twenty-first century.

Part 1: How Children's Rights Developed

Children's rights arose during the nineteenth century in Europe and the United States largely in response to the social conditions produced by the Industrial Revolution. Now, at the end of the twentieth century, children's rights have achieved worldwide recognition, but at the beginning of the century the idea of specific rights for children, as distinct from other groups, would have been met by surprise. European and North American children were seen as in need of discipline or protection, perhaps even as the beneficiaries of charity or welfare, but not as possessing specific rights of their own. Legally, those children could inherit property, and their governments, in the role of "superparent," could determine their futures if they were considered criminals or if social service staff declared them to be abused or neglected (Mason, 1994). Public education was directed toward forming an orderly, democratic society rather than emphasizing each child's potential for growth. Even though Swedish children's advocate Ellen Key predicted that the twentieth century would be "the century of the child" (Hawes, 1991, 25), children in Europe and the United States were seen at best as objects to be provided for and protected. Until the devastation of World War II brought about changes in the world's conception of human rights, children had no significant voice in society. Now, although much change has occurred since the beginning of the twentieth century, and particularly since 1948, children have rights, but those rights are not widely implemented.

Today, children's rights are divided into three categories:

- protection rights, which are legal safeguards against exploitative and other harms
- provision rights, which require some kind of positive action, usually the provision of social services or social security
- participation rights, which grant the child an increasingly active role as a citizen in his or her society.

Early Concepts of Children's Rights

Philosophically and legally, children's rights are part of the post–World War II codification of human rights. Human rights arise from two sources: *moral rights* attributed to human beings by philosophers and theologians, and *legal rights,* which are formulated by legislative bodies deriving their power from the consent of the governed (Levin, 1982, 11). Children's rights are now conceptualized in the United Nations Convention on the Rights of the Child (CRC), which was adopted in 1989. They grew as a separate category of human rights because the drafters of the UN treaty and the large numbers of nongovernmental organizations (NGOs) consulting in their creation were convinced that children deserved special rights due to their vulnerability and their roles as the inheritors of the future.

Although political rights in the English-speaking world have a long history, they have always been limited in some way. In the Magna Carta, free subjects of the king received rights, while in 1689 the Parliament was the official recipient of rights from the sovereign. In the United States, the 1789 Bill of Rights applied to "all men" except slaves and Native Americans; the 1789 French Declaration of the Rights of Man and Citizen omitted reference to slavery. The United Nations created the modern conception of human rights after World War II, when the Universal Declaration of Human Rights proclaimed in 1948 that "All human beings are born free and equal in dignity and rights." This declaration, which became the cornerstone of the International Bill of Rights, referred to all people, but specific groups, such as women or children, who might need or deserve additional rights were not specifically named. The United Nations later drafted a series of legally enforceable international human rights instruments, called conventions, to address this absence.[1]

Besides the development of ideas, this book is also concerned with the actions of historical individuals and groups who gave rise to the moral and legal philosophy of children's rights. Recognizing limitations of space, the focus is primarily on the evolution of children's rights in the United States and those that were formulated by the United Nations. Children's rights are not specific to the United States or Europe; not only is Islamic law represented in the CRC, but regional documents such as the African Charter on the Rights and Welfare of the Child demonstrate that children's rights are perceived differently through the lens of non-Western cultures (Van Bueren, 1995, xxi).

Children's rights emerged in the United States largely through the efforts of social movements that were active in four historical periods (Hawes and Hiner, 1985). The first included organizations such as the New York Children's Aid Society, founded in New York in 1853, and the National Society for the Prevention of Cruelty to

Children, which began in the United States and later expanded to Great Britain. These organizations tried to intervene in the lives of poor children in the hope of either saving society from potential future criminals or saving children themselves from abuse or neglect. The now infamous "orphan trains" of the mid-nineteenth century relocated children in rural areas of the United States, far from the "evils" of urban industrial society. These organizations were founded and supported by upper- and middle-class reformers whom Anthony Platt calls the "child-savers."

A second source of contemporary children's rights was the social movement to end child labor. Relying on a romantic image of poor children, Tory aristocrats brought about passage of the English Factory Acts by Parliament in 1833. In the United States, the banner for child labor rights was taken up by Populists and the largely middle-class reformers of the Progressive Era (1890–1920), who sought legislation to limit work hours and ameliorate working conditions for children. In the United States, Progressive reformers such as Florence Kelley, Mother Jones, and the Abbott sisters sought to save children from the worst conditions of industrialism by advocating federal minimum-hour laws, building upon those passed by states in the 1880s and 1890s.

A third source for contemporary children's rights was the movement to reform the legal system's treatment of juveniles. The first juvenile court was established in the state of Illinois in 1899. Whereas U.S. courts had recognized the legal principle "the best interests of the child" since the early nineteenth century (Mason, 1994), the juvenile justice reform movement sought to realize it by removing children from the consequences of the adult penal system, thereby facilitating development of the perception that children possess actual rights of their own.

A fourth source of children's rights was the American interest in educating children to be responsible citizens in a democratic society. The Progressive Movement produced considerable interest in the reform and expansion of public schooling to assist in the creation of a more stable, democratic social order as well as help young people adapt effectively to the tensions and uncertainties created by an emerging urban, industrial civilization. The Progressive emphasis on child-centered pedagogy, which was linked by theoreticians like John Dewey to the creation of responsible citizens in a democracy, significantly transformed the schooling experience in the United States. However, by the 1970s, child liberationists like John Holt were advocating greater freedom for children to learn in less bureaucratic settings, where adults had far less control and children could investigate and inquire much more on their own terms. Also influenced by the substantial changes generated by the civil rights movement of the 1950s and 1960s, the school remained a central focus of activity for the expansion of children's rights during the second half of the twentieth century.[2]

Now there is a fifth generation of children's advocates in the United States who support the application of international legal standards for children. Amnesty International and Human Rights Watch are but two of these. Law schools, like those at the University of Minnesota and the University of California, Berkeley, are adding international human rights, including children's rights, to their curricula. The United States lags behind other nations in requiring the study of human rights in primary and secondary schools, although states like New Jersey and California have mandated teaching about genocide, and individual schoolteachers in public and private schools have introduced lessons of their own, employing materials from such organizations as Amnesty International and Save the Children.

Conceptions of Children's Rights

Children's rights are conceptualized in three main categories: rights of protection, provision, and participation, similar to the rights given to all people by the United Nations Universal Declaration of Human Rights.[3] Children's rights are more extensive than adult rights, however, because children cannot fend for themselves from birth. For the purpose of this book, "the child" will be defined according to the 1989 United Nations Convention on the Rights of the Child (CRC): "anyone who has not yet reached the age of 18 who has also not been declared an adult in a nation's laws" (Article I, CRC). This book traces mainly the twentieth-century paths that lead to human rights for children, noting important dates, pioneers, benchmark legislation, and the work of the organizations that both formed and carry on children's rights advocacy.[4]

Developing Protective Rights

In the United States the grass-roots activism of the Populists and the Progressives produced child regulatory legislation primarily on the state level; the first federal legislation mandating shorter work hours, the Keating-Owens Act of 1916, was declared unconstitutional by the U.S. Supreme Court in 1918 *(Hammer v. Dagenhart)*.

The Progressives also sought to protect children from abandonment, abuse, and neglect by establishing "orderly" institutions such as the orphanage to replace the early-nineteenth-century workhouse, which made children virtually indentured laborers until the ages of 18 (females) and 21 (males). The movement to establish juvenile courts in the United States gained currency at the end of the nineteenth century, separating children from the adult penal system with a focus toward the moral and social rehabilitation of the child. Efforts to protect children from workplace hazards heightened during the New Deal of the 1930s, and continue today.

Middle-class children were in need of protection along with the working-class child. One of the forerunners in redefining the view of the child was Ellen Key, the nineteenth-century Swedish lecturer who argued that children had distinct personalities and were entitled to education and a loving, nurturing home. At the turn of the twentieth century, the "child-saving" Progressive reformers who focused on creating a better environment for children began to lose ground to another group of child-savers, sometimes called the "Professionals" (Hawes and Hiner, 1985, 6–11). The Professionals concentrated on the "normal child," who could be discovered through scholarly research. Thus the idea that child development was worthy of social scientific study came into prominence, and education became an academic discipline in and of itself. Efforts to understand the child were directed by psychologists and sociologists. At the end of the nineteenth century, many social scientists had begun to view children from a developmental perspective, which conceptualized child growth as proceeding through observable and distinct stages. The adoption of this view by major social scientists and educational theorists contributed to the acceptance of the "right to develop" as a fundamental category of children's rights, one in which a child's civil rights include the right to education and moral and spiritual nurture. The U.S. Children's Bureau, established in 1912, is a product of this belief.

Protecting Children

The protection of children was another intent of the child labor movement. In 1904 the National Child Labor Committee was established to lobby for child labor reform. The organization hired Lewis Hine to travel throughout the South and photograph children at work in textile mills and at their homes. There was good reason to send Hine into the South: by 1900, 25 percent of southern mill workers were children between the ages of 10 and 16 (Kemp, 1986, 8). Hine's photographs documented the long hours children worked, as well as the poverty in which they lived. Although U.S. children did not have federal legislation regulating their conditions of work until the Wagner Act of 1935, the first intergovernmental regulations made on behalf of working children were formulated in 1919 by the International Labour Organization (ILO), the agency associated with the League of Nations. Later, the ILO participated constructively in the drafting of the United Nations' instruments, including the 1989 CRC.

Providing for the Child

The concept of the state providing for the child in the United States derives from the European acceptance of social security. Economic rights for children were advocated in England in the nineteenth century, and by 1920 children had access to social security and social services under national law. U.S. Progressives joined European reformers in asserting that children deserved decent childhoods, but no lasting federal social security legislation was passed in the United States until the Social Security Act of 1935. Disabled children were also provided for in this law. The Declaration of Geneva, promulgated as the Declaration of the Rights of the Child by the League of Nations in 1924, made the first international case for rights of provision.

In the United States, poor and disabled children received an increase in benefits resulting from amendments to the Social Security Act in 1973. The 1960s War on Poverty also produced expanded entitlements in the area of education, child health, and child nutrition. Laws are not rights, however. Laws can be repealed and their allocations diminished or rescinded by the Congress. It is in the international legal sphere that social, cultural, and economic rights are guaranteed for children.

Making Active Citizens through Participation Rights

Participation rights refer to those rights that allow the child to develop into an active citizen in a democratic society. In the United States, participation rights, or civil and political rights, have been extended to children through decisions of the Supreme Court. Many of the cases that interpret children as having special rights result from the modern civil rights movement, which is usually dated from the Warren Court's *Brown v. Board of Education of Topeka, Kansas* decision in 1954. In this case, all children, irrespective of race, were granted the right to equal educational opportunity by the Fourteenth Amendment to the U.S. Constitution. Subsequent cases give children the same basic rights as adults when they are subject to the juvenile court system (*In Re Gault,* 1969). Other participation rights in the United States include rights to freedom of self-expression (*Tinker v. Des Moines Independent School District,* 1969), although subsequent decisions have defined student rights to freedom of expression in school settings more strictly (*Hazelwood School District et al. v. Cathy Kuhlmeier et al.,* 1988). The children's liberation movement of the 1970s, which found expression primarily in the area of education, is another source for participation rights of children, articulated in such declarations as the Rights of Youth from the White House Conferences of 1970 and 1971 and the Manifesto of the Children's Legal Centre, London, in 1987 and 1992.

Creating International Rights for Children

According to Nigel Cantwell, former director of Defense for Children International, the path toward international children's rights began with five principles published by Britain's Save the Children International Union in 1923. The League of Nations was then persuaded by Eglantyne Jebb, the union's founder, to issue the 1924 Declaration of Geneva, which in turn was expanded by the United Nations into seven basic principles of children's rights in 1948 (Cantwell, 1992, 207) after Europe's devastation during World War II. In 1959, the United Nations proclaimed the Declaration of the Rights of the Child, stating that the child belonged to a special category to which "mankind owes . . . the best it has to give." The ten principles were devoted to the child's rights to develop and grow in a safe and healthy world. Written in a climate of superpower conflict and confrontation, the Declaration of the Rights of the Child focused on those rights that protected and provided for children, omitting any notion of civil and political rights. In contrast, no tradition of economic, social, and cultural rights as human rights existed in the United States, where civil and political rights had a history of recognition. The declaration's omission of civil and political rights for children was not its major weakness in the eyes of many nations, however. In international law, a declaration is not a legally enforceable instrument, and therefore a convention was considered desirable to replace and update the Declaration of the Rights of the Child.

Drafting and Adopting the UN Convention on the Rights of the Child

In 1979, the government of Poland presented the United Nations Commission on Human Rights with the draft of a legally binding instrument based on the Declaration of the Rights of the Child. Following United Nations procedure, the commission asked the UN secretariat to gather comments from other nations, intergovernmental agencies, and nongovernmental organizations. The 46 replies as well as hundreds of later submissions made by these and additional participants were used constructively in the drafting by the unanimously elected chairman of the CRC's working group, Adam Lopatka of Poland (Van Bueren, 1995, 14).

The UN Commission on Human Rights set up the working group on the drafting of the CRC in 1979. The group used, among others, a draft from Canada as the basis of the incorporation of participation rights for children, adding to the rights of protection and provision that came from the 1959 Declaration of the Rights of the Child. The treaty writers also incorporated advanced UN standards such as the "Beijing Rules." In 1983, in order to make more effective and efficient use of the expertise of nongovernmental organizations, the NGOs formed an Ad Hoc Working Group of their own and negotiated with the chairman to allow one NGO to represent them during the formal drafting. While unassociated NGOs were also given the floor during the drafting procedure, the Ad Hoc NGO Working Group represented a unique cooperation between delegate nations and consulting "competent bodies" whose task was to make children's rights explicit and legally binding in the world. By allowing nongovernmental organizations an important role in formal and informal drafting sessions, the chairman permitted the working group to forge rights that came from the expertise of hands-on experts as well as national delegates.[5]

Human rights activists point out that the CRC was drafted by the process of consensus: If any of the drafting nations, which represented the dominant world cultures, found a clause in the treaty objectionable, the clause was rewritten or dropped so that nations would have no difficulty in ratifying the final draft. Each article was therefore shaped and adopted by a process assuring that controversial interpretations of children's rights were softened or omitted. Claims that the CRC represents "Western imperialism" are tempered by these facts. But, because of its consensual nature, the CRC must be read as containing only the *minimum* standards of children's rights. Recognizing, however, that rights are an evolving reality in international law, the drafters included Article 41 of the CRC, giving children the highest standard of national or international legal rights that exists in their particular situation.

The CRC was completed and adopted by the United Nations General Assembly in 1989. It was open for signature in early 1990, and by September 1990 it had entered into force (i.e., 20 nations had completed the ratification process). The CRC was more than ten years in the making, and is significant not only because it represents an enforceable legal consensus of world experts and over 175 nations, but also because it is the highest international legal source for the basic principles and standards constituting the rights of a child. The CRC brings together international law, which protects, provides for, and enables children to participate in society, both as a vulnerable group deserving special consideration and as young human beings possessing their own rights. Although it represents only the minimum standards for nations to follow when enacting laws and making decisions about children, the CRC is nonetheless a watershed in 200 years of efforts on their behalf.

Significance of the CRC

Three basic categories of children's rights, "protection, provision, and participation," are defined in the convention. Protection articles stem from the belief that children are entitled to more safeguards than adults because they are more vulnerable. Provision rights refer to the States Parties, who must assure that children get their rights by law and sometimes by allocation of funds. By adding participation rights—the rights to develop and participate in society—not only are children as a collective group recognized as having rights, so is the individual child. All of these rights are enforceable in the UN system when a nation (State Party) ratifies the CRC.

A nation that ratifies the CRC guarantees all children their rights whether or not they or their parents are citizens of that nation, and contracts to act at all times "in the child's best interests" (Article 3). Additionally, for the first time, the child must be listened to in matters affecting his or her own future (Article 12). Children are now entitled to rehabilitation after abuse (Article 39), and nations must work to prevent traditional practices that harm the child's health (Article 24).

The Convention on the Rights of the Child begins with a preamble, which states the philosophy and spirit in which it was written. Five important "umbrella articles" follow; these define the age of the child (Article 1), nondiscrimination (Article 2), the basic principle of the "child's best interests" (Article 3), and include two other articles that explain the implementation process for ratifying nations. Umbrella Article 4 allows nations to implement the convention to "the maximum extent of their available resources," thereby recognizing that nations do not have the resources to put all of the rights into effect on the date of ratification. Article 5 concerns "evolving capacities." Interpretation varies, but it provides for the gradual assumption of a child's exercise of his or her rights and a gradual diminishing of parental guidance; it is left to individual nations to determine when each child can exercise which rights. The entire CRC is qualified by the umbrella articles; thus, all rights must be granted in such a manner as to avoid discrimination and with the child's best interests paramount.[6]

Following the umbrella articles are the enumerated rights of the child. The drafting group broke the convention into sections that define rights of "protection, participation, and provision," but there are overlapping and even apparently contradictory rights. Different groups categorize the rights in the CRC in different ways; some prefer to list the so-called "participation" articles with the education articles, among others, arriving at "development" articles, which emphasize a psychosocial developmental interpretation of the convention. The United Nations Children's Fund (UNICEF), formerly the United Nations International Children's Emergency Fund, is among other organizations that emphasize prevention, or the right of children to survive. Whatever the grouping of rights, the convention translates into law fundamental understandings of what children need and deserve in order to grow into adulthood.

Enforcing Children's Rights

Enforcement is done by a treaty-monitoring body, the Committee on the Rights of the Child, which oversees each ratifying nation's compliance on a two-year, then five-year basis. Implementation procedures are covered in part II of the CRC. The committee is one of 12 UN treaty-monitoring bodies. It is comprised of "ten experts of high moral standing and recognized competence in the field" of children's rights who serve for terms of four years (Article 43 of the CRC). The experts are selected by the UN Human Rights Commission and come from countries within the United Nations' five world areas. The first Committee on the Rights of the Child met in Geneva in September 1991 and has developed a schedule for preparatory meetings in the five world areas in addition to three

three-week sessions each year in Geneva. The committee's mandate is to develop standards for monitoring the CRC and then to examine the reports submitted by nations (States) that ratify the convention to see if the States are implementing children's rights within their jurisdiction. The committee has been particularly directed to "encourage international cooperation in the field covered by the Convention" (Article 45), and to that end it may call upon the assistance of UN agencies such as UNICEF and "other competent bodies" (taken to mean nongovernmental organizations). Nongovernmental organizations (NGOs) have proven to be invaluable in drafting the convention, setting standards for children's rights, and providing evidence of compliance.

The committee serves as a central point, or clearinghouse, for information on how reporting nations are enforcing children's rights and for resources to help them in their task. Furthermore, the committee has the power to require countries to demonstrate improvement in the situation of children in their jurisdiction; subtle or overt pressure from the committee can result in the invitation of children's rights organizations or experts to recommend changes or donate resources. Essentially, though, its ultimate power is the power of publicity: by making a country's poor record of implementation a public matter, it can embarrass nations into making improvements. The committee's major focus, however, is to bring about changes in the condition of children, emphasizing cooperation and the bringing together of need on the part of a reporting country and the resources available through international organizations.

Children's Rights Are Still Being Created

Many nations agree that the CRC needs amending or enlarging, and in the 1990s two optional protocols are being drafted, one to raise the age of soldiers to 18, thus eliminating child soldiers, and another to prevent the sale and trafficking of children and child prostitution. There are other omissions, too. The CRC omits reference to medical experimentation, for example, and an addition to the nondiscrimination clause (Article 2) outlawing discrimination because of gender preference.

Part 2: Current Issues in Children's Rights

This book places U.S. children's rights in the context of their international rights. How children exercise their rights varies according to cultural norms, socioeconomic standing, the constraints of the natural and built environments, and other factors, yet everywhere children possess the same rights: those in the United Nations Convention on the Rights of the Child. A strong argument in international law says that because an overwhelming number of nations in the world accept the provisions of the CRC, the unchallenged articles have become international customary human rights law (Van Bueren, 1995; Newman and Weissbrodt, 1990), and therefore are enforceable everywhere. Here are some of the problematic areas in children's rights today in the United States and some indication of how these issues exist globally.

Child Health and Welfare

The efforts of the UN World Health Organization (WHO), UNICEF, and nongovernmental organizations such as Save the Children have helped to produce an improvement in child health in developing nations. Smallpox has been eradicated and, provided children are inoculated, the same fate may soon befall polio. The number of children surviving their first year has increased more than 50 percent between 1960 and 1992 (chapter 6, table 8). Yet, improvement in health and the child's ability to grow and thrive depends on the eradication of poverty. One-sixth of the world's children now live in poverty; in the United States, 14 million children live below the poverty line, the largest number being African-American children (chapter 6, table 3). Many U.S. children rely on federally funded nutrition programs such as the Women, Infants, and Children Program, along with reduced-cost school breakfasts and lunches, which are in jeopardy due to the current assault on federal entitlements.

In the Convention on the Rights of the Child, all children are recognized as having the rights to "the highest attainable standard of health and to facilities for the treatment of illness and rehabilitation of health," as enumerated in clauses of the article (Article 24). Article 26 of the CRC gives the child the right to benefit from social security and Article 27 recognizes the child's right to "a standard of living adequate for the child's physical, spiritual, moral and social development." Read in the context of umbrella Article 4, nations are not mandated to meet the requirements of these articles overnight, but are urged to address problems of poverty and want to "the maximum extent of their available resources." All nations recognize the importance of basic economic and social rights, or rights they must provide for children, but this issue often arises: How much of the annual budget is meant by "the maximum extent"?

Education

Education is an indicator of the basic quality of life in a nation (*see* chapter 6, table 8). Nearly all children of the appropriate age are enrolled in primary school in developed countries (free and compulsory primary education is recognized in the International Bill of Rights and the CRC), but in the least-developed countries less than half are enrolled. The figures alter dramatically when the girl child in both developing and the least-developed nations is considered; in developing countries only 62 percent are enrolled, and in the least-developed countries only 23 percent (chapter 6, table 8). The double standard in education results from both cultural norms and economic needs. When a family is poor and in need of labor, should children be removed from school to promote economic survival? Should the girl child be kept in the home to help her mother, thus perpetuating cultural norms? The CRC reflects the concerns of developed and developing countries when the right to education (Article 28) is directed toward the prevention of dropouts as well as increasing the availability of secondary education.

Cultural norms in the goals of education are respected in Article 29, as are respect for the family, human rights, peace, and the natural environment. Education is also to be directed to all forms of equality and to life in a free society. Do these articles adequately cover the goals of education?

Children of ethnic, religious, or linguistic minorities, or those who are members of indigenous societies, are entitled to learn their own culture and profess and practice their own religion and language (Article 30). Should these minority rights be extended to public education? If so, by what standards? In the United States, has the movement since the 1960s to provide bilingual education provided cultural, ethnic, and linguistic minorities with an appropriate education that satisfies this aspect of the CRC?

Children and the Law

Children throughout the world encounter the law in different contexts than do adults. In many societies, because of their age and vulnerability, legal systems treat children separately from adults. In fewer than five other countries (the United States is one at this writing), children can legally receive the death penalty for grave crimes. The reality is, however, that children die because of contact with the law in many more. In many countries, children can be imprisoned with adults. Second, many times family conflict causes children to be the subject of legal opinions and judicial decisions. Child abuse, neglect, domestic violence, divorce, and custodial care are situations in which children can become directly involved with the law; consequently, important considerations are raised about the best interests of the child. Third, during the many stages of their development, children participate in activities that are regulated by laws at various levels of government. Children in the work force are often subject to stipulations of when, where, how much, and how long they can work. Similarly, children enrolled in schools must comply with compulsory attendance laws and a myriad of legal restrictions concerning behavior and conduct and the acquisition of credentials toward further education or employment.

Various international instruments have set procedures for the treatment of children when they come in contact with the law; most notably, there are the "Beijing Rules" (the UN Standard Minimum Rules for the Administration of Juvenile Justice) and the UN Rules for the Protection of Juveniles Deprived of Their Liberty. The Convention on the Rights of the Child, in Articles 37, 38, 39, and 40, is careful to refer to these guidelines; some of these concepts have been incorporated into the treaty, thus giving children the right to these protections. The convention is worded to protect children from the moment they come in contact with authorities and throughout a legal system. The CRC repeats the Civil and Political Covenant's proscription against torture and "cruel, inhuman, or degrading treatment or punishment," thus providing a higher standard than current U.S. law, which does not regard "degrading" or "treatment" in terms of rights. In countries where there are higher standards for the treatment of children by authorities, the CRC is careful to invoke those higher standards in Article 41.

The complex issue of children and the death penalty is raised today. In some countries, children have received the death penalty before their teenage years. In the CRC, a child is defined in Article 1 as still a minor until the age of 18. In the United States, it is possible to impose the death sentence on adolescents who commit capital crimes at the ages of 16 and 17, but not below the age of 16 *(Thompson v. Oklahoma)*. The U.S. Supreme Court has upheld the constitutionality of such death sentences *(Stanford v. Kentucky)*; if the United States continues to permit the use of capital punishment, is a conflict with the CRC inevitable? In this case, should the

United States submit a qualification (or reservation) when ratifying, stating that it will not uphold that clause of the treaty? To do so would take away one of the fundamental rights guaranteed to young people by international law. At this writing the United States is one of only seven countries worldwide known to have executed juvenile offenders during the period 1980–1991 (Amnesty International, 1991, 1).

Chapter 5 contains significant Supreme Court cases that delineate the relationship between children and the law in the United States. Since the 1960s, children's rights have been expanded by Supreme Court interpretation of the Bill of Rights *(see In Re Gault)* to include protections that were formerly seen as applying only to adults. However, since the early 1980s increasing restrictions on the freedom of expression and privacy of young people in school settings have been imposed by the U.S. Supreme Court, the most recent being their decision to permit random drug tests for student athletes in *Vernonia School District v. Acton* (*New York Times*, 27 June 1995, B3).

Children and Violence

Violence is a prevalent factor at the end of the twentieth century, in the United States and worldwide. The effects of violence—whether from war, armed conflict between groups, or violence in the streets of a town or city—have terrible effects on children. Robert Coles's writings confirm this trauma. Here is an issue that overlaps human rights, because when people are deprived of human rights they can resort to violence to restore them, and authorities can use violence to keep down opposition. This process in the microcosm of cities becomes a cycle of violence between warring gangs, drug dealers, and others.

Humanitarian law, the product of the Geneva Conventions, is an area of law that verges on human rights law. Given the actuality of war, the International Committee of the Red Cross (the politically neutral monitoring body for the conventions) seeks to mitigate the effects of war on civilians and to forbid the waging of war by children. In recent history, children as young as ten years of age have been conscripted as soldiers by nations or armed groups who believe they should fight. The Geneva Conventions prohibit the participation of children under the age of 16 in armed conflict and regulate recruitment so that older ones are inducted into armies first. The CRC now makes 15 the age at which children can be recruited into armed conflict. The Committee on the Rights of the Child is attempting to raise the age of soldiers to 18 by writing an optional protocol, or amendment, that nations can ratify. Should the United States, which allows young men to enlist at the age of 16, sign this protocol? What is the difference between allowing recruitment into the armed forces and conscripting a young person into a guerrilla army or an independence movement? These are some of the issues that arise around children and the violence of armed conflict. Does the guaranteeing of children's rights require an end to all violence?

Civilian children also are protected by the humanitarian law of the Geneva Conventions, as are adult civilians. But what should nations do to help children who have experienced the violence of war? The United Nations has instituted a worldwide campaign against the placing of land mines, which are documented to be one of the most frequent ways children become disabled apart from disease. The United States has ordered a partial ban on the placing of new land mines, and nongovernmental organizations are now campaigning for the total ban.

What does society owe children who have experienced any kind of violence—armed conflict, gang-related violence, or even the domestic violence that can result in the child's removal from the home? Many of the symptoms of trauma faced by the children are the same, irrespective of the situation in which violence has occurred. The Convention on the Rights of the Child states that children have a right to rehabilitation. In Article 39, States Parties are held accountable for "promoting physical and psychological recovery" of children who have experienced violence and the critically important factor of the "social reintegration of a child victim. . . ." The concept of rehabilitation as a right has been articulated before, but in the CRC it is mandated for the first time. It is also mandated to take place "in an environment which fosters the health, self-respect and dignity of the child."

Child Refugees

The legal status of refugee is given to people who flee armed conflict or political persecution. The number of refugees throughout the world is now estimated at 18 million people, 7 million of whom are children. Refugees have rights (Article 22, CRC); the UN High Commissioner for Refugees is charged with caring for many of these refugees. Nongovernmental organizations such as Save the

Children and the International Committee of the Red Cross provide needed services in cooperation with UN agencies.

But families are forced to leave their homes for other reasons, too. By what equation can children who are displaced because of drought or economic want be placed in a different category than people who cross borders to escape political persecution or the ravages of armed conflict? And, should children who lose their homes because of natural disaster but who do not cross international borders be denied aid because they are merely "internally displaced"? In another example, the undocumented alien is in a precarious situation: Should his or her child be denied basic needs because of uncertain legal status within a country and thereby, through no fault of the child, fall through the legal cracks of a national legal system? The Convention on the Rights of the Child contains an answer to the moral and often economic dilemma that these situations present: *All* children are entitled to the rights in the convention, and all children have the right to a name and a nationality (Articles 7 and 8). States Parties have the obligation, within the capacities of their situation (Article 4), to extend rights to the refugee child or the child who would be stateless except for the Convention on the Rights of the Child.

Children and the Family

From time to time U.S. newspapers report that children have been separated from their parents who have been deported after raids on sweatshops. These children, like those in Rwandan refugee camps, where thousands of children have appeared without their parents, fall into the category of "unaccompanied minors." Once children have reached the shelter of the UN High Commissioner for Refugees, the commissioner cooperates with organizations such as Save the Children and the International Committee of the Red Cross to find their relatives. But what of the child who is stranded in a country that has been entered illegally by his or her parents? Even those children possess rights, one of which is the right to be reunified with his or her parents if separated, even if the family is separated by borders (Article 22). The CRC strongly upholds the child's right to be raised in a family environment (unless this environment is proven not "in the best interests of the child"). Both parents are recognized as having a role in the upbringing of the child (Article 18). Other issues that have arisen about the child and the family are covered in the CRC; for example, the goals of education include respect for the family (Article 29). The CRC also recognizes that parents or guardians have a primary role in raising children, consistent with the evolving capacities of the child (Article 5). Articles 7, 8, and 14 also recognize the parental role in raising children.

Children and Sexual Exploitation

The sexual exploitation of children is a worldwide problem that takes various forms in different countries. The sale of children has been outlawed since the International Convention for the Suppression of the Traffic in Women and Children was signed in Geneva in 1922 (*see* chapter 4), but the problem has not appreciably diminished. The sale and trafficking of children encompasses the issues of sale for prostitution or domestic servitude and the trade in body parts, as the film *The Body Parts Business* by children's rights activist Bruce Harris illustrates (*see* chapter 9). Children have now become the victims of international sex tourism. The Norwegian government showed a film at a recent antislavery working group graphically depicting sex tourism in the United States, the Philippines, and Thailand, a problem well documented in the work of organizations such as the International Catholic Child Bureau and Defense for Children International (*see* chapter 7). In Europe, the United States, and Asia, tours promising male or female prostitutes are advertised among legitimate tours in newspapers; by reading the advertisements carefully, a client can discern the difference.

Those who exploit children have adapted their methods to modern conditions, and the Committee on the Rights of the Child has recognized that Article 34 needs elucidation and greater protections for children against all forms of sexual exploitation and sexual abuse. An optional protocol on the sale and trafficking of children is now being drafted with contemporary conditions in mind.

Child Labor

The United States has federally regulated child labor since the 1920s, but children still face exploitation in this country and throughout the world. In the United States, for example, undocumented or documented sweatshop workers often bring their children to work because there is no one to care for them. Better known in the West are the conditions of bonded labor in Asia: children are sold to factory owners in return for a small loan to the child's family. The factory owners force the children to work long hours to purchase their freedom while being paid substandard wages. Children are forced to work in hazardous conditions making glass or weaving carpets, as was Iqbal Masih of Pakistan (*see* chapter 3). There is little education and often no escape for the children until they reach the age of majority.

The International Labour Organization, one of the United Nations' agencies, has long crusaded for better working conditions for children. ILO representatives aided in the drafting of Article 32 of the CRC in which children are protected from work that can prevent them from learning and growing. There is no proscription on child labor in the CRC because children are seen as part of the economic unit of the family in many cultures, and their help is needed in bringing in a harvest or weaving material. Article 32, however, states that children should be "protected from economic exploitation and from performing any work that is likely to be hazardous or to interfere with the child's education, or to be harmful to the child's health or physical, mental, spiritual or social development." Furthermore, in the CRC children are granted the right to rest and leisure (Article 31), which can apply to all aspects of the child's life and learning. Are these protections enough for the child? Or do the workplace hazards documented in chapter 6, table 15, persist due to indifference and lack of government regulation and enforcement, or through the continuity of poverty and the overwhelming need for families to survive?

Part 3: Implications for Children's Rights in the United States

Status of the UN Convention on the Rights of the Child in the United States

Despite the holding of the 1990 World Summit for Children at the United Nations in New York City, the United States did not instruct U.S. ambassador to the United Nations, Madeline Albright, to sign the Convention on the Rights of the Child until February 1995, thereby honoring the commitment made by Hillary Clinton at the memorial service for UNICEF's James Grant. The UN Convention on the Rights of the Child is second only to the UN Charter as the most widely adopted UN treaty in history. When the

United States at last signed the CRC, it took a major step toward joining the international community in making children's rights a priority for action.

Along with the 1995 signing of the CRC, the Clinton administration's stated commitment to forward it to the U.S. Senate for ratification within the advise-and-consent clause of the U.S. Constitution suggests that more in-depth federal consideration of this far-reaching landmark document is imminent. But would U.S. ratification of the CRC and the subsequent reconciliation of U.S. law with the CRC improve the condition of children in the United States? First, U.S. ratification would likely have a very significant impact by making children's issues front-burner items for legislative action at the federal and possibly state levels of government. U.S. law would have to be reconciled with the high standards for child welfare established in the CRC; this would generate momentum to increase state government commitments in the area of provision rights to a higher minimum level than currently exists. As an example, simple comparisons of two states (Alabama and New Hampshire) in the areas of infant mortality and reading proficiency demonstrate the wide disparity in addressing child health needs, which could be positively influenced by raising minimum provisions of education and health care to reduce infant mortality. Whereas in Alabama the infant mortality rate per 1,000 live births was 10.5 infants (ranked forty-ninth in the United States), in New Hampshire the infant mortality rate was 5.9 (ranked second). Concerning reading proficiency, 52 percent of Alabama's fourth-grade public school students lacked basic reading proficiency, compared to 27 percent for New Hampshire, almost one-half the rate in Alabama (Children's Defense Fund, 1995a). More effective minimum standards of provision for children could provide incentives for improving the condition of all children, while encouraging states with already good standards to do even better.

Second, ratification may demonstrate to the nation's children that the rhetoric of empowerment, which is often included in political appeals for youth participation in government and citizen action, is supported by the commitment of the federal government. The participation rights of the CRC embody the potential to mobilize children as active and thoughtful citizens in their families, schools, and communities. Reflecting in many ways the philosophical framework of pioneers in children's rights such as Ellen Key and Janusz Korczak, the spirit of the CRC's participation rights emphasizes child empowerment, which helps them learn the skills and attitudes critical for effective democratic citizenship. Although parents and other authority figures might feel threatened or intimidated by the prospect of children expressing their participation rights at home, in school, or in the larger community, this is only one possible effect. In contrast, parents could recognize that enhanced child participation in decision making under effective adult supervision can broaden the commitment of young people to democratic institutions, and possibly increase the involvement of young people in formal democratic procedures such as voting, political party activity, and the operation of government.

Third, CRC ratification would provide a strong incentive to embody the three major aspects of that document—provision, participation, and protection—in all areas of child policy throughout the United States. Historically, the concept of protection has dominated child policy efforts in the United States, as witnessed in early federal and state efforts to enact laws in the areas of child labor and child health during the Progressive Era. Combining the historic U.S. commitment to child protection with the CRC's strong emphases on provision and participation offers an opportunity to serve the best interests of the whole child, with an overt emphasis on how children can grow and develop within the context of family life. In many ways, the recommendations of the National Commission on Children (*see* chapter 5) are consistent with the CRC's emphases, notably in the commission's recommendations for universal health care, the strengthening of families by revision of the tax structure, and increased support services for families in need, as well as the expansion of opportunities for children to engage in community service. The influence of the CRC in promoting comparable policy recommendations at the federal and state levels in the United States could be very significant, particularly with the strong advocacy of the executive branch.

Creation of a National Ombudsperson for Children

Early in the twentieth century the U.S. Children's Bureau focused on developing a voice for children in selected areas of child protection, specifically child labor and child health, which were special emphases of Progressive Era social reform activity. The first two directors of the U.S. Children's Bureau, Julia Lathrop and Grace Abbott, were vigorous and tireless advocates of children during a period when the role of the federal government in enacting and implementing policy for children was very limited. With the expansion of the federal government's role concerning both child protection and provision during the 1930s, and the massive expansion of federal government programs affecting children's issues during the 1960s and 1970s, the traditional functions of the U.S. Children's Bureau were dispersed among many federal agencies. Today, there is no one individual or federal agency whose mandate is solely the advocacy of children in the United States.

Following the model established in Norway by Malfrid Grude Flekkoy (*see* chapter 3), one option for the United States would involve creation of a federal cabinet level post of ombudsperson for children. Guidelines for the development and implementation of such a position already exist, as conceptualized by Malfrid Flekkoy based on her work in Norway, and with the UNICEF International Child Development Center in Florence, Italy. The dispersion of children's programs throughout the federal government has made it difficult to coordinate and integrate their emphases and functions, as reported by the National Commission on Children in 1991 (National Commission on Children, 1991, 81). One strong voice for children at the cabinet level could effectively develop interagency collaboration that would streamline the delivery of important services to children, coordinate federal/state-level activity on behalf of children, and provide a consistent, powerful voice for children at the highest levels of the state. Additionally, this person would be able to work closely with intergovernmental and nongovernmental children's rights organizations (*see* chapter 7), as well as with the Department of State and other cabinet-level agencies that address children's issues on the international level. Most importantly, though, the primary role of an ombudsperson for children—to advocate improvements in the quality of life for children in the United States—could bring a powerful coherence to the arguments in favor of making provision, protection, and participation three essential dimensions in all state and federal children's policies.

Enactment of Recommendations Made by the National Commission for Children

The lack of commitment to fulfill the promise of the National Commission for Children's recommendations in their final report, *Beyond Rhetoric: A New American Agenda for Children and Families*, may be overcome if the United States desires to improve the quality of life for children in the foreseeable future. Developed by a bipartisan commission spanning the ideological spectrum, the National Commission followed in the distinguished tradition of White House Conferences on Children begun in the early twentieth century by President Theodore Roosevelt and continuing throughout the twentieth century (*see* selected White House Conference documents in chapter 5). Recognizing that improving the condition of children's lives could not realistically be achieved without placing child welfare in the context of strengthened families, the commission's recommendations are family-centered, as is the UN Convention on the Rights of the Child.

The National Commission's most far-reaching recommendations concern the over 20 percent of all children who live in poverty in the United States (Children's Defense Fund, 1995b, 17). The proposed revision of the tax code to incorporate a $1,000 tax credit for children is an expensive proposition, but far more expensive is the continuing erosion of children's lives by the grinding effects of poverty, which has debilitating impacts on child growth and development, family relationships, education, and child health. Tied to the tax-reform proposal is the commission's advocacy of employee-based health insurance coverage for workers and the provision of universal health insurance for all children and pregnant mothers. Despite the failure of the Clinton administration's health reform initiative during 1993–1994, renewed scrutiny of the National Commission's recommendations is timely, not only because of the serious needs they would address but also because of the recognition by the commission and many other experts that the problems of children and families are interrelated. Simultaneously improving the health care of children and offering family planning services to prospective parents, both of which are commission recommendations, make good sense by having federal, state, and community levels of government work together to strengthen children's lives within the family environment.

Recognizing that its recommendations would cost money, the committee offered six different funding options, all adhering to three guiding principles: deficit neutrality (not adding to the federal deficit), progressive (placing the greater burden of revenue generation on those most able to pay), and growth (using sources of revenue likely to grow over time). In light of the shifts in legislative affiliations resulting from the 1994 congressional elections, these six financing options require a fresh look, but none should be rejected simply because the new Congress was not seated when the commission published its report. Rather, the fiscal requirements of the commission's recommendations are meager compared to the cost to society if the quality of life for children and families does not improve.

Enforcement of Existing Laws and Regulations through Enhanced International, Federal, State, and Local Cooperation

An impressive body of laws, regulations, policies, and practices designed to improve the quality of life for children has emerged in the twentieth century. Many of these enactments address problems that recognize no boundaries of time and space, and require a coordinated, comprehensive response to mitigate their effects. One example is the sexual exploitation of children, which was the focus of an International Labour Organization Convention in 1922 and which persists today in the widespread practices of child prostitution and sex tourism.

Street children in many urban areas are particularly vulnerable to this form of exploitation, as are homeless and destitute children, particularly females. Patterns of substance abuse are often connected to sexual exploitation of street children, which multiplies the difficulties faced by governmental and nongovernmental organizations in addressing this multifaceted problem (Defense for Children International, 1989, 23–24).

Similarly, the persistence of child labor throughout the globe, much of it in extremely exploitative situations, heightens the need for enhanced collaboration and coordination of policy initiatives. As has been pointed out, "The multiple aspects of child labour require a multi-pronged approach to the problem, including not only legislation and law enforcement but also action in such areas as incomes and employment, formal and non-formal education, welfare and the promotion of children's rights" (Bequele and Boyden, 1988, 170). When a consumer in the United States purchases a product made by the hands of a ten-year-old bonded laborer in Southwest Asia, the reality is that profits are being made for businesses that regularly violate both international child labor standards and the fundamental rights of the children they employ. The actions of people all over the world, and at every level of government, can have significant influences on the condition of children, making imperative not only the need for improved education about children but direct action on their behalf. And such action can only be truly effective if done in a coordinated fashion.

One example is the use of the power of publicity to demonstrate to the world community how children's rights are being denied. Using the mass media to improve the visibility of children's rights issues has enormous potential for displaying the problems encountered by children to a global audience, with the hope that deliberation and action can then result (*see* the biography of Iqbal Masih in chapter 3). Coordination of world law enforcement activities focused on reducing child sexual exploitation is generating some significant results, notably in the area of sex tourism. If an aggressive program was implemented to educate children about their rights using the UN Convention on the Rights of the Child as the framework, such efforts might help children resist efforts to exploit them in the sex tourism trade (Ould, 1994, 20).

One possible effect of U.S. ratification of the CRC is the bringing into conformity of U.S. domestic laws with the articles of the convention. Although a time-consuming process dependent on close coordination of legislative, judicial, and executive branches at the federal and state levels, such changes could focus the considerable moral, financial, and intellectual resources of government directly on the problems facing children. The difficulty of accomplishing this task rests in fashioning comprehensive approaches to problems (such as the health and education status of children) that are currently addressed by a wide variety of federal and state agencies, but which have not been effectively solved nationwide. Raising the level of federal commitment to the high minimum standards established in the CRC could provide the impetus for a systematic national initiative placing the condition of children at the center of federal and state domestic policy making.

At the same time, even if the United States delays ratification of the CRC, improved coordination and cooperation at all levels of government to address the problems faced by children is possible. Consistent with the recommendations of the National Commission on Children, federal, state, and local governments and nongovernmental organizations can improve their efforts to bring children's issues to the attention of the mass media, develop programs emphasizing prevention and proactive intervention in the areas of child health and welfare, and act to strengthen support services for families so that U.S. children are less likely to fall into poverty, suffer from the effects of homelessness, and endure the debilitating effects of poor health and substandard education.

Summary

The discussion of implications for children's rights in the United States envisions an activist role for the federal government concerning improvement of the quality of life for children. The efforts of the congressional majority elected in 1994 to limit the size and scope of government programs, particularly in the interests of simultaneously balancing the federal budget and returning more discretionary power to the states concerning social welfare programs, run counter to this activist role. As the Congress and the Clinton administration debate the pros and cons of budgetary priorities that restructure the federal government's role concerning the status of children, the outcome of their deliberations remains unclear. However, there is no doubt that the complexity of issues in the area of children's rights will continue to occupy the attention of U.S. policymakers, most notably because of the interdependent nature of these issues and the systematic efforts of the world community to address them with the standards of the CRC and the UN system.

Notes

1. The International Bill of Rights contains the Universal Declaration of Human Rights, two legally enforceable covenants: the International Covenant on Civil and Political Rights and the International Covenant on Economic, Social, and Cultural Rights, and an Optional Protocol on Civil and Political Rights, which creates machinery to enforce the first covenant. The idea of two covenants arose during the Cold War; the original framers had no intention of dividing rights into categories, as reported in "Fact Sheet No. 2," Center for Human Rights, United Nations Office at Geneva, 8–4, Avenue de la Paix, 1211 Geneva 10 Switzerland.

2. The following works were also consulted in the preparation of this chapter: Bruce Bellingham, "The Unspeakable Blessing: Street Children, Reform Rhetoric and Misery in Early Industrial Capitalism," *Politics and Society* 12:3 (1983), 303–330; R. Dingwall and J. M. Eekelaar, "Families and the State: An Historical Perspective on the Public Relations of Private Conflict," *Law and Policy* 10:4 (October 1988), 341–361; Clark Nardinelli, *Child Labor and the Industrial Revolution* (Bloomington: Indiana University Press, 1990); Paul C. Taylor, *The ABC-CLIO Companion to the American Labor Movement* (Santa Barbara, CA: ABC-CLIO, 1993); and Walter I. Trattner, *Crusade for the Children: A History of the National Child Labor Committee and Child Labor Reform in America* (Chicago: Quadrangle Books, 1970).

3. Van Bueren explains that a new "P," "the Prevention of harm to children," has been added to the traditional categorization of rights and is beginning to take hold. She explains ". . . it is arguable that protection in literal terms includes prevention, however, the reality is very different. Much of human rights implementation on both a governmental and nongovernmental level has not focused on prevention. . . . The preventive role in the form of technical advice and assistance has largely been overshadowed, although this is now slowly beginning to change" (Van Bueren, 1995, 15).

4. For a fuller discussion of the moral and legal framework for children's rights, see Van Bueren, chapter 1.

5. For a more detailed description of the role of nongovernmental organizations in the drafting process, see Michael Longford, "NGOs and the Rights of the Child" in *"The Conscience of the World": The Influence of Non-Governmental Organisations in the U.N. System*, edited by Peter Willets, London: Hurst & Co., 1996, 21–40.

6. For a fuller discussion of issues surrounding who is a child, see Van Bueren, chapter 2.

References

Amnesty International USA. *The Death Penalty and Juvenile Offenders.* New York: Amnesty International USA, 1991.

Bequele, Assefa, and Jo Boyden. "Working Children: Current Trends and Policy Responses." *International Labour Review* 127:2 (1988), 153–172.

Cantwell, Nigel. "Conventionally Theirs: An Overview of the Origins, Content, and Significance of the Convention on the Rights of the Child," *Social Education* 56:4 (April/May 1992), 207–210.

Children's Defense Fund. *Children in the States.* Washington, DC: Children's Defense Fund, 1995a.

Children's Defense Fund. *The State of America's Children Yearbook 1995.* Washington, DC: Children's Defense Fund, 1995b.

Defense for Children International. *International Investigation into the Rights of Abandoned Children.* Geneva, Switzerland: Defense for Children International, 1989.

Grant, James P. *The State of the World's Children 1995.* Oxford: Oxford University Press, 1995.

Hawes, Joseph N. *The Children's Rights Movement: A History of Advocacy and Protection.* Boston: Twayne Publishers, 1991.

Hawes, Joseph N., and N. Ray Hiner, eds. *American Childhood: A Research Guide and Historical Handbook.* Westport, CT: Greenwood Press, 1985.

Kemp, John R., ed. *Lewis Hine: Photographs of Child Labor in the New South.* Jackson: University Press of Mississippi, 1986.

Levin, Leah. *Human Rights: Questions and Answers.* Paris, France: UNESCO, 1982.

Mason, Mary Ann. *From Father's Property to Children's Rights: The History of Child Custody in the United States.* New York: Columbia University Press, 1994.

National Commission on Children. *Beyond Rhetoric: A New American Agenda for Children and Families. Executive Summary.* Washington, DC: U.S. Government Printing Office, 1991.

New York Times. "Excerpts from the Opinions on Random Drug Testing for Student Athletes." *New York Times,* 27 June 1995, B3.

Newman, Frank, and David Weissbrodt. *International Human Rights: Law, Policy, Process.* Cincinnati: Anderson Publishing, 1990.

Ould, David. "The Fight against Sex Tourism." *Anti-Slavery Reporter* 13:9 (1994), 20.

Van Bueren, Geraldine. *The International Law on the Rights of the Child.* Dordrecht, the Netherlands: Martinus Nijhoff, 1995.

Chronology 2

The items listed in this chronology represent major events of the twentieth century concerning children's rights, with special emphasis on the United States. They have been chosen using one or more of these criteria: (1) They illustrate historic milestones and/or trends in the development of laws, legislation, and policy regarding the protection and advocacy of children; (2) they highlight the development of international agreements and treaties in the area of children's rights; (3) they identify critically important rulings of the U.S. Supreme Court related to children's rights; and (4) they identify major activities of individuals, groups, and organizations that have played central roles in raising awareness about children's rights in the United States and internationally.

1892 Kate Douglas Wiggan, author of *Rebecca of Sunnybrook Farm*, publishes *Children's Rights*, in which she advocates a realistic attitude toward children and a milder approach to discipline.

1894 William T. Stead's *If Christ Came to Chicago* is published; this muckraking book contributes to development of the juvenile court movement.

1896 John Dewey establishes the Laboratory School at the University of Chicago to scientifically study child development.

1897 The National Congress of Parents and Teachers is created from an existing organization, the National Congress of Mothers. This advocacy organization dedicates itself to improving parental education, with the aim of bettering the lives of children.

1899 The Illinois Juvenile Court Act establishes the first juvenile court in the United States, giving the state's courts vast powers to act in the best interests of children under age 16 who had violated the law.

The National Federation of Consumers' Leagues are founded, with Florence Kelley spearheading the organization's anti–child labor campaign.

John Dewey publishes *The School and Society,* the first major statement of Progressive educational theory in the United States.

1900 Ellen Key publishes *The Century of the Child,* in which she advocates the humane treatment of children consistent with her view of children as basically good.

1903 The first children's march for reform in the twentieth century occurs from 7–27 July when Mary Harris Jones (Mother Jones) leads working children on a march from Kensington, Pennsylvania, to Oyster Bay, New York, home of President Theodore Roosevelt, to demand federal laws regulating child labor. President Roosevelt responds by sending a representative who rejects the children's cause.

1904 The International Association of Labour Legislation issues the International Agreement for the Suppression of the White Slave Traffic, an attempt to end "the procuring of women or girls for immoral purposes abroad."

The National Child Labor Committee, the first effective lobbying group for reforming child labor conditions, is established in the United States.

1905 The Pennsylvania Supreme Court decides juvenile courts are legal in *Commonwealth v. Fisher.*

1906 The Playground and Recreation Association of America is established, advocating that children have the right to play in safe areas.

Senator Albert J. Beveridge of Indiana introduces the first bill in the U.S. Congress to regulate child labor.

1909 The first White House Conference on Care of Dependent Children is held in Washington, D.C., during the administration of President William Howard Taft.

1910 The Boy Scouts of America and the Campfire Girls are founded in Washington, D.C., and Lake Sebago, Maine, respectively.

1912 The Girl Scouts of America is founded in Savannah, Georgia.

The first federal agency devoted expressly to the welfare of children, the U.S. Children's Bureau, is founded.

1916 The U.S. Congress passes and President Woodrow Wilson signs the Keating-Owens Act, the first federal legislation regulating child labor.

1918 In *Hammer v. Dagenhart,* the U.S. Supreme Court declares the Keating-Owens Act unconstitutional.

Mississippi becomes the last state in the United States to mandate compulsory public education.

1919 The International Labour Organization adopts the Convention Fixing the Minimum Age for Admission

1919 *cont.* of Children to Industrial Employment and the Convention Concerning the Night Work of Young Persons Employed in Industry, which establish minimum employment ages for children in specific industries and places of employment on an international level. Lower minimum ages for child workers in Japan and India are included in both conventions.

Eglantyne Jebb founds the Save the Children Fund in Great Britain.

1920 The Child Welfare League of America is chartered.

1921 The Sheppard-Towner Act is signed into law as the first federal-state program for maternal and child health, establishing the principle of shared federal-state responsibility for health and social welfare concerns about children.

1922 The Young Workers International and the International Union of Socialist Youth Organizations proclaim the Declaration of the Rights of the Adolescent, a set of guidelines for the employment of youth and adolescents, with specific restrictions proposed for the workday, prohibitions on work during preschool and compulsory school age, compulsory medical examinations for young persons prior to employment, and reform of the apprenticeship system.

The International Council of Women issues its Children's Charter, a declaration based on initial resolutions by Women's Councils in Italy and the United States calling for the development of a charter embodying minimum rights of children in all countries. The Children's Charter includes seven sections: prenatal care, care of mothers and children up to school age, children of school age, children in employment, delinquent children, children's state departments, and international conferences.

1923 The American Child Health Association is established.

1923–1924 The Declaration of Geneva is presented by representatives of the Save the Children International Union to a representative of the government of the canton of Geneva, Switzerland. The result of two years of work under the leadership of Eglantyne Jebb and colleagues in the Save the Children International Union, this five-part Declaration of the Rights of the Child is the forerunner of other major international statements on children's rights in the twentieth century. Soon after its proclamation in Switzerland, the declaration is discussed and adopted by the Assembly of the League of Nations, marking the first time that a major international organization endorsed fundamental rights for every child.

1929 The U.S. Congress fails to renew the Sheppard-Towner Act, primarily because of lobbying by the American Medical Association.

1930 Delegates to the White House Conference on Child Health and Protection prepare the Children's Charter, a set of 19 principles that summarized the recommendations of the conference deliberations and reports. Under the guidance of President Herbert Hoover, the Children's Charter contained key principles in the areas of education, child labor, vocational training, recreation, family welfare, health, growth and development, disabled children, and related areas, including the Bill of Rights for the Handicapped Child.

1931 The Wickersham Commission publishes the first national study on the condition of juvenile delinquents who violate federal laws.

1933 U.S. First Lady Eleanor Roosevelt continues her lobbying for child labor laws.

The New Deal of Franklin Delano Roosevelt includes legislation to employ unmarried men as young as age 17 in the Civilian Conservation Corps, while the National Recovery Act, a voluntary law, includes a prohibition on labor by children under the age of 16.

1935 The Social Security Act establishes the Aid to Families with Dependent Children program, and incorporates U.S. Children's Bureau recommendations on maternal and child health, entitlements for handicapped children, and child welfare services, establishing the foundation of contemporary federal welfare programs for children.

Franklin D. Roosevelt creates the National Youth Administration, which develops specific programs for youth in the United States.

1936 The Walsh-Healy Act is signed into law, becoming the first legally binding federal legislation to prevent the use of child labor in companies with federal contracts.

1938 The Fair Labor Standards Act is signed into law by President Franklin D. Roosevelt; it prohibits the interstate shipment of goods made in firms that employ children under the age of 16, or children under the age of 18 in hazardous occupations.

Federal law establishes that persons under the age of 18 who commit federal crimes are to be tried as juveniles.

Mary McLeod Bethune reports to the National Youth Administration about the continuing problems plaguing African-American youth.

1940 The White House Conference on Children and Youth in a Democracy emphasizes prevention of juvenile crime.

The U.S. Supreme Court rules that First Amendment rights are not violated by state laws requiring children to salute the flag in the case of *Minersville School District v. Gobitis.*

1941 The U.S. Supreme Court upholds the provisions of the Fair Labor Standards Act concerning child labor prohibitions in the case of *United States v. Darby.*

1942 Delegates from 21 Western Hemisphere countries prepare the Declaration of Opportunities for Children as part of the Eighth Pan American Child Congress, held in Washington, D.C., in April and May. The declaration focuses on three major issues: guaranteeing that the needs of children would be met, in peacetime and wartime; guidelines for planning child welfare after the end of World War II; and developing avenues for cooperation in the Western Hemisphere to address the pressing needs of children and their overall welfare.

1943 The U.S. Supreme Court reverses its position as stated in the ruling on *Minersville School District v. Gobitis* (1940), asserting in *West Virginia Board of Education v. Barnette* that First Amendment rights are indeed violated by state laws requiring children to salute the flag in the public schools.

Child labor laws are relaxed to allow teenagers to work in wartime factories; by 1944, 2.9 million are employed.

1944 In *Prince v. Massachusetts*, the U.S. Supreme Court rules that the states have the right to intervene on behalf of the well-being of a youth.

1945 The United Nations is founded and holds its first meetings in San Francisco, California.

1946 The United Nations Children's Fund (UNICEF) is established with a mandate to provide relief to children suffering in the aftermath of World War II.

The U.S. Congress passes and President Harry Truman signs into law the provisions of the National School Lunch Act, which provides for federal subsidies to provide reduced-cost lunches to children in public schools.

1946–1959 The International Union for Child Welfare initiates the process of seeking adoption by the United Nations of a slightly amended version of the 1924

1946–1959 *cont.*	Declaration of Geneva. Between 1946 and 1958, lobbying and deliberation continue within the Economic and Social Council of the United Nations as well as the UN Commission on Human Rights. Negotiations continue until October 1959, when debate on the "Concept—Declaration on the Rights of the Child" is closed.
1948	The United Nations General Assembly unanimously approves the Universal Declaration of Human Rights.
1949	World diplomats gathered in Geneva, Switzerland, approve the Convention for the Protection of Civilian Persons in Time of War, including two additional protocols specifically addressing the needs of children in time of war.
1950	Participants in the Mid-Century Conference on Children and Youth prepare the Pledge to Children, a 19-paragraph set of commitments by adults to children. Continuing the tradition of earlier U.S. public declarations about child welfare, the Pledge to Children contains commitments by adults to children in the areas of promoting education, strengthening family life, safeguarding civil equality and nondiscrimination, improving workplace conditions, enhancing democratic citizenship and institutions, and advocating the development of the child's individual talents and potential.
1951	The government of Japan proclaims the Children's Charter on 5 May 1951. Three general principles are included: respect for the child as a human being, due regard for the child as a member of society, and the necessity of providing a good environment for the child's upbringing. Created as a document complementing the new Japanese constitution of the post–World War II era, the Children's Charter contains 12 sections emphasizing government's responsibility to children and the safeguarding of their rights. It provides greater autonomy for the child's individual

decision making than has been traditional in Japanese culture, yet balances the individual's prerogatives with sustaining the historic cultural Japanese imperative of group cohesion and solidarity.

1954 In a unanimous ruling, the U.S. Supreme Court overturns the doctrine of "separate but equal" in the landmark decision *Brown v. Board of Education of Topeka, Kansas,* which establishes the constitutional justification for the abolition of segregated public education in the United States.

1955 In the *Brown II* decision, the U.S. Supreme Court establishes guidelines for the desegregation of public schooling, indicating that "appropriate relief" should be provided with "all deliberate speed."

1957 President Dwight Eisenhower orders federal troops to assist with the desegregation of public schools in Little Rock, Arkansas.

1959 The General Assembly of the United Nations unanimously adopts the Declaration on the Rights of the Child. Expanded beyond the scope of the 1924 Declaration of Geneva, the UN declaration places children's rights within the context of fundamental universal human rights, beginning with the preamble and continuing with ten principles. The preamble establishes the historical foundations of the UN declaration and sets forth the need to provide for children in the best manner possible.

1961 C. Henry Kempe introduces and describes the concept of the battered child syndrome at a conference of the American Academy of Pediatrics.

1964 The U.S. Congress passes and President Lyndon Johnson signs into law the Civil Rights Act of 1964. Title IV of this act reinforces the federal government's commitment to school desegregation, permitting the U.S. attorney general to file lawsuits to help desegregate public schools and colleges.

1965 The U.S. Congress passes and President Lyndon Johnson signs into law the most comprehensive public education assistance act in the history of the United States: the Elementary and Secondary Education Act of 1965.

The U.S. Congress passes and President Lyndon Johnson signs into law the Economic Opportunity Amendments of 1965, which establish many federal antipoverty programs. Included in this legislation is the Head Start program to assist preschool children from deprived families in making an effective transition to schooling at the kindergarten or first-grade levels.

1966 The U.S. Congress passes and President Lyndon Johnson signs into law the Child Nutrition Act, which expands the federal food aid program for children to include a school breakfast program.

1967 In the case of *In Re Gault*, the U.S. Supreme Court rules that minors are entitled to the civil and political rights embodied in the U.S. Constitution.

1968 The U.S. Supreme Court rules in the case of *Levy v. Louisiana* that illegitimate children have the right to equal protection of the laws.

1969 The U.S. Supreme Court rules in the case of *Tinker v. Des Moines Independent School District* that guarantees of First Amendment rights for students should be maintained in the public schools.

1970s Influenced by the writings of A. S. Neill, John Holt, and David Gottlieb, the children's liberation movement gains momentum and influences both theory and practice in educational settings nationwide.

1970 The White House Conference on Children issues a six-point declaration entitled the Children's Bill of Rights. Emerging from the work of approximately

3,700 delegates at the weeklong conference, this Bill of Rights represents the key points from the deliberations of Forum 22, which identifies six specific rights of children as "central to a child's well-being," including the following: the right to growth and development, the right to be born healthy and wanted through childhood, the right to nurturing by affectionate parents, the right to make choices in the process of maturation and development and have a meaningful voice in the community, the right to be educated to one's full potential, and the right to have societal mechanisms to enforce these rights.

The National Center for Youth Law is founded in San Francisco, California.

1971 In April, the White House Conference on Youth issues a Declaration on the Rights of Youth, focusing on adolescents age 14–24. The conference declaration recognizes the need to reinterpret the rights of the U.S. Declaration of Independence and the U.S. Constitution, and includes four additional rights statements specifically dealing with youth: the right to adequate food, clothing, and a decent home; the right of the individual to do his/her thing, so long as it does not interfere with another's rights; the right to preserve and cultivate ethnic and cultural heritages; and the right to do whatever is necessary to preserve these rights. The document also includes nine grievances of youth, ranging from denial of equal opportunity to development of a climate of fear among societal groups that impedes cooperation toward common goals.

1972 The U.S. Supreme Court rules in *Wisconsin v. Yoder* that Amish parents can restrict their children's access to public education when faced with compulsory education laws in order to facilitate the religious development of their children.

1973 The Children's Defense Fund is founded in Washington, D.C.

1973 *cont.* The International Labour Organization calls on member states to ratify and implement the provisions of the Minimum Age Convention, ILO Convention 138, which requires all ratifying countries to specify a minimum age for admission to employment or work and to raise that minimum age to a level consistent "with the fullest physical and mental development of young persons."

The federal Rehabilitation Act of 1973 contains entitlements for handicapped children.

1974 John Holt publishes *Escape from Childhood,* which articulates the perspective of child liberation.

The Federal Child Abuse Prevention Treatment Act is passed by the U.S. Congress and signed into law by President Gerald Ford, requiring that states appoint guardians to represent children in all civil judicial proceedings involving abuse and neglect. It also establishes the National Center on Child Abuse and Neglect and programs for abused children.

The passage and signing into law by President Gerald Ford of the Family Educational Rights and Privacy Act, part of the reauthorization of many federal educational programs by the U.S. Congress, establishes parents' access to student records. Subsequent amendments clarify the scope of privacy retained by students and educational institutions.

The U.S. Congress passes and President Gerald Ford signs into law the Juvenile Justice and Delinquency Act, which authorizes the Law Enforcement Assistance Administration to administer juvenile delinquency programs and appropriates $10.5 million to address the problems of runaway youth. It also establishes basic procedural rights for juveniles under federal jurisdiction, including notification of rights of the accused, the right to a speedy trial, and safeguards on the disclosure of juvenile records.

1975 The U.S. National Association of Social Workers (NASW) issues the Children and Youth Bill of Rights, which begins with a background section stating "It is essential that public social policy recognize children as individuals with rights, including the right to be part of family." The 12 rights statements that follow emphasize the significant role government must play to protect children, provide for their basic needs, and advocate their legal rights.

The Education for All Handicapped Children Act requires "free" and "appropriate" public education for disabled children that must be comparable to educational opportunities offered other children in the public schools.

Legislation is passed by the U.S. Congress and signed into law by President Gerald Ford establishing specific requirements for education of handicapped children, including the use of individualized educational programs, along with strengthening due-process protections for the rights of handicapped children.

1976 The first National Conference on Child Abuse and Neglect is held in Atlanta, Georgia.

1978 The Child Abuse Prevention and Adoption Reform Act extends abuse and treatment programs while adding new emphases on prevention and treatment of child sexual abuse.

1978–1989 After Poland calls for a UN treaty to mark the International Year of the Child (1979), deliberations commence in 1978 within the Commission on Human Rights to frame a UN Convention on the Rights of the Child. The Open-Ended Working Group on the Draft Convention on the Rights of the Child is established in 1979 and works for ten years, consulting with interested member states of the UN, intergovernmental agencies such as the International Labour Organization, UNICEF, and the UN High Commissioner for Refugees, along with nongovernmental

1978–1989 *cont.* organizations such as Defence for Children International. In March 1989, the draft convention is sent to the Committee on Human Rights of the UN Economic and Social Council, which forwards it to the United Nations General Assembly in the fall of 1989.

1979 The International Association of School Psychologists adopts the Declaration of the Psychological Rights of the Child, which contains three areas, each with three specific rights statements. Area 1 deals with love and freedom from fear. Area 2 emphasizes rights to personal identity and expression, to opportunities for spiritual and moral development, and to have satisfying interpersonal relationships and group memberships. Area 3 includes the rights to education; full opportunity for play, recreation, and fantasy; and optimum physical and psychological development.

The United Nations declares 1979 the International Year of the Child.

The United Nations Open-Ended Working Group on the Draft Convention on the Rights of the Child is formed in Geneva.

Defense for Children International is established in Geneva, Switzerland.

1980 UNICEF issues the first of its annual *State of the World's Children* reports, providing a summary of the worldwide condition of children.

The Adoption Assistance and Federal Welfare Act is signed into law by President Jimmy Carter, requiring that every child have a "case plan" that aims toward permanent placement, a six-month review of each case, and deadlines for permanent placement.

1981 Norway appoints the world's first Commissioner for Children (Children's Ombudsman), Malfrid Grude Flekkoy.

1982 In the case of *Plyler v. Doe,* the U.S. Supreme Court establishes that public education should be accessible to children of illegal aliens.

1983 The Thirteenth World Congress of the International Confederation of Free Trade Unions (ICFTU) adopts the Youth Charter. Primarily concerned with labor, employment, and education rights, the Youth Charter also addresses concerns regarding marriage and maternity, establishes age 18 as the point at which young people should be considered adults, and advocates the ongoing development of free trade unions and social justice worldwide.

The Ad Hoc NGO Working Group on the UN Draft Convention on the Rights of the Child is formed with Defense for Children International as the secretariat, signaling a unique cooperation between drafters and NGO consultants.

1984 The Child Abuse Amendment of 1984 establishes responsibility for disabled infants and guidelines for health care providers.

The Office of Child and Family Service Advocacy is founded in Ontario, Canada.

The British section of Amnesty International asks for rules for the treatment of children deprived of their liberty.

1985 Children's Law Shops are founded in Amsterdam, the Netherlands.

The United Nations publishes the Standard Minimum Rules for the Administration of Juvenile Justice ("Beijing Rules").

1986 The United Nations General Assembly unanimously adopts the UN Declaration Relating to Foster Placement and Adoption. The declaration contains detailed guidelines in four sections: a preamble

1986 *cont.* containing references to preceding UN initiatives concerning the welfare of children, Section A (General Family and Child Welfare), Section B (Foster Placement), and Section C (Adoption).

In the case of *State of New Jersey v. T.L.O.,* the U.S. Supreme Court rules that guidelines restricting unreasonable searches and seizures by school officials of students in the public schools can be modified to adhere to a less restrictive "reasonable suspicion" standard.

1987 The Manifesto of the Children's Legal Centre of London is published, emphasizing the empowerment of children.

The Charter on the Rights of the Arab Child is adopted by the League of Arab States, detailing Islamic principles for children's rights.

1988 The U.S. Supreme Court, in the case of *Hazelwood School District et al. v. Cathy Kuhlmeier et al.,* rules that public school officials have the authority to restrict the content of school publications when the publications are curriculum-related and school-sponsored.

In the case of *Thompson v. Oklahoma,* the U.S. Supreme Court rules that executions of offenders age 15 and younger at the time of their crimes are unconstitutional.

1989 In the case of *Stanford v. Kentucky,* the U.S. Supreme Court rules that the Eighth Amendment prohibitions against cruel and unusual punishments do not prohibit the death penalty for crimes committed at the ages of 16 or 17.

The U.S. Supreme Court rules in the case of *Bethel v. Fraser* that public school officials have the authority to restrict student speech.

The UN Convention on the Rights of the Child is adopted by the United Nations General Assembly on 20 November, now recognized as International Children's Rights Day.

1990 The American Civil Liberties Union Children's Rights Project initiates litigation on behalf of child victims of social welfare services.

The UN Convention on the Rights of the Child is open for signature and ratification. Nepal is the first member state to ratify.

The Organization of African Unity adopts the Charter on the Rights and Welfare of the African Child.

The UN Convention on the Rights of the Child enters into force, marking the shortest time between signature and ratification for any UN treaty except the UN Charter, and the first Committee on the Rights of the Child is chosen.

The first World Summit for Children is held at UNICEF headquarters in New York City. The World Declaration on the Survival, Protection, and Development of Children is issued based on the proceedings of the conference.

The world community begins to hear about the substandard condition of children in Romanian orphanages.

The United Nations' Rules for the Protection of Juveniles Deprived of Their Liberty extends the Beijing Rules standards to children held in government or other institutions.

The General Assembly adopts the United Nations Rules for the Protection of Juveniles Deprived of Their Liberty. In its first fundamental principle, the rules state that the "juvenile justice system should uphold the rights and safety and promote the physical and mental well-being of juveniles. Imprisonment should be used as a last resort."

1991 Vititt Muntarbhorn of Thailand is chosen Special Rapporteur on Children by the UN Human Rights Commission, and subsequently publishes two comprehensive reports.

The first meeting of the Committee on the Rights of the Child takes place at the UN Human Rights Center in Geneva, Switzerland.

The U.S. National Commission on Children publishes its final report, *Beyond Rhetoric: A New American Agenda for Children and Families,* calling for substantial federal efforts to reduce the number of children in poverty, strengthen families, improve the health care of all children, and establish a stronger commitment to improving educational performance at all levels of schooling.

1992 The 13 National Coordinating Bodies To Monitor the Implementation of the Convention of the Rights of the Child in Latin America meet in Lima, Peru, and issue the Declaration of Lima, a statement that assesses the progress and problems faced by Latin American societies in implementing the convention.

1993 The Committee on the Rights of the Child examines the first country reports of States Parties to the CRC.

UNESCO revises its guidelines on teaching human rights, including children's rights.

The Committee on the Rights of the Child meets in Latin America under the auspices of UNICEF to hear local NGOs describe children's conditions on that continent.

The Hague Convention on Intercountry Adoption is completed, containing detailed rules for qualification when placing children outside their native countries and strict follow-up procedures.

1994 The Narino Accord is published by ministers and representatives of Latin American and Caribbean governments attending the Second Meeting on Children and Social Policy in the Americas, held in Santa Fe de Bogotá, Colombia. The Narino Accord identifies mid-decade goals to improve the lives of children in the region consistent with those stated at the World Summit for Children in 1990, as well as follow-up mechanisms to assist in their achievement.

Hillary Rodham Clinton, wife of President William Jefferson Clinton, announces at the memorial service for UNICEF Executive Director James Grant that the United States intends to sign the Convention on the Rights of the Child.

1995 U.S. A mbassador to the United Nations Madeline Albright signs the UN Convention on the Rights of the Child on behalf of the United States.

The U.S. Supreme Court rules in *Vernonia School District v. Acton* that random drug tests of student athletes are constitutional.

1996 On June 1, over 200,000 people rally under the leadership of the Children's Defense Fund in Washington, D.C., on behalf of child advocacy, protesting efforts in the U.S. Congress to reduce federal support for children's programs in health, education, and human services.

3 Biographical Sketches

The individuals chosen for this chapter have been identified as major figures in the historical and contemporary development of children's rights theory and practice. Their activities have contributed to increased awareness and advocacy of children's rights in many contexts: as theorists of children's rights (Janusz Korczak and Ellen Key), participants in the development and implementation of international children's rights instruments and law (Thomas Hammarberg and the Committee on the Rights of the Child), grass-roots activists (Bruce Harris of Casa Alianza and Iqbal Masih), or as social reformers and human services practitioners advocating the rights of children to diverse audiences (Eglantyne Jebb, Marian Wright Edelman, and Grace Abbott). In one case (Janusz Korczak), the theorist became a martyr and died for his principles. In many cases, the work of the individuals included in this chapter ranges across varied dimensions of children's rights, demonstrating that rigid boundaries between theory and practice often disappear in the daily struggle on behalf of children worldwide.

Grace Abbott (1878–1939)

Grace Abbott was born in 1878 in Grand Island, Nebraska. She received her undergraduate degree from Grand Island College and her master's degree in political science from the University of Chicago in 1909. In 1908 Abbott joined the team of social reformers at Hull House in Chicago, where she lived while directing the Immigrants' Protective League. Although her work on behalf of immigrants included the welfare of children, her critical work for them occurred during her tenure as chief of the federal Children's Bureau from 1921 to 1934. Under her direction, the Children's Bureau implemented federal child labor regulations, administered the Sheppard-Towner Act—the first federal maternal and infant health legislation—and conducted wide-ranging studies on child working conditions, the impact of unemployment on children, child delinquency, child malnutrition, and child neglect. Abbott also worked internationally on behalf of child welfare, representing the United States on the League of Nations' Advisory Committee on Traffic in Women and Children, and as the first U.S. delegate to the International Labor Organization, successfully advocating a recommendation raising the minimum age for employment to 15 years. From 1934 to 1939, she taught at the University of Chicago's School of Social Service Administration and authored major books about the history of child welfare and public welfare services. Abbott died of anemia at the age of 60 in 1939.

Melba Patillo Beals (1942–)

Melba Patillo was 15 years old when she and eight other African-American children integrated the public schools in Little Rock, Arkansas. Known in history books as "the Little Rock Nine," six young women and three young men, escorted by U. S. Army paratroopers and the nationalized Arkansas National Guard, braved mobs of segregationists to attend Central High School in 1957. Of that group, the senior Ernest Green was the first African-American to graduate, doing so in the spring of 1958. The other members of the Little Rock Nine were Minniejean Brown, Elizabeth Eckford, Thelma Mothershed, Gloria Ray, Terrance Roberts, Jefferson Thomas, and Carlotta Walls, who was the only other of the students to return to Central High School and graduate after all Little Rock schools were closed by Governor Orville Faubus during the 1958–1959 academic year.

Melba Patillo, whose book *Warriors Don't Cry* painfully traces the painful process of integrating Central High and its effects on her life, embodied the strength of will and character to endure her junior year against the taunts and threats of segregationists. Her book also describes the legal support provided by the National Association for the Advancement of Colored People (NAACP) during the struggle. When Governor Faubus closed the Little Rock schools to forestall further integration, Patillo accepted an invitation through the NAACP to live with a Quaker family in Santa Rosa, California, in order to complete her high school education. There, although at first frightened to find the Quaker McCabe family was white, she was greeted with love and encouraged to complete her high school education and then to enroll at San Francisco State University, from which she received a bachelor's degree in 1962. Currently residing in the San Francisco Bay area, Melba Patillo Beals is a practicing journalist and writer whose courageous work as a pioneer of school integration makes her a pioneer of children's rights.

T. Berry Brazelton (1918–)

Considered the most influential pediatrician of the post-1960 era, T. Berry Brazelton has advocated the rights of children and families for over 30 years. Educated at Princeton University and Columbia, from which he received his medical degree in 1943, Brazelton developed early an interest in child psychiatry, which he applied in his pediatric practice in Cambridge, Massachusetts, as well as in his work as an instructor at the Harvard Medical School.

Based upon his ongoing research with infants in the Boston area, Brazelton developed the Neonatal Behavioral Assessment Scale. First published in 1973, later revised in 1984, this diagnostic test has been praised and implemented worldwide as a clinical and research tool to help physicians and parents understand and relate to newborns. In 1972, Brazelton and his colleague Edward Tronick established the Child Development Unit at Children's Hospital Medical Center in Boston. This groundbreaking facility provides medical students and child-care professionals, along with physicians, opportunities to conduct research on early child development and to gain experience in clinical work with children and parents.

Since 1969, Brazelton has published over two dozen books, including *Infants and Mothers: Individual Differences in Development*, which has sold more than 1 million copies and been translated into 18 languages. In his books, Brazelton has emphasized the need to support parents and families, particularly given the stress modern families face in meeting the complex demands of the workplace and changing role definitions, notably of females of all ages.

By the late 1980s, Brazelton had become critical of the unwillingness of the federal government to institute policies supporting families and children, such as widespread quality day care and services designed to help the growing number of children in poverty. He formed Parent Action in 1988, a grass-roots lobby designed to influence government policy favorably in areas of great concern to families: day care, education, and health insurance, among others.

Serving on the National Commission for Children, Brazelton toured the United States in the early 1990s, garnering support for national family leave legislation. Although vetoed by President George Bush, Brazelton saw this legislation reintroduced, passed by Congress, and signed into law by President William Clinton in February 1993. Believing that much more must be done to address the problems of working families trying to raise children, Brazelton asserts that the United States is unfortunately "one of the least child-oriented societies in the world."

Recipient of numerous awards and honors, Brazelton holds the post of professor emeritus at the Harvard Medical School, where in 1990 the T. Berry Brazelton chair in child development was established, the first academic post emphasizing normal development to be created at any medical school.

Nigel Cantwell (1946–)

Nigel Cantwell's realization that there was no effective international organization that "dealt with child maltreatment" led to the 5 July 1979 founding of Defense for Children International (DCI), the first international nongovernmental organization (NGO) to advocate specifically for children who are jailed, tortured, or denied proper care after incarceration.

Nigel Cantwell was born in Epsom, a town south of London, in 1946. He won a place at Cambridge University and later took a postgraduate degree in applied society (social work) at Nottingham University, from which he graduated in 1969. He worked in

Newcastle for one year as a probation officer, a social worker charged with the aftercare of juvenile offenders, before moving to Geneva, Switzerland, to marry and raise a family. He was working for the International Union for Child Welfare in Geneva when he realized that its policy of "active neutrality" was not enough to improve the treatment of children by governments, and therefore founded DCI.

The UN General Assembly declared 1979 the "International Year of the Child," and the Human Rights Commission established the open-ended working group whose task was to formulate children's rights into international human rights law (*see* chapter 1). Nigel Cantwell quickly became a valued NGO consultant at the drafting, in part because of his hands-on experience as a social worker. In 1983, DCI was chosen by other NGOs to coordinate their activities in an attempt to speed up the drafting process and keep distant NGOs in touch with the treaty's progress. Cantwell was able to elicit cooperation from more than 25 organizations, coordinating activities so that relevant interventions would be made by one, possibly two, NGO representatives during discussion of an article. Drafters have said more than once that it was Nigel Cantwell's sincerity and eloquence at working-group sessions that pushed the convention toward stronger rights for children.

In addition to its work on the CRC, DCI under Cantwell's direction arranged for a children's rights advocate to be present in an Iraqi camp for Iranian boy prisoners of war (1985–1986), exposed and negotiated an end to international trafficking and sale of children in Romania and Albania, and worked on the Hague Convention on Inter-Country Adoption. He is currently under contract with UNICEF to develop a new area of its work, juvenile justice.

Robert Coles (1929–)

Robert Coles was born on 12 October 1929 in Boston and attended Harvard University, where he received his bachelor's degree in 1950. He received his M.D. degree from Columbia University in 1954, completing his internship at the University of Chicago clinics in 1955 and later serving a residency in psychiatry between 1955 and 1958. Following his service as a psychiatrist in the U.S. Air Force, Coles married Jane Hallowell and moved to Georgia, where his interest in the lives of children was nurtured during the emerging civil rights movement. Coles initiated studies of young

African-American children who were experiencing the trauma of the civil rights conflicts in the South and published his first major work, *Children of Crisis*, volume 1, in 1967. As the first installment in a massive five-volume work, Coles's study illuminated the lives of young children and the discrimination and hardships they encountered in a hostile environment. Continuing the series with volumes on other groups of children, ranging from migrant workers to Eskimos to the children of wealthy parents, Coles developed detailed portraits of the emotional lives of children that shed light on their fears, aspirations, and feelings toward others.

Coles continued his work in child psychiatry with books on the political life of children and the moral life of children, drawing upon interviews from a global cross section of societies. In his writing and teaching, Coles draws heavily upon the humanities to inform his understanding of human behavior, following the example of his mentor, poet and physician William Carlos Williams. Coles continues to write prolifically, and his studies in child psychology and the literary imagination are linked by his commitment to social justice and the ongoing examination of moral and spiritual values in American society.

Committee on the Rights of the Child

Elected every four years by the UN Economic and Social Council, the members of the Committee on the Rights of the Child come from the five major United Nations areas and have similar records of achievement working for children's rights. In addition to Thomas Hammarberg and Marta Santos Pais, original drafters of the Convention on the Rights of the Child, the current committee comsists of chairperson Hoda Badran (Egypt), Akila Belembaogo (Burkina Faso), Flora Corpuz-Eufemio (Philippines), Judith Karp (Israel), Youri Kolosov (Russia), Sandra Mason (Barbados), Swithun Mombeshora (Zimbabwe), and Marilia Sardenberg (Brazil).

Marian Wright Edelman (1939–)

Marian Wright Edelman, founder of the Washington-based Children's Defense Fund, is the leading African-American advocate for children's rights in the United States. Her approach of working through the U.S. legal and political systems has expanded existing entitlements to millions of children and kept the issue of racial and child poverty on the top burner of national administrations for two decades.

Marian Wright was born in the small town of Bennettsville, South Carolina, to Baptist minister Arthur Jerome Wright and Maggie Leola Bowen Wright. She graduated from Spelman College in Atlanta in 1960, after a junior year abroad, and then from Yale Law School in 1963. Crediting her father's inspiration and her own experience fighting injustices and unequal treatment of Negroes by whites, she chose an activist's career after her education was completed.

Her personal involvement with the second civil rights movement in the United States began when she helped to organize a sit-in in Atlanta during her senior year at Spelman. An internship with the NAACP Legal Defense and Educational Fund resulted in her going to Charlotte, North Carolina, where she opened a legal office for the organization and passed her bar examination. She then traveled to Jackson, Mississippi, to work with the SNCC Mississippi Summer Project in 1964, where she reexperienced the violence that had accompanied a previous trip to the state.

In 1965, having become convinced that community activism brought positive change, she founded the Child Development Group of Mississippi, an organization that managed to win Head Start entitlements for 12,000 poor children in its first year. After marrying Peter Edelman, a member of Senator Robert Kennedy's staff and now a law professor, she founded two projects to research and publicize the plight of poor and minority children before creating the Children's Defense Fund (CDF) in 1973. Under her directorship, the CDF has led the struggle for federally funded child care (Act for Better Child Care, 1988), achieved the expansion of existing federal entitlements under the Head Start and Job Partnership Training Act, advocated raising the minimum age at which children could work, and campaigned for the eradication of poverty in America. Her efforts helped bring the extension of Medicare health insurance to millions of children. The annual reports of the Children's Defense Fund provide statistics and other data that confront Americans with the increasing gap between rich and poor children in the 1980s and 1990s.

Marian Wright Edelman continued her activism by writing three notable books along with hundreds of articles on children's rights. Her first book, *Black and White Children in America* (1983), made teenage pregnancy a focus of U.S. policy. In 1987, she wrote *Families in Peril,* which exposed the effects of federal budget cuts on children, and in 1992 she published the best-selling *Measure of Our Success: A Letter to My Children and Yours,* which she wrote as a "spiritual and family dowry" for her three sons, and which highlights her belief in family and community.[1]

Malfrid Grude Flekkoy (1936–)

Norway's first commissioner (ombudsman) for children, Malfrid Grude Flekkoy is a psychologist of note in her country and the world. Born in Oslo in 1936, Malfrid Grude Skard became bilingual when she was evacuated to the United States due to the German occupation of Norway (1940–1945). Specializing in clinical child psychology, she graduated from the University of Oslo in 1967 and received her doctorate in education. Her clinical training was done in Oslo at the Nic Waals Institute for Child and Adolescent Psychiatry from 1969 to 1972; she returned to the Institute as chief psychologist in 1991.

Flekkoy was always interested in children and young people; she began her career teaching preschoolers and remained active as a leader in the Girl Scouts until she graduated from the University of Oslo. She married and had three children who were born during and after her university career. She returned to the United States to practice at the Eastern Pennsylvania Psychiatric Institute in Philadelphia between 1972 and 1983. She has also worked with mentally disabled children and youth. Author of numerous publications on child psychology, she began her career in what she later saw to be the developmental psychology division of children's rights in the late 1960s. Her book, *Your Child Is Growing,* written with her mother, Ase Grude Skard, and Phyllis M. Pickard of the World Organization for Early Childhood Development (OMEP), became the primer for developing countries and convinced UNESCO to incorporate early childhood education into its work. Flekkoy later became acting secretary-general of OMEP between 1964 and 1969. In subsequent years, she went on to work with other professional organizations specializing in child and adolescent psychology.

Flekkoy's role as Commissioner for Children in Norway in 1981 turned into a personal campaign to spread the idea of an ombudsman's office. Her intent is to ensure that children receive their rights and do not slip between the cracks of national legal and social service systems. She notes two achievements during her term in office: first, that as she left office in 1989, public opinion in Norway was so strong that the office was continued in spite of attempts to abolish it, and second, a Norwegian law that mandates that every municipality must consider children's needs when zoning or building is undertaken. She also lobbied for Norway's law against corporal punishment, which she says raises awareness about the treatment of children since Norwegian law already provides penal sanctions for maltreatment. As the world's first ombudsman for children, Flekkoy is the world's model for the office, for which she later defined international standards as a senior fellow at the UNICEF International Child Development Center in Florence, Italy (1989–1991). Flekkoy continues to work with and on behalf of children at the Nic Waals Institute and as a visiting professor in Europe and the United States, where she plans to work on the issue of a child's "evolving capacities" (Article 5 of the Convention on the Rights of the Child) from the perspective of developmental psychology.

James P. Grant (1922–1995)

James P. Grant became the third executive director of the United Nations Children's Fund (UNICEF) in 1980 and led the organization through an important period in its history. He is well known for his leadership of the UNICEF campaign called "Child Survival and Development Revolution" and perhaps best known for organizing the World Summit for Children after the passage of the Convention on the Rights of the Child. James Grant died of cancer in 1995, and it was at his memorial service that Hillary Clinton announced that the United States would sign the Convention on the Rights of the Child.

UNICEF estimates that the Child Survival and Development Revolution, Grant's campaign that began in the early 1980s, has saved 25 million children's lives. Carried on throughout the developing world and in conjunction with other UN agencies such as the World Health Organization, the program concentrated on "simple, low-cost and practical methods" for improving child survival and health, such as oral rehydration using a small, inexpensive packet of essential salts to overcome the effects of diarrhea. The program also emphasized breast-feeding and immunizing 80 percent of the world's children against six of the main child-killer diseases. UNICEF is currently joining UNESCO and the United Nations Population Fund in expanding basic education opportunities for out-of-school children and continues to publish *The State of the World's Children*, begun under Grant's tenure in 1980.

Grant was born in Beijing, China, in 1922, where his father was a pioneer in the field of public health. He graduated from the University of California, Berkeley, in 1943 and received a doctorate in jurisprudence from Harvard University in 1951. He spent the early years of his career at the U.S. State Department, working first as a legal officer. In the 1960s he joined the U.S. Agency for International Development (US AID), for which he headed various programs in Southeast and Southwest Asia, rising to assistant administrator of the agency in 1967. Grant then founded the Overseas Development Council in 1969, and remained there as president and chief executive officer until he was nominated by the United States to head UNICEF.

During Grant's tenure, UNICEF achieved another high point: UNICEF decided to support the drafting of the Convention on the Rights of the Child and Grant insisted upon a major international summit to highlight its significance. The World Summit for Children (1990) focused nations on the importance of the full range of rights given in the CRC and undoubtedly spurred nations to sign and ratify the convention. UNICEF's subsequent Plan of Action to implement the Declaration of the World Summit for Children (1990) outlined goals for realizing children's rights for the rest of the decade. Grant received many awards from countries around the world for his work at UNICEF.

Thomas Hammarberg (1942–)

Thomas Hammarberg has been committed to helping children throughout his life. He claims that "all people have the ability to do good things," but as secretary-general of Rädda Barnen (the Save the Children affiliate in Sweden), drafter of the Convention on the Rights of the Child, and now a founding member of the Committee on the Rights of the Child, Hammarberg has set an uncompromising standard for children's advocacy.

Hammarberg was born in Ornskolsvik, Sweden, in 1942. He worked as a foreign correspondent and columnist for Swedish newspapers after his graduation from the Stockholm School of Economics in 1973. In 1980 he was chosen secretary-general of Amnesty International and led the world's most prominent human rights NGO until 1986, when he became secretary-general of Rädda Barnen. During his years at Amnesty International, he fought for the lives of political prisoners and was personally responsible in at least one instance for achieving a pardon for a condemned member of an overthrown African government. His belief is that if a person has achieved the position in life where it is possible to help others, it is his or her obligation to use that power to bring about human rights.

As head of Rädda Barnen, Hammarberg helped establish an international office for the Save the Children organizations in Geneva and appointed Simone Ek, a highly effective children's advocate from Rädda Barnen, to assist in the drafting of the CRC. Rädda Barnen made numerous contributions to strengthening the rights in the CRC, not the least of which was Hammarberg's own attendance at the drafting, during which he began a crusade to raise the age of children who could be recruited into a nation's military from 15 years of age, as it is in the CRC, to an age of 18. The protocol that is now in its second year of drafting owes much to his efforts in concert with those of other NGOs, notably the Quaker United Nations Office. A stern questioner of nations reporting to the Committee on the Rights of the Child, he is also noted for his "quiet diplomacy" work to alleviate the harshness of famine and war on its youngest victims. His years at Rädda Barnen resulted in expanded international activities for the organization as well as stronger Swedish national law regarding children.

Hammarberg has written numerous articles on human and children's rights and is now working on a book on children's rights.

Bruce Harris (1955–)

Currently working as executive director of Latin American Programs for Covenant House, a major privately funded child care agency, Bruce Harris has been a children's rights activist in Latin America since 1985. From 1985 to 1989, he was the Bolivian field office director for the Save the Children Foundation, initiating rural community development programs and antipoverty programs for slum children in La Paz. For his work Harris was awarded the "Gran Orden Boliviano de la Educación," the second-highest civilian award given by Bolivia. Since assuming his post with Covenant House, Harris has worked to protect and guarantee the rights of street children in four Latin American countries, most notably Guatemala. His work to safeguard street children from repression, torture, and murder by government security forces and death squads earned him and Covenant House worldwide acclaim, along with numerous death threats from those opposed to his work. Awarded the Cardinal Carter Award for Human Rights in Toronto, Canada, in 1992 for his work on behalf of Guatemalan street children, Harris continues his children's rights advocacy from the Covenant House Latin America headquarters (Casa Alianza) in San José , Costa Rica. In addition to safeguarding the rights of street children, he has also participated in production of television documentaries on illegal trafficking of children and human body parts, many of which were extracted from kidnapped or "disappeared" children in Latin America and other world regions.

Asma Jahangir (1952–)

Like many advocates around the world, Asma Jahangir believes that human rights, women's rights, and children's rights are interconnected. Born into a political household in Pakistan in 1952, she took an active part in human rights from her student days. In 1977 she received her law degree and started a law practice in early 1980. Since then she has risen to be an advocate at the Supreme Court in Pakistan and is chairperson of the Human Rights Commission of Pakistan, an NGO independent of the government.

During her career, Jahangir has made significant contributions regarding the rights of bonded laborers, women, and children at both the domestic and international levels. Jahangir has acted as lawyer for individual women and children whose human rights were violated, and through her personal concern and great energy, she has helped change the course of many lives. Her efforts to end child bonded labor reached the international level in Asia in 1984. In 1986, she worked to improve the conditions of abandoned children and was chosen vice-chairperson of Defense for Children International, a position she held until 1989. She is currently on the board of international human rights organizations in addition to her work as head of the Human Rights Commission of Pakistan.

Jahangir has written numerous papers on children's rights, as well as two books. *Hudood Ordinance: A Divine Sanction?* is a detailed analysis of the social and legal impacts of the Islamic penal laws, with special reference to rape statutes, while her latest book, *Children of a Lesser God: Child Prisoners of Pakistan* (written with Canadian lawyer Mark Doucet), chronicles the exploitation and neglect of millions of children in Pakistan and recommends detailed reforms for the juvenile justice system to align it with international laws and standards.

Eglantyne Jebb (1876–1928)

Eglantyne Jebb was born 25 August 1876 in Ellesmere, England. The fourth child in a wealthy family, she was educated at home and then read modern history at Oxford, graduating in 1898. She spent one year at Stockwell Training College preparing for teaching in elementary education, which she did for one year, resigning due to poor health in 1900.

Jebb's social conscience developed during the period between 1900 and 1914, through her work on behalf of Macedonian peasants during the Second Balkan War. As World War I ensued and eventually concluded, Jebb became committed to the defense of powerless victims of war, notably children, founding the Fight-the-Famine Council with her sister, Mrs. C. R. Buxton, in 1919. Soon thereafter, this organization was renamed the Save the Children Fund. The immediate problem of working on behalf of between 4 and 5 million children in danger of starvation throughout Europe inspired Jebb to rally support from other British philanthropists and the general public, and Save the Children rapidly expanded its focus by 1921 into the Soviet Union, where a famine threatened the lives of thousands of children, and on behalf of Armenian orphans made destitute by the genocide implemented by Turks against Armenians between 1915 and 1923.

From the outset of her work in the Save the Children Fund, Jebb advocated a universal set of rights for children, embodying child protection in the fields of child labor, child marriage, and social and economic concerns. She defended the idea of protecting children irrespective of their nationality, even during times of war, by quoting George Bernard Shaw, who said "I have no enemies under the age of seven." In 1923, she formulated the text of the "Children's Charter" after having developed the organizational framework for the Save the Children International Union, headquartered in Geneva. In 1924, the Children's Charter was retitled the Declaration of the Rights of the Child, and was adopted by the League of Nations, becoming the forerunner of all subsequent major international children's rights instruments. Eglantyne Jebb continued her efforts on behalf of children at Geneva, but through exhaustion and overwork fell ill and died there on 17 December 1928.

Ellen Key (1849–1926)

Ellen Key was born into an aristocratic family in Sundsholm, Sweden, on 11 December 1849. She received a broad-based education and later traveled widely in Europe, beginning her career as an essayist about topics in art history. After assuming a teaching position in Stockholm in 1870, Key began lecturing and writing about the three topics that were to constitute her life's work: education, feminism, and the rights of children. Key advocated the conscious education of children by parents whose marriages were forged in true love, and whose children were conceived and nurtured in homes dominated by a love ethic based upon loyalty and self-discipline.

In her most influential book on children, *The Century of the Child,* Key argued that children had the right to choose their parents wisely, or that parents should very carefully consider whether they should have children at all. As a forerunner of family planning, Key also advocated day care for children, a situation that would help women maintain roles in the economy outside of the home. She also argued for a radical transformation of education, arguing that children had real personalities that had to be nurtured so that their potential for cultivating good could be realized. This "New Education Movement" was very influential in reshaping the fundamental assumptions of educators regarding the child's educational growth and development, and Key's essays had wide impact in Europe both during and after her lifetime. Key died in 1926, widely regarded at her death as one of the most significant female literary figures in Swedish history.

Janusz Korczak (1878–1942)

Janusz Korczak, the pen name of Henryk Goldszmit, was born in Warsaw in 1878 into a successful Jewish family of professionals. Before Korczak reached the age of 12, his father succumbed to mental illness, an issue often cited in Korczak's own writings. At Warsaw University, Korczak studied medicine and was drawn to the ideas of liberal educators and writers. Soon after beginning his medical practice, Korczak wrote his first books, *Children of the Streets* (1901) and *A Child in the Salon* (1904).

Following service in the Russian army as a doctor, Korczak returned to Poland and began to work with children, treating them in a Jewish children's hospital, developing programs for children's summer camps, and eventually assuming the directorship of a Jewish orphanage in Warsaw in 1912. Korczak authored major works on the education of children, emphasizing the dignity and respect that children warranted from adults based upon their individual characteristics and their unique emotional lives. Rejecting the view that children were to be socialized and educated solely to meet adult expectations and needs, Korczak argued in *The Child's Right to Respect* (1929) that reform of the educational system would require the relinquishing of total control and power over children by adults. Korczak implemented many of his theoretical ideas at the two orphanages he administered, providing children with institutions of self-government (such as a court system) and a public forum for their own writing in a weekly supplement to the Jewish daily *Nasz Przeglad.*

As an advocate of children's rights, Korczak's most significant contribution was putting forth the idea that children have a right to respect from adults, rather than, solely, a duty to respect their elders. Janusz Korczak continued his advocacy of children and the direction of the Jewish orphanage in Warsaw despite the Nazi occupation of Poland and the implementation of the Holocaust. Joined by his devoted colleague Stefania Wilczynska, Korczak refused to leave his children when the Nazis ordered their deportation in 1942, and he marched to the train with his children, holding the hands of two orphans as they embarked for Treblinka, where they all perished.

Iqbal Masih (1982–1995)

Iqbal Masih was born in a small village in Pakistan in 1982, the sixth child of a poor farmer. When he was four years old, his father sold him into bonded labor for the equivalent of 600 rupees, money the family wanted to pay for the wedding of an older brother. Iqbal's courage in challenging Pakistan's child bonded labor system won him a Reebok Youth Action Award in 1994, but may also have contributed to his murder in 1995.

Iqbal was one of 7.5 million Pakistani children forced to work until they pay off exorbitant interest on small sums, the only "loans" available to poor families. Bonded child labor is deeply ingrained in the economy of Pakistan and some other Asian countries. Iqbal's particular "contract" was with a carpet factory owner, who sometimes chained him to a loom when Iqbal tried to flee. Children sold into bonded labor work up to ten hours daily and are lucky if they receive two hours of schooling per week. Iqbal suffered from a form of dwarfism that was not genetic, but which resulted from substandard working conditions.

At the age of ten in 1992, Iqbal defied the carpet factory owner and attended a freedom day celebration held by the Bonded Labor Liberation Front (BLLF), an organization that fights bonded labor in part by teaching laborers about their human rights. Iqbal was so moved at this meeting that he stood up and spoke about the life he and other children were forced to endure; Iqbal's testimony was reported in the newspaper the following day. Once the newspaper article appeared, Iqbal refused to return to the carpet factory and instead sought help from the BLLF. The organization gave him a "letter of freedom" written by a BLLF lawyer, and accepted him into a school that the organization runs for former bonded laborer children. An excellent speaker, Iqbal exposed the realities of bonded labor to large audiences in Pakistan, and was nominated for the Reebok Youth Freedom Award, which he received in December 1994. The "debt" that he had incurred had by then reached 13,000 rupees, and was subsequently paid to the carpet factory owner by some of Iqbal's well-wishers. Iqbal wanted to pursue a legal career, and with the Reebok Award, he had the money to finance his higher education.

On 12 April 1995, Iqbal (whose family name means "Christian") returned to his village for Easter Sunday with his family. While riding on the handlebars of a friend's bicycle, Iqbal was shot and died instantly. The BLLF claims that he was murdered by a "carpet Mafia," and the Pakistani authorities claim he was accidentally killed because he witnessed a crime or because he was caught in the cross fire of a feud. Investigations have not yet reconciled the differing accounts of his death.

Iqbal displayed courage through his willingness to expose an exploitative child labor system and demonstrated even greater courage in his persistent efforts to defy the bonded labor system throughout Pakistan. Schoolchildren are responding in Europe and in the United States to his work by raising funds to contribute to projects such as schools built in his name.

John F. O'Toole (1949–)

An activist by conviction and temperament, John F. O'Toole works for children's rights because "when you represent children, and you're able to do some things when they're younger, it might actually make a difference in their lives—it might actually turn their lives around."[2] O'Toole has been head of the National Center for Youth Law (NCYL) in San Francisco since 1981 and is credited with building the organization into the only national legal support group for children's issues in the country at a time when national politicians were dismantling federally funded poverty law programs.

O'Toole was born in 1949 in Englewood, New Jersey. During his college years at the University of California, Los Angeles, from which he graduated cum laude in 1971, O'Toole discovered a passion for helping the poor help themselves. After a summer of community organizing in Chicago and campaigning for Robert Kennedy in 1968, he won an internship with his hero, Congresswoman Shirley Chisholm. At this time, O'Toole became convinced that social change could be effected through legal advocacy, and he enrolled in Boalt Law School at the University of California, Berkeley. Spending most of his time working for the Legal Aid Society of Alameda County while studying law, his legal skills were forged by practice rather than in the abstract. He graduated from Boalt in 1974 and went to work immediately for California Rural Legal Assistance in Marysville, California, where he acted on behalf of farm workers and other poor clients in matters such as civil rights and welfare benefits.

Under O'Toole's leadership, the NCYL continues to specialize in large-scale impact litigation, the sort of legal cases that force governments to improve conditions or deliver legislated mandates for thousands of people. In *Angela R. v. Clinton,* acting on behalf of many abused and neglected children, the NCYL won a judgment that ordered the state of Arkansas to reform its child welfare system; another case, *David C. v. Leavitt,* did the same in the state of Utah. *Johnson v. Upchurch* ordered reform of the Arizona juvenile corrections system, in which children had been treated like adult felons.

O'Toole recognizes that social change is a slow process, and yet he and his organization have already gained rights for a significant number of American children through their advocacy.

Nelia Sancho Liao (1951–)

Nelia Sancho Liao became a pioneer for children's rights after having been an early advocate for women's rights in Asia. Born in 1951 in Pandan, Antigue, Philippines, Nelia Sancho Liao attended the University of the Philippines in Diliman from 1968 to 1972. There she studied mass communications and majored in journalism. Sancho Liao is married and has two teenage children.

Believing emphatically that the full range of human rights must embody civil and political rights, as well as economic, social, and cultural rights, Sancho Liao contends that all are necessary for the emancipation of women and children. She advocates the full range of human rights by helping to establish and direct nongovernmental organizations whose mandates reflect her passion for righting societal wrongs. She is presently convenor and coordinator of AMISTAD (the Philippine-Cuba Friendship Society) and women's desk coordinator of Bagong Alyansang Makabayan, an alliance of progressive people's and nongovernmental organizations in the Philippines. Previously in the area of women's rights, she founded and was secretary general of GABRIELA, an alliance of feminist organizations in the Philippines with chapters in different parts of the world. She is also regional coordinator of the Asian Women's Human Rights Council—an Asia-wide network of women's human rights programs, centers, organizations, and individuals—and was chairperson and coordinator of LILA-Filipina, an organization created to bring comfort to women and achieve just compensation for survivors of families who have suffered from human rights violations.

Sancho Liao was moved to anger by the situation of children who were internally displaced by civil war and children who were victims of poverty and injustice, so she became vice president for Asia for Defense for Children International (DCI), and used her years on the international board of directors to publicize and raise funds for children's relief throughout the world. Sancho Liao was a pioneer in the "South to South" exchange of experts from one developing country to another when she arranged for a delegation from DCI-Colombia to work on children's rights in Manila. She also founded the GABRIELA Commission on Children and the Family and is a consultant and president of the board of directors of Street Children and Child Workers Support Center, a social service organization. Aiding children through their families, she helped to found Parent's Alternative, Inc., an institution that promotes parenting development, support systems for parents, and early childhood education. She promoted women's and children's rights at worldwide United Nations conferences between 1993 and 1995.

Marta Santos Pais (1952–)

Marta Santos Pais is a leader in children's rights as an original drafter of the Convention on the Rights of the Child and a founding member of its Committee on the Rights of the Child. Born in Lisbon in 1952, she credits her father's courageous work on behalf of political prisoners during the years of the dictatorship as the inspiration for her own accomplishments in the field of international children's rights. She remembers particularly visiting a client of her father's, a four-year-old child who was imprisoned for running away from home, and deciding then that she would dedicate herself to children's rights.

Pais explains that she is but one of a generation who grew up without freedom of speech and recognized the opportunity to build a legal framework for grass-roots democracy and social justice when the dictator, Antonio Salazar, was overthrown. For that reason, when she graduated from the Law Faculty at University of Lisbon in 1976, she joined the democratically elected Portuguese government first as a legal adviser and then as lawyer for the Office of Documentation and Comparative Law. She followed her university studies with courses in human rights law at the Rene Cassin Institute of Human Rights, Strasbourg, France, in 1983 and the United Nations Center for Human Rights in Geneva. She understands law in three languages—Portuguese, English, and French—and also speaks Spanish.

During the drafting of the Convention on the Rights of the Child, Pais acted as Portuguese government representative; one of her achievements then was to lead other delegates to the strongest wording possible for the rights of children deprived of their liberty in what is now Article 40. She continues her tireless work on behalf of children as she consults with governments around the world on how to incorporate the highest standards of children's rights into their constitutions. The Committee on the Rights of the Child chose her as rapporteur (the person who summarizes the committee's findings), and she instituted a system for making their reports more accessible to NGOs and the general public. Her questions to the reporting countries are astute and flow from a concern for cooperation with them in their efforts to realize children's rights. She has written nearly 100 journal and news articles on the convention and has spoken on children's rights in Europe, Asia, Africa, and Latin America.

Notes

1. Jason DeParle, "The Transition; Clinton Social Policy Camps: Bill's vs. Hillary's," *New York Times,* 20 December 1992, 1; and Calvin Tomkins, "A Sense of Urgency," *The New Yorker,* 27 March 1989, 48–74.

2. Chris Palamountain and Adam Culbreath, "A Fish Is Only as Good as Its Head," *Youth Law News,* May–June 1994, 11–13.

4 International Instruments, Declarations, Guidelines, and Charters

This chapter includes international instruments that illustrate the increasing global and domestic concern about children's rights. The contents are restricted to materials produced during the twentieth century, when major children's rights initiatives focusing on the unique evolving roles of children both within and outside the family gained momentum in Europe and North America. The influence of these trends emerged somewhat later in the century in Africa, Asia, and Latin America, where children are seen primarily within the context of the entire family structure.

International instruments (declarations and conventions) are the framework within which standards and guarantees for children's rights are set forth to the world community. Complete texts of the most significant international instruments are provided, while relevant sections of other international instruments, such as the Geneva Conventions and Protocols, are excerpted.

The emergence of nongovernmental organizations (NGOs) as powerful voices for children's rights is a phenomenon beginning in the late nineteenth century, brought to the federal level in the United States during the

Progressive Era, beginning soon thereafter in Europe and other world societies, and continuing with increasing activity to the present. This chapter includes materials from a diverse group of NGOs that have made very significant contributions to increasing global awareness of the problems faced by children, pressuring governments and international organizations to guarantee children fundamental rights.

Because of the dynamic nature of children's rights activity worldwide, much of it stimulated by the development of the Convention on the Rights of the Child and its placement into force as a binding international instrument in the early 1990s, this compendium of relevant documents about children's rights is necessarily incomplete. The authors urge readers to carefully examine the contents of this chapter and pursue their interests in the ongoing debate on children's rights through contacts with the agencies and organizations listed in chapter 7, as well as through study of emergent international agreements, federal and state legislation, and domestic and international judicial decisions.

The first international recognition of children's rights by an intergovernmental body appears in the regulations of the International Labour Organization; prior to this, child labor and child protection were subjects for national law or state, then national law in the United States. Several nongovernmental organizations had already advocated for children's rights within the national sphere, but it was Eglantyne Jebb's work with the organization now called Save the Children that brought about the first general international declaration of children's rights (the Declaration of Geneva, 1924). The real work in what is now termed "international human rights law" took place after World War II, under the auspices of the UN Human Rights Commission. Children appear as a general category of victims of war in the Geneva Conventions of 1949 and as a targeted population in the two protocols to the Geneva Conventions of 1977. The latter instruments are considered part of "humanitarian law" and are separate from the UN system of law; the Geneva Conventions and Protocols are monitored by an important nongovernmental organization, the International Committee of the Red Cross.

Various declarations, charters, and regulations were made in the middle years of the twentieth century, but the real international interest about children as a specially targeted group began again in 1979 with the ten-year drafting of the Convention on the Rights of the Child. During the 1980s, NGOs and various UN bodies issued important guidelines and regulations, such as the Standard Minimum Rules for the Administration of Juvenile Justice (the "Beijing Rules" of 1985 and its related United Nations Rules for the Protection of Juveniles Deprived of Their Liberty, 1990). These serve as international standards required of States Parties in Article 41 of the Convention on the Rights of the Child for young people who have been taken into custody by agents of governments.

UNICEF published the World Declaration for the Survival, Protection, and Development of Children (1990) after the World Summit for Children, celebrating the adoption of the UN Convention on the Rights of the Child (CRC) by the General Assembly, 20 November 1989 (now called International Children's Rights Day), and guidelines for children's rights by the UN High Commissioner for Refugees office were completed in 1993. UNESCO revised its guidelines on teaching human rights in 1993, and these are important for children's rights in the specific context of Article 42 of the CRC, which requires States Parties to "make the principles and provisions of the Convention widely known. . . ." The Human Rights Commission is currently working on the "Optional Protocol on the Involvement of Children in Armed Conflicts," as well as one on the international crime of child prostitution.

Preferring to define children's rights in terms of non-Western cultures, the League of Arab States published their Charter on the Rights of the Child in the late 1980s, and the Organization of African Unity promulgated the Charter on the Rights and Welfare of the African Child in 1990; both are important regional documents. More recently, the Declaration of Lima (1992) represents a progress report about efforts in one world region concerning the monitoring and implementation of the Convention on the Rights of the Child.

ILO Convention Fixing the Minimum Age for Admission of Children to Industrial Employment (1919)

Convention 5

The General Conference of the International Labour Organisation, having been convened by the Government of the United States of America at Washington on the 29th day of October 1919, and having decided upon the adoption of certain proposals with regard to the "employment of children: minimum age of employment," which is part of the fourth item in the agenda for the Washington meeting of the Conference, and having determined that these proposals shall take the form of an International Convention, adopts the following Convention, which may be cited as the Minimum Age (Industry) Convention, 1919, for ratification by the Members of the International Labour Organisation in accordance with the provisions of the Constitution of the International Labour Organisation:

Article 1.

1. For the purpose of this Convention, the term "industrial undertaking" includes particularly—
   (a) mines, quarries, and other works for the extraction of minerals from the earth;
   (b) industries in which articles are manufactured, altered, cleaned, repaired, ornamented, finished, adapted for sale, broken up or demolished, or in which materials are transformed; including ship-building, and the generation, transformation, and transmission of electricity and motive power of any kind;
   (c) construction, reconstruction, maintenance, repair, alteration or demolition of any building, railway, tramway, harbour, dock, pier, canal, inland waterway, road, tunnel, bridge, viaduct, sewer, drain, well, telegraphic or telephonic installation, electrical undertaking, gas work, water work, or other work of construction, as well as the preparation for or laying the foundations of any work or structure;
   (d) transport of passengers or goods by road or rail or inland waterway, including the handling of goods at docks, quays, wharves, and warehouses, but excluding transport by hand.
2. The competent authority in each country shall define the line of division which separates industry from commerce and agriculture.

Article 2.

Children under the age of fourteen years shall not be employed or work in any public or private industrial undertaking, or in any branch thereof, other than an undertaking in which only members of the same family are employed.

Article 3.

The provisions of Article 2 shall not apply to work done by children in technical schools, provided that such work is approved and supervised by public authority.

Article 4.

In order to facilitate the enforcement of the provisions of this Convention, every employer in an industrial undertaking shall be required to keep a register of all persons under the age of sixteen years employed by him, and of the dates of their births.

Article 5.

1. In connection with the application of this Convention to Japan, the following modifications of Article 2 may be made:
   (a) children over twelve years of age may be admitted into employment if they have finished the course in the elementary school;
   (b) as regards children between the ages of twelve and fourteen already employed, transitional regulations may be made.
2. The provisions in the present Japanese law admitting children under the age of twelve years to certain light and easy employments shall be repealed.

ILO Convention Concerning the Night Work of Young Persons Employed in Industry (1919)

Convention 6

The General Conference of the International Labour Organisation, having been convened by the Government of the United States of America at Washington, on the 29th day of October 1919, and having decided upon the adoption of certain proposals with regard to the "employment of children: during the night," which is part of the fourth item in the agenda for the Washington meeting of the Conference, and having determined that these proposals shall take the form of an international Convention, adopts the following Convention, which may be cited as the Night Work of Young Persons (Industry) Convention, 1919, for ratification by the Members of the International Labour Organisation in accordance with the Provisions of the Constitution of the International Labour Organisation:

Article 1.

1. For the purpose of this Convention, the term "industrial undertaking" includes particularly—
   (a) mines, quarries, and other works for the extraction of minerals from the earth;
   (b) industries in which articles are manufactured, altered, cleaned, repaired, ornamented, finished, adapted for sale, broken up, or demolished, or in which materials are transformed; including ship building, and the generation, transformation, and transmission of electricity or motive power of any kind;
   (c) construction, reconstruction, maintenance, repair, alteration or demolition of any building, railway, tramway, harbour, dock, pier, canal, inland waterway, road, tunnel, bridge, viaduct, sewer, drain, well, telegraphic or telephonic installation, electrical undertaking, gas work, water work, or other work of construction as well as the preparation for or laying the foundations of any such work or structure;
   (d) transport of passengers or goods by road or rail, including the handling of goods at docks, quays, wharves, and warehouses, but excluding transport by hand.
2. The competent authority in each country shall define the line of division which separates industry from commerce and agriculture.

Article 2.

1. Young persons under eighteen years of age shall not be employed during the night in any public or private industrial undertaking, or in any branch thereof, other than an undertaking in which only members of the same family are employed, except as hereinafter provided for.
2. Young persons over the age of sixteen may be employed during the night in the following industrial undertakings on work which, by reasons of the nature of the process, is required to be carried on continuously day and night:

(a) manufacture of iron and steel; processes in which reverberatory or regenerative furnaces are used, and galvanising of sheet metal or wire (except the pickling process);
(b) glass work;
(c) manufacture of paper;
(d) manufacture of raw sugar;
(e) gold mining reduction work.

Article 3.

1. For the purpose of this Convention, the term "night" signifies a period of at least eleven consecutive hours, including the interval between ten o'clock in the evening and five o'clock in the morning.
2. In coal and lignite mines work may be carried on in the interval between ten o'clock in the evening and five o'clock in the morning, if an interval of ordinarily fifteen hours, and in no case of less than thirteen hours, separates two periods of work.
3. Where night work in the baking industry is prohibited for all workers, the interval between nine o'clock in the evening and four o'clock in the morning may be substituted in the baking industry for the interval between ten o'clock in the evening and five o'clock in the morning.
4. In those tropical countries in which work is suspended during the middle of the day, the night period may be shorter than eleven hours if compensatory rest is accorded during the day.

Article 4.

The provisions of Articles 2 and 3 shall not apply to the night work of young persons between the ages of sixteen and eighteen years in case of emergencies which could not have been controlled or foreseen, which are not of a periodical character, and which interfere with the normal working of the industrial undertaking.

Article 5.

In the application of this convention to Japan, until 1 July 1925, Article 2 shall apply only to young persons under fifteen years of age and thereafter it shall apply only to young persons under sixteen years of age.

Article 6.

In the application of this Convention to India, the term "industrial undertaking" shall include only "factories" as defined in the

Indian Factory Act, and Article 2 shall not apply to male young persons over fourteen years of age.

Article 7.

The prohibition of night work may be suspended by the Government, for young persons between the ages of sixteen and eighteen years, when in case of serious emergency the public interest demands it.

Article 8.

1. The formal ratifications of this Convention, under the conditions set forth in the Constitution of the International Labour Organisation, shall be communicated to the Director-General of the International Labour Office for registration.

Article 9.

1. Each member of the International Labour Organisation which ratifies this Convention engages to apply it to its colonies, protectorates and possessions which are not fully self-governing—
   (a) except where owing to the local conditions its provisions are inapplicable; or
   (b) subject to such modifications as may be necessary to adapt its provisions to local conditions.
2. Each Member shall notify to the International Labour Office the action taken in respect to each of its colonies, protectorates and possessions which are not fully self-governing.

Article 10.

As soon as the ratifications of two Members of the International Labour Organisation have been registered with the International Labour Office, the Director-General of the International Labour Office shall so notify all the Members of the International Labour Organisation.

Article 11.

This Convention shall come into force at the date on which such notification is issued by the Director-General of the International Labour Office, and it shall then be binding only upon those Members which have registered their ratifications with the International Labour Office. Thereafter this Convention will come into force for any other Member at the date on which its ratification is registered with the International Labour Office.

Article 12.

Each member which ratifies this Convention agrees to bring its provisions into operation not later than 1 July 1922, and to take such action as may be necessary to make these provisions effective.

Article 13.

A Member which has ratified this Convention may denounce it after the expiration of ten years from the date on which the Convention first comes into force, by an act communicated to the Director-General of the International Labour Office for registration. Such denunciation shall not take effect until one year after the date on which it is registered with the International Labour Office.

Article 14.

At least once in ten years the Governing Body of the International Labour Office shall present to the General Conference a report on the working of this Convention, and shall consider the desirability of placing on the agenda of the Conference the question of its revision or modification.

Article 15.

The French and English texts of this Convention shall both be authentic.

International Convention for the Suppression of the Traffic in Women and Children (1922)

Opened for Signature at Geneva from 20 September 1921 to 31 March 1922.

Article 1.

The High Contracting Parties agree that, in the event of their not being already parties to the Agreement of the 18th May, 1904, and the Convention of the 4th May, 1910, mentioned above, they will transmit, with the least possible delay, their ratifications of, or adhesions to, those instruments in the manner laid down therein.

Article 2.

The High Contracting Parties agree to take all measures to discover and prosecute persons who are engaged in the traffic in children of both sexes and who commit offenses within the meaning of Article 1 of the Convention of the 4th May, 1910.

Article 3.

The High Contracting Parties agree to take the necessary steps to secure the punishment of attempts to commit, and, within legal limits, of acts preparatory to the commission of, the offenses specified in Articles 1 and 2 of the Convention of the 4th May, 1910.

Article 4.

The High Contracting Parties agree that, in cases where there are no extradition Conventions in force between them, they will take all measures within their power to extradite or provide for the extradition of persons accused or convicted of the offenses specified in Articles 1 and 2 of the Convention of the 4th May, 1910.

Article 5.

In paragraph B of the final Protocol of the Convention of 1910, the words "twenty completed years of age" shall be replaced by the words "twenty-one completed years of age."

Article 6.

The High Contracting Parties agree, in case they have not already taken legislative or administrative measures regarding licensing and supervision of employment agencies and offices, to prescribe such regulations as are required to ensure the protection of women and children seeking employment in another country.

Article 7.

The High Contracting Parties undertake in connection with immigration and emigration to adopt such administrative and legislative measures as are required to check the traffic in women and children. In particular, they undertake to make such relations as are required for the protection of women and children travelling on emigrant ships, not only at the points of departure and arrival, but also during the journey, and to arrange for the exhibition in railway stations and in ports, of notices warning women and children of the traffic and indicating the places where they can obtain accommodation and assistance.

Article 8.

The present Convention, of which the French and the English texts are both authentic, shall bear this day's date, and shall be open for signature until the 31st March, 1922.

Article 9.

The present Convention is subject to ratification. The instruments of ratification shall be transmitted to the Secretary-General of the League of Nations, who will notify the receipt of them to the other Members of the League and to States admitted to sign the Convention. The instruments of ratification shall be deposited in the archives of the Secretariat.

In order to comply with the provisions of Article 18 of the Covenant of the League of Nations, the Secretary-General will register the present Convention upon the deposit of the first ratification.

Article 10.

Members of the League of Nations which have not signed the present Convention before the 1st April, 1922, may accede to it.

The same applies to States not Members of the League to which the Council of the League may decide officially to communicate the present Convention.

Accession will be notified to the Secretary-General of the League, who will notify all Powers concerned of the accession and of the date on which it was notified.

Article 11.

The present Convention shall come into force in respect of each Party on the date of the deposit of its ratification or act of accession.

Article 12.

The present Convention may be denounced by any Member of the League or by any State which is a party thereto, on giving twelve months' notice of its intention to denounce. Denunciation shall be effected by notification in writing addressed to the Secretary-General of the League of Nations. Copies of such notification shall be transmitted forthwith by him to all other Parties, notifying them of the date it was received.

The denunciation shall take effect one year after the date on which it was notified to the Secretary-General, and shall operate only in respect of the notifying Power.

Article 13.

A special record shall be kept by the Secretary-General of the League of Nations, showing which of the Parties have signed, ratified, acceded to or denounced the present Convention. This record shall be open to the Members of the League at all times; it shall be published as often as possible, in accordance with the directions of the Council.

Article 14.

Any Member of State signing the present Convention may declare that the signature does not include any or all of its colonies, overseas possessions, protectorates or territories under its sovereignty or authority, and may subsequently adhere separately on behalf of any such colony, overseas possession, protectorate or territory so excluded in its declaration.

Denunciation may also be made separately in respect of any such colony, overseas possession, protectorate or territory under its sovereignty or authority, and provisions of Article 12 shall apply to any such denunciation.

Done at Geneva, the 30th day of September, 1921, in a single copy, which shall remain deposited in the archives of the League of Nations.

Declaration of Geneva (1924)

By the present Declaration of the Rights of the Child, commonly known as the "Declaration of Geneva," men and women of all nations, recognising that mankind owes to the Child the best that it has to give, declare and accept it as their duty that, beyond and above all considerations of race, nationality or creed:

1. The child must be given the means requisite for its normal development, both materially and spiritually.

2. The child that is hungry must be fed; the child that is sick must be nursed; the child that is backward must be helped; the delinquent child must be reclaimed; and the orphan and the waif must be sheltered and succored.
3. The child must be the first to receive relief in times of distress.
4. The child must be put in a position to earn a livelihood, and must be protected against every form of exploitation.
5. The child must be brought up in the consciousness that its talents must be devoted to the service of its fellow-men.

Geneva Convention Relative to the Protection of Civilian Persons in Time of War (12 August 1949)

Only selected excerpts from the Geneva Convention of 1949 directly related to children's rights are included.

Part I
GENERAL PROVISIONS

Article 1

The High Contracting Parties undertake to respect and to ensure respect for the present Convention in all circumstances.

Article 2

In addition to the provisions which shall be implemented in peacetime, the present Convention shall apply to all cases of declared war or of any other armed conflict which may arise between two or more of the High Contracting Parties, even if the state of war is not recognized by one of them. They shall furthermore be bound by the Convention in relation to the said Power, if the latter accepts and applies the provisions thereof.

Article 3

In the case of armed conflict not of an international character occurring in the territory of one of the High Contracting Parties, each Party to the conflict shall be bound to apply, as a minimum, the following provisions:

(1) Persons taking no active part in the hostilities, including members of armed forces who have laid down their arms and those placed hors de combat by sickness, wounds, detention,

or any other cause, shall in all circumstances be treated humanely, without any adverse distinction founded on race, colour, religion or faith, sex, birth or wealth, or any other similar criteria. To this end the following acts are and shall remain prohibited at any time and in any place whatsoever with respect to the above-mentioned persons:

(a) violence to life and person, in particular murder of all kinds, mutilation, cruel treatment and torture;

(b) taking of hostages;

(c) outrages upon personal dignity, in particular humiliating and degrading treatment;

(d) the passing of sentences and the carrying out of executions without previous judgment pronounced by a regularly constituted court, affording all the judicial guarantees which are recognized as indispensable by civilized peoples.

(2) The wounded and sick shall be collected and cared for. An impartial humanitarian body, such as the International Committee of the Red Cross, may offer its services to the Parties to the conflict.

The Parties to the conflict should further endeavour to bring into force, by means of special agreements, all or part of the other provisions of the present Convention.

The application of the preceding provisions shall not affect the legal status of the Parties to the conflict.

Article 4

Persons protected by the Convention are those who, at a given moment and in any manner whatsoever, find themselves, in case of a conflict or occupation, in the hands of a Party to the conflict or Occupying Power of which they are not nationals.

Nationals of a State which is not bound by the Convention are not protected by it. Nationals of a neutral State who find themselves in the territory of a belligerent State, and nationals of a co-belligerent State, shall not be regarded as protected persons while the State of which they are nationals has normal diplomatic representation in the State in whose hands they are.

The provisions of Part II are, however, wider in application, as defined in Article 13.

Persons protected by the Geneva Convention for the Amelioration of the Condition of the Wounded and Sick in Armed Forces in the Field of 12 August 1949, or by the Geneva Convention for the Amelioration of the Condition of Wounded, Sick and Shipwrecked Members of Armed Forces at Sea of 12 August 1949, or by the Geneva Convention relative to the Treatment of Prisoners of War of 12 August 1949, shall not be considered as protected persons within the meaning of the present Convention.

Article 5

Where in the territory of a Party to the conflict, the latter is satisfied that an individual protected person is definitely suspected of or engaged in activities hostile to the security of the State, such individual person shall not be entitled to claim such rights and privileges under the present Convention as would, if exercised in the favour of such individual person, be prejudicial to the security of such State.

Where in occupied territory an individual protected person is detained as a spy or saboteur, or as a person under definite suspicion of activity hostile to the security of the Occupying Power, such person shall, in those cases where absolute military security so requires, be regarded as having forfeited rights of communication under the present Convention.

In each case, such persons shall nevertheless be treated with humanity and, in case of trial, shall not be deprived of the rights of fair and regular trial prescribed by the present Convention. They shall also be granted the full rights and privileges of a protected person under the present Convention at the earliest date consistent with the security of the State or Occupying Power, as the case may be.

Article 6

The present Convention shall apply from the outset of any conflict or occupation mentioned in Article 2.

In the territory of Parties to the conflict, the application of the present Convention shall cease on the general close of military operations.

In the case of occupied territory, the application of the present Convention shall cease one year after the general close of military operations; however, the Occupying Power shall be bound, for the duration of the occupation, to the extent that such Power exercises the functions of government in such territory, by the provisions of the following Articles of the present Convention: 1 to 12, 27, 29 to 34, 47, 49, 51, 52, 53, 59, 61 to 77, 143.

Protected persons whose release, repatriation or re-establishment may take place after such dates shall meanwhile continue to benefit by the present Convention.

Article 7

In addition to the agreements expressly provided for in Articles 11, 14, 15, 17, 36, 108, 109, 132, 133 and 149, the High Contracting Parties may conclude other special agreements for all matters concerning which they may deem it suitable to make separate provision. No special agreement shall adversely affect the situation of protected persons, as defined by the present Convention, nor restrict the rights which it confers upon them.

Protected persons shall continue to have the benefit of such agreements as long as the Convention is applicable to them, except where express provisions to the contrary are contained in the aforesaid or in subsequent agreements, or where more favourable measures have been taken with regard to them by one or other of the Parties to the conflict.

Article 8

Protected persons may in no circumstances renounce in part or in entirety the rights secured to them by the present Convention, and by the special agreements referred to in the foregoing Article, if such there be.

Article 9

The present Convention shall be applied with the cooperation and under the scrutiny of the Protecting Powers whose duty it is to safeguard the interests of the Parties to the conflict. For this purpose, the Protecting Powers may appoint, apart from their diplomatic or consular staff, delegates from amongst their own nationals or the nationals of other neutral Powers. The said delegates shall be subject to the approval of the Power with which they are to carry out their duties.

The Parties to the conflict shall facilitate to the greatest extent possible the task of the representatives or delegates of the Protecting Powers.

The representatives or delegates of the Protecting Powers shall not in any case exceed their mission under the present Convention.

They shall, in particular, take account of the imperative necessities of security of the State wherein they carry out their duties.

Article 10

The provisions of the present Convention constitute no obstacle to the humanitarian activities which the International Committee of the Red Cross or any other impartial humanitarian organization may, subject to the consent of the Parties to the conflict concerned, undertake for the protection of civilian persons and for their relief.

Article 11

The High Contracting Parties may at any time agree to entrust to an international organization which offers all guarantees of impartiality and efficacy the duties incumbent on the Protecting Powers by virtue of the present Convention.

When persons protected by the present Convention do not benefit or cease to benefit, no matter for what reason, by the activities of a Protecting Power or of an organization provided for in the first paragraph above, the Detaining Power shall request a neutral State, or such an organization, to undertake the functions performed under the present Convention by a Protecting Power designated by the Parties to a conflict.

If protection cannot be arranged accordingly, the Detaining Power shall request or shall accept, subject to the provisions of this Article, the offer of the services of a humanitarian organization, such as the International Committee of the Red Cross, to assume the humanitarian functions performed by Protecting Powers under the present Convention.

Any neutral Power or any organization invited by the Power concerned or offering itself for these purposes, shall be required to act with a sense of responsibility towards the Party to the conflict on which persons protected by the present Convention depend, and shall be required to furnish sufficient assurances that it is in a position to undertake the appropriate functions and to discharge them impartially.

No derogation from the preceding provisions shall be made by special agreements between Powers one of which is restricted, even temporarily, in its freedom to negotiate with the other Power or its allies by reason of military events, more particularly where the whole, or a substantial part, of the territory of the said Power is occupied.

Whenever in the present Convention mention is made of a Protecting Power, such mention applies to substitute organizations in the sense of the present Article.

The provisions of this Article shall extend and be adapted to cases of nationals of a neutral State who are in occupied territory or who find themselves in the territory of a belligerent State in which the State of which they are nationals has not normal diplomatic representation.

Article 12

In cases where they deem it advisable in the interest of protected persons, particularly in cases of disagreement between the Parties to the conflict as to the application or interpretation of the provisions of the present Convention, the Protecting Powers shall lend their good offices with a view to settling the disagreement.

For this purpose, each of the Protecting Powers may, either at the invitation of one Party or on its own initiative, propose to the Parties to the conflict a meeting of their representatives, and in particular of the authorities responsible for protected persons, possibly on neutral territory suitably chosen. The Parties to the conflict shall be bound to give effect to the proposals made to them for this purpose. The Protecting Powers may, if necessary, propose for approval by the Parties to the conflict a person belonging to a neutral Power, or delegated by the International Committee of the Red Cross, who shall be invited to take part in such a meeting.

The Convention shall also apply to all cases of partial or total occupation of the territory of a High Contracting Party, even if the said occupation meets with no armed resistance.

Although one of the Powers in conflict may not be a party to the present Convention, the Powers who are parties thereto shall remain bound by it in their mutual relations.

Part II

GENERAL PROTECTION OF POPULATIONS AGAINST CERTAIN CONSEQUENCES OF WAR

Article 13

The provisions of Part II cover the whole of the populations of the countries in conflict, without any adverse distinction based in particular on race, nationality, religion or political opinion, and are intended to alleviate the sufferings caused by war.

Article 14

In time of peace, the High Contracting Parties and, after the outbreak of hostilities, the Parties thereto, may establish in their own territory and, if the need arises, in occupied areas, hospital and safety zones and localities so organized as to protect from the effects of war, wounded, sick and aged persons, children under fifteen, expectant mothers and mothers of children under seven.

Upon the outbreak and during the course of hostilities, the Parties concerned may conclude agreements on mutual recognition of the zones and localities they have created. They may for this purpose implement the provisions of the Draft Agreement annexed to the present Convention, with such amendments as they may consider necessary.

The Protecting Powers and the International Committee of the Red Cross are invited to lend their good offices in order to facilitate the institution and recognition of these hospital and safety zones and localities.

Article 15

Any Party to the conflict may, either direct or through a neutral State or some humanitarian organization, propose to the adverse Party to establish, in the regions where fighting is taking place, neutralized zones intended to shelter from the effects of war the following persons, without distinction:

(a) wounded and sick combatants or non-combatants;
(b) civilian persons who take no part in hostilities, and who, while they reside in the zones, perform no work of a military character.

When the Parties concerned have agreed upon the geographic position, administration, food supply and supervision of the proposed neutralized zone, a written agreement shall be concluded and signed by the representatives of the Parties to the conflict. The agreement shall fix the beginning and the duration of the neutralization of the zone.

Article 17

The Parties to the conflict shall endeavour to conclude local agreements for the removal from besieged or encircled areas, of wounded, sick, infirm and aged persons, children and maternity cases, and for the passage of ministers of all religions, medical personnel and medical equipment on their way to such areas.

Article 23

Each High Contracting Party shall allow the free passage of all consignments of medical and hospital stores and objects necessary for religious worship intended only for civilians of another High Contracting Party, even if the latter is its adversary. It shall likewise permit the free passage of all consignments of essential foodstuffs, clothing and tonics intended for children under fifteen, expectant mothers and maternity cases.

The obligation of a High Contracting Party to allow the free passage of the consignments indicated in the preceding paragraph is subject to the condition that this Party is satisfied that there are no serious reasons for fearing:

(a) that the consignments may be diverted from their destination,
(b) that the control may not be effective, or
(c) that a definite advantage may accrue to the military efforts or economy of the enemy through the substitution of the above-mentioned consignments for goods which would otherwise be provided or produced by the enemy or through the release of such material, services or facilities as would otherwise be required for the production of such goods.

The Power which allows the passage of the consignments indicated in the first paragraph of this Article may make such permission conditional on the distribution to the persons benefited thereby being made under the local supervision of the Protecting Powers.

Such consignments shall be forwarded as rapidly as possible, and the Power which permits their free passage shall have the right to prescribe the technical arrangements under which such passage is allowed.

Article 24

The Parties to the conflict shall take the necessary measures to ensure that children under fifteen, who are orphaned or are separated from their families as a result of the war, are not left to their own resources, and that their maintenance, the exercise of their religion and their education are facilitated in all circumstances. Their education shall, as far as possible, be entrusted to persons of a similar cultural tradition.

The Parties to the conflict shall facilitate the reception of such children in a neutral country for the duration of the conflict with the consent of the Protecting Power, if any and under due safeguards for the observance of the principles stated in the first paragraph.

They shall, furthermore, endeavour to arrange for all children under twelve to be identified by the wearing of identity discs, or by some other means.

Article 26

Each Party to the conflict shall facilitate enquiries made by members of families dispersed owing to the war, with the object of renewing contact with one another and of meeting, if possible. It shall encourage, in particular, the work of organizations engaged in this task provided they are acceptable to it and conform to its security regulations.

Article 38

With the exception of special measures authorized by the present Convention, in particular by Articles 27 and 41 thereof, the situation of protected persons shall continue to be regulated, in principle, by the provisions concerning aliens in time of peace. In any case, the following rights shall be granted to them:

(1) They shall be enabled to receive the individual or collective relief that may be sent to them.
(2) They shall, if their state of health so requires, receive medical attention and hospital treatment to the same extent as the nationals of the State concerned.
(3) They shall be allowed to practise their religion and to receive spiritual assistance from ministers of their faith.
(4) If they reside in an area particularly exposed to the dangers of war, they shall be authorized to move from that area to the same extent as the nationals of the State concerned.
(5) Children under fifteen years, pregnant women and mothers of children under seven years shall benefit by any preferential treatment or to the same extent as the nationals of the State concerned.

Article 49

Individual or mass forcible transfers, as well as deportations of protected persons from occupied territory to the territory of the

Occupying Power or to that of any other country, occupied or not, are prohibited, regardless of their motive.

Nevertheless, the Occupying Power may undertake total or partial evacuation of a given area if the security of the population or imperative military reasons so demand. Such evacuations may not involve the displacement of protected persons outside the bounds of the occupied territory except when for material reasons it is impossible to avoid such displacement. Persons thus evacuated shall be transferred back to their homes as soon as hostilities in the area in question have ceased.

The Occupying Power undertaking such transfers or evaluations shall ensure, to the greatest practicable extent, that proper accommodation is provided to receive the protected persons, that the removals are effected in satisfactory conditions of hygiene, health, safety and nutrition, and that members of the same family are not separated.

The Protecting Power shall be informed of any transfers and evaluations as soon as they have taken place.

The Occupying Power shall not detain protected persons in an area particularly exposed to the dangers of war unless the security of the population or imperative military reasons so demand.

The Occupying Power shall not deport or transfer parts of its own civilian population into the territory it occupies.

Article 50

The Occupying Power shall, with the cooperation of the national and local authorities, facilitate the proper working of all institutions devoted to the care and education of children.

The Occupying Power shall take all necessary steps to facilitate the identification of children and the registration of their parentage. It may not, in any case, change their personal status, nor enlist them in formations or organizations subordinate to it.

Should the local institutions be inadequate for the purpose, the Occupying Power shall make arrangements for the maintenance and education, if possible by persons of their own nationality, language and religions, or children who are orphaned or separated from their parents as a result of the war and who cannot be adequately cared for by a near relative or friend.

A special section of the Bureau set up in accordance with Article 136 shall be responsible for taking all necessary steps to identify children whose identity is in doubt. Particulars of their parents or other near relatives should always be recorded if available.

The Occupying Power shall not hinder the application of any preferential measures in regard to food, medical care and protection against the effects of war, which may have been adopted prior to the occupation in favour of children under fifteen years, expectant mothers, and mothers of children under seven years.

Article 51

The Occupying Power may not compel protected persons to serve in its armed or auxiliary forces. No pressure or propaganda which aims at securing voluntary enlistment is permitted.

The Occupying Power may not compel protected persons to work unless they are over eighteen years of age, and then only on work which is necessary either for the needs of the army of occupation, or for the public utility services, or for the feeding, sheltering, clothing, transportation or health of the population of the occupied country. Protected persons may not be compelled to undertake any work which would involve them in the obligation of taking part in military operations. The Occupying Power may not compel protected persons to employ forcible means to ensure the security of the installations where they are performing compulsory labour.

The work shall be carried out only in the occupied territory where the persons whose services have been requisitioned are. Every such person shall, so far as possible, be kept in his usual place of employment. Workers shall be paid a fair wage and the work shall be proportionate to their physical and intellectual capacities. The legislation in force in the occupied country concerning working conditions, and safeguards as regards, in particular, such matters as wages, hours of work, equipment, preliminary training and compensation for occupational accidents and diseases, shall be applicable to the protected persons assigned to the work referred to in this Article.

In no case shall requisition of labour lead to a mobilization of workers in an organization of a military or semi-military character.

Article 68

Protected persons who commit an offence which is solely intended to harm the Occupying Power, but which does not constitute an attempt on the life or limb of members of the occupying forces or administration, nor a grave collective danger, nor seriously damage the property of the occupying forces or administration or the installations used by them, shall be liable to internment of simple imprisonment, provided the duration of such internment or imprisonment is proportionate to the offence committed. Furthermore, internment or imprisonment shall, for such offences, be the only measure adopted for depriving protected persons of liberty. The courts provided for under Article 66 of the present Convention may at their discretion convert a sentence of imprisonment to one of internment for the same period.

The penal provisions promulgated by the Occupying Power in accordance with Articles 64 and 65 may impose the death penalty on a protected person only in cases where the person is guilty of espionage, of serious acts of sabotage against the military installations of the occupying Power or of intentional offences which have caused the death of one or more persons, provided that such offences were punishable by death under the law of the occupied territory in force before the occupation began.

The death penalty may not be pronounced against a protected person unless the attention of the court has been particularly called to the fact that since the accused is not a national of the Occupying Power, he is not bound to it by any duty of allegiance.

In any case, the death penalty may not be pronounced against a protected person who was under eighteen years of age at the time of the offence.

Article 76

Protected persons accused of offences shall be detained in the occupied country, and if convicted they shall serve their sentences therein. They shall, if possible, be separated from other detainees and shall enjoy conditions of food and hygiene which will be sufficient to keep them in good health, and which will be at least equal to those obtaining in prisons in the occupied country.

They shall receive the medical attention required by their state of health.

They shall also have the right to receive any spiritual assistance which they may require.

Women shall be confined in separate quarters and shall be under the direct supervision of women.

Proper regard shall be paid to the special treatment due to minors.

Protected persons who are detained shall have the right to be visited by delegates of the Protecting Power and of the International Committee of the Red Cross, in accordance with the provisions of Article 143.

Such persons shall have the right to receive at least one relief parcel monthly.

Regulations for the Treatment of Internees

General Provisions

Article 81

Parties to the conflict who intern protected persons shall be bound to provide free of charge for their maintenance, and to grant them also the medical attention required by their state of health.

No deduction from the allowances, salaries, or credits due to the internees shall be made for the repayment of those costs.

The Detaining Power shall provide for the support of those dependent on the internees, if such dependents are without adequate means of support or are unable to earn a living.

Article 82

The Detaining Power shall, as far as possible, accommodate the internees according to their nationality, language and customs. Internees who are nationals of the same country shall not be separated merely because they have different languages.

Throughout the duration of their internment, members of the same family, and in particular parents and children, shall be lodged together in the same place of internment, except when separation of a temporary nature is necessitated for reasons of employment or health or for the purposes of enforcement of the provisions of Chapter IX of the present Section. Internees may request that their children who are left at liberty without parental care shall be interned with them.

Wherever possible, interned members of the same family shall be housed in the same premises and given separate accommodation from other internees, together with facilities for leading a proper family life.

Article 89

Daily food rations for internees shall be sufficient in quantity, quality and variety to keep internees in a good state of health and prevent the development of nutritional deficiencies. Account shall also be taken of the customary diet of the internees.

Internees shall also be given the means by which they can prepare for themselves any additional food in their possession.

Sufficient drinking water shall be supplied to internees. The use of tobacco shall be permitted.

Internees who work shall receive additional rations in proportion to the kind of labour which they perform.

Expectant and nursing mothers and children under fifteen years of age, shall be given additional food, in proportion to their physiological needs.

Article 94

The Detaining Power shall encourage intellectual, educational and recreational pursuits, sports and games amongst internees, whilst leaving them free to take part in them or not. It shall take all practicable measures to ensure the exercise thereof, in particular by providing suitable premises.

All possible facilities shall be granted to internees to continue their studies or take up new subjects. The education of children and young people shall be ensured; they shall be allowed to attend schools either within the place of internment or outside.

Internees shall be given opportunities for physical exercise, sports and outdoor games. For this purpose, sufficient open spaces shall be set aside in all places of internment. Special playgrounds shall be reserved for children and young people.

Article 132

Each interned person shall be released by the Detaining Power as soon as the reasons which necessitated his internment no longer exist.

The Parties to the conflict shall, moreover, endeavour during the course of hostilities, to conclude agreements for the release, the repatriation, the return to places of residence or the accommodation in a neutral country of certain classes of internees, in particular children, pregnant women and mothers with infants and young children, wounded and sick, and internees who have been detained for a long time.

Protocol I of 8 June 1977

Protocol Additional to the Geneva Conventions of 12 August 1949, and Relating to the Protection of Victims of International Armed Conflicts (Protocol I)

The High Contracting Parties, proclaiming their earnest wish to see peace prevail among peoples, recalling that every State has the duty, in conformity with the Charter of the United Nations, to refrain in its international relations from the threat or use of force against the sovereignty, territorial integrity or political independence of any State, or in any other manner inconsistent with the purposes of the United Nations, believing it necessary nevertheless to reaffirm and develop the provisions protecting the victims of armed conflicts and to supplement measures intended to reinforce their applications, expressing their conviction that nothing in this Protocol or in the Geneva Conventions of 12 August 1949 can be construed as legitimizing or authorizing any act of aggression or any other use of force inconsistent with the Charter of the United Nations, reaffirming further that the provisions of the Geneva Conventions of 12 August 1949 and of this Protocol must be fully applied in all circumstances to all persons who are protected by those instruments, without any adverse distinction based on the nature or origin of the armed conflict or on the causes espoused by or attributed to the Parties to the conflict, have agreed on the following:

PART II

Wounded, Sick and Shipwrecked

Section I—General Protection

Article 8—Terminology

For the purposes of this Protocol:

(a) "wounded" and "sick" mean persons, whether military or civilian, who, because of trauma, disease or other physical or mental disorder or disability are in need of medical assistance or care and who refrain from any act of hostility. These terms also cover maternity cases, new-born babies and other persons who may be in need of immediate medical assistance or care, such as the infirm or expectant mothers, and who refrain from any act of hostility. . . .

Article 70—Relief Actions

1. If the civilian population of any territory under the control of a Party to the conflict, other than occupied territory is not adequately provided with the supplies mentioned in Article 69, relief actions which are humanitarian and impartial in character and conducted without any adverse distinction shall be undertaken, subject to the agreement of the Parties concerned in such relief actions. Offers of such relief shall not be regarded as interference in the armed conflict or as unfriendly acts. In the distribution of relief consignments, priority shall be given to those persons, such as children, expectant mothers, maternity cases and nursing mothers, who, under the Fourth Convention or under this Protocol, are to be accorded privileged treatment or special protection.
2. The Parties to the conflict and each High Contracting Party shall allow and facilitate rapid and unimpeded passage of all relief consignments, equipment and personnel provided in accordance with this Section, even if such assistance is destined for the civilian population of the adverse Party.
3. The Parties to the conflict and each High Contracting Party which allow the passage of relief consignments, equipment and personnel in accordance with paragraph 2:
   (a) shall have the right to prescribe the technical arrangements, including search, under which such passage is permitted;
   (b) may make such permission conditional on the distribution of this assistance being made under the local supervision of a Protecting Power;
   (c) shall, in no way whatsoever, divert relief consignments from the purpose for which they are intended nor delay their forwarding, except in cases of urgent necessity in the interest of the civilian population concerned.
4. The Parties to the conflict shall protect relief consignments and facilitate their rapid distribution.
5. The Parties to the conflict and each High Contracting Party concerned shall encourage and facilitate effective international co-ordination of the relief actions referred to in paragraph 1.

Section III—Treatment of Persons in the Power of a Party to the Conflict

Article 74—Reunion of Dispersed Families

The High Contracting Parties and the Parties to the conflict shall facilitate in every possible way the reunion of families dispersed as a result of armed conflicts and shall encourage in particular the work of the humanitarian organizations engaged in this task in accordance with the provisions of the Conventions and of this Protocol and in conformity with their respective security regulations.

Article 75—Fundamental Guarantees

1. In so far as they are affected by a situation referred to in Article 1 of this Protocol, persons who are in the power of a Party to the conflict and who do not benefit from more favourable treatment under the conventions or under this Protocol shall be treated humanely in all circumstances and shall enjoy, as a minimum, the protection provided by this Article without any adverse distinction based upon race, colour, sex, language, religion or belief, political or other opinion, national or social origin, wealth, birth or other status, or on any other similar criteria. Each Party shall respect the person, honour, convictions and religious practices of all such persons.
2. The following acts are and shall remain prohibited at any time and in any place whatsoever, whether committed by civilian or by military agents:
   (a) violence to the life, health, or physical or mental well-being or persons, in particular:
      (i) murder;
      (ii) torture of all kinds, whether physical or mental;
      (iii) corporal punishment; and
      (iv) mutilation;
   (b) outrages upon personal dignity, in particular humiliating and degrading treatment, enforced prostitution and any form of indecent assault;
   (c) the taking of hostages;
   (d) collective punishments; and
   (e) threats to commit any of the foregoing acts.

5. Women whose liberty has been restricted for reasons related to the armed conflict shall be held in quarters separated from men's quarters. They shall be under the immediate supervision of women. Nevertheless, in cases where families are detained or interned, they shall, whenever possible, be held in the same place and accommodated as family units.

Article 77—Protection of Children

1. Children shall be the object of special respect and shall be protected against any form of indecent assault. The Parties to the conflict shall provide them with the care and aid they require, whether because of their age or for any other reason.
2. The Parties to the conflict shall take all feasible measures in order that children who have not attained the age of fifteen years do not take a direct part in hostilities and, in particular, they shall refrain from recruiting them into their armed forces. In recruiting among those persons who have attained the age of fifteen years but who have not attained the age of eighteen years, the Parties to the conflict shall endeavour to give priority to those who are oldest.
3. If, in exceptional cases, despite the provisions of paragraph 2, children who have not attained the age of fifteen years take a direct part in hostilities and fall into the power of an adverse Party, they shall continue to benefit from the special protection accorded by this Article, whether or not they are prisoners of war.
4. If arrested, detained or interned for reasons related to the armed conflict, children shall be held in quarters separate from the quarters of adults, except where families are accommodated as family units as provided in Article 75, paragraph 5.
5. The death penalty for an offence related to the armed conflict shall not be executed on persons who had not attained the age of eighteen years at the time the offence was committed.

Article 78—Evacuation of Children

1. No Party to the conflict shall arrange for the evacuation of children, other than its own nationals, to a foreign country except for a temporary evacuation where compelling reasons of the health or medical treatment of the children, or except in occupied territory, their safety, so require. Where the parents or legal guardians can be found, their written consent to such evacuation is required. If these persons cannot be found, the

written consent to such evaluation of the persons who by law or custom are primarily responsible for the care of the children is required. Any such evacuation shall be supervised by the Protecting Power in agreement with the Parties concerned, namely, the Party arranging for the evacuation, the Party receiving the children and any Parties whose nationals are being evacuated. In each case, all Parties to the conflict shall take all feasible precautions to avoid endangering the evacuation.

2. Whenever an evacuation occurs pursuant to paragraph 1, each child's education, including his religious and moral education as his parents desire, shall be provided while he is away with the greatest possible continuity.
3. With a view to facilitating the return to their families and country of children evacuated pursuant to this Article, the authorities of the Party arranging for the evacuation and, as appropriate, the authorities of the receiving country shall establish for each child a card with photographs, which they shall send to the Central Tracing Agency of the International Committee of the Red Cross. Each card shall bear, whenever possible, and whenever it involves no risk of harm to the child, the following information:
   (a) surname(s) of the child;
   (b) the child's first name(s);
   (c) the child's sex;
   (d) the place and date of birth (or if that date is not known, the approximate age);
   (e) the father's full name;
   (f) the mother's full name and her maiden name;
   (g) the child's next-of-kin;
   (h) the child's nationality;
   (i) the child's native language, and any other languages he speaks;
   (j) the address of the child's family;
   (k) any identification number for the child;
   (l) the child's state of health;
   (m) the child's blood group;
   (n) any distinguishing features;
   (o) the date on which and the place where the child was found;
   (p) the date on which and the place from which the child left the country;

(q) the child's religion, if any;
(r) the child's present address in the receiving country;
(s) should the child die before his return, the date, place and circumstances of death and place of internment.

Protocol II of 8 June 1977

Protocol Additional to the Geneva Conventions of 12 August 1949, and Relating to the Protection of Victims of Non-International Armed Conflicts (Protocol II)

Preamble

The High Contracting parties, recalling that the humanitarian principles enshrined in Article 3 common to the Geneva Conventions of 12 August 1949, constitute the foundation of respect for the human person in cases of armed conflict not of an international character, recalling furthermore that international instruments relating to human rights offer a basic protection to the human person, emphasizing the need to ensure a better protection for the victims of those armed conflicts, recalling that, in cases not covered by the law in force, the human person remains under the protection of the principles of humanity and the dictates of the public conscience, have agreed on the following:

Part II

Humane Treatment

Article 4—Fundamental Guarantees

1. All persons who do not take a direct part or who have ceased to take part in hostilities, whether or not their liberty has been restricted, are entitled to respect for their person, honour and convictions and religious practices. They shall in all circumstances be treated humanely, without any adverse distinction. It is prohibited to order that there shall be no survivors.
2. Without prejudice to the generality of the foregoing, the following acts against the persons referred to in paragraph 1 are and shall remain prohibited at any time and in any place whatsoever:
   (a) violence to the life, health, and physical or mental well-being of persons, in particular murder as well as cruel treatment such as torture, mutilation or any form of corporal punishment;

(b) collective punishments;
(c) taking of hostages;
(d) acts of terrorism;
(e) outrages upon personal dignity, in particular humiliating and degrading treatment, rape, enforced prostitution and any form of indecent assault;
(f) slavery and the slave trade in all their forms;
(g) pillage;
(h) threats to commit any of the foregoing acts.

3. Children shall be provided with the care and aid they require, and in particular:
   (a) they shall receive an education, including religious and moral education, in keeping with the wishes of their parents, or in the absence of parents, of those responsible for their care;
   (b) all appropriate steps shall be taken to facilitate the reunion of families temporarily separated;
   (c) children who have not attained the age of fifteen years shall neither be recruited in the armed forces of groups nor allowed to take part in hostilities;
   (d) the special protection provided by this Article to children who have not attained the age of fifteen years shall remain applicable to them if they take a direct part in hostilities despite the provisions of sub-paragraph (c) and are captured;
   (e) measures shall be taken, if necessary, and whenever possible with the consent of their parents or persons who by law or custom are primarily responsible for their care, to remove children temporarily from the area in which hostilities are taking place to a safer area within the country and ensure that they are accompanied by persons responsible for their safety and well-being.

Article 6—Penal Prosecutions

4. The death penalty shall not be pronounced on persons who were under the age of eighteen years at the time of the offence and shall not be carried out on pregnant women or mothers of young children.

The Children's Charter of Japan (1951)

Proclaimed on 5 May 1951.

Preamble

We, the people of Japan, in accordance with the spirit of the Constitution, do adopt this Charter to establish correct ideas toward children and thus bring about the well-being of all children.

General Principles

The child shall be respected as a human being.
The child shall be given due regard as a member of society.
The child shall be brought up in a good environment.

Text

1 All children shall be assured healthy minds and bodies and shall be guaranteed freedom from want.
2. All children shall be entitled to be brought up in their own homes with proper love, knowledge and skill. Those children not having homes shall be brought up in an environment having similar advantages.
3. All children shall be provided with adequate nourishment, housing and clothing and shall be protected against disease and injury.
4. All children shall be educated in accordance with their individuality and capacity and so guided that they will honestly and independently discharge their responsibilities as members of society.
5. All children shall be so guided that they may love nature, respect science and art, and accept the virtues of morality.
6. All children shall be assured access to schooling and be provided with complete educational facilities.
7. All children shall be provided with opportunity to receive vocational guidance and training.
8. All children shall be fully protected against exploitation in labour that their mental and physical development shall not be retarded, their opportunities to receive education not be lost and that their lives as children not be hampered.
9. All children shall be assured access to wholesome recreational and cultural resources and be protected against evil environments.

10. All children shall be protected against abuse, exploitation, neglect and other harmful treatment. Children who have committed wrongful acts shall be provided with adequate protection and guidance.
11. All children who are mentally or physically handicapped shall be provided with appropriate medical care, education and protection.
12. All children shall be so guided that they may be united with one another in the spirit of love and sincerity and as good citizens devote themselves to the peace and culture of mankind.

Reprinted from Philip E. Veerman, *The Rights of the Child and the Changing Image of Childhood* (Dordrecht, the Netherlands: Martinus Nijhoff, 1992), pp. 463–464. Reprinted by permission of Kluwer Academic Publishers.

Declaration of the Rights of the Child (1959)

Proclaimed by the General Assembly resolution 1386 (XIV) of 20 November 1959.

Preamble

Whereas the peoples of the United Nations have, in the Charter, reaffirmed their faith in fundamental human rights and in the dignity and worth of the human person, and have determined to promote social progress and better standards of life in larger freedom,

Whereas the United Nations has, in the Universal Declaration of Human Rights, proclaimed that everyone is entitled to all the rights and freedoms set forth therein, without distinction of any kind, such as race, colour, sex, language, religion, political or other opinion, national or social origin, property, birth or other status,

Whereas the child, by reason of his physical and mental immaturity, needs special safeguards and care, including appropriate legal protection, before as well as after birth,

Whereas the need for such special safeguards has been stated in the Geneva Declaration of the Rights of the Child of 1924, and recognized in the Universal Declaration of Human Rights and in the statutes of specialized agencies and international organizations concerned with the welfare of children,

Whereas mankind owes to the child the best it has to give,

Now therefore, the General Assembly proclaims this Declaration of the Rights of the Child to the end that he may have a happy childhood and enjoy for his own good and for the good of society the rights and freedoms herein set forth, and calls upon parents, upon men and women as individuals, and upon voluntary organizations, local authorities and national Governments to recognize these rights and strive for their observance by legislative and other measures progressively taken in accordance with the following principles:

Principle 1

The child shall enjoy all the rights set forth in this Declaration. Every child, without any exception whatsoever, shall be entitled to these rights, without distinction or discrimination on account of race, colour, sex, language, religion, political or other opinion, national or social origin, property, birth or other status, whether of himself or of his family.

Principle 2

The child shall enjoy special protection, and shall be given opportunities and facilities, by law and by other means, to enable him to develop physically, mentally, morally, spiritually and socially in a healthy and normal manner and in conditions of freedom and dignity. In the enactment of laws for this purpose, the best interests of the child shall be the paramount consideration.

Principle 3

The child shall be entitled from his birth to a name and a nationality.

Principle 4

The child shall enjoy the benefits of social security. He shall be entitled to grow and develop in health; to this end, special care and protection shall be provided to him and to his mother, including adequate pre-natal and post-natal care. The child shall have the right to adequate nutrition, housing, recreation and medical services.

Principle 5

The child who is physically, mentally or socially handicapped shall be given the special treatment, education and care required by his particular condition.

Principle 6

The child, for the full and harmonious development of his personality, needs love and understanding. He shall, wherever possible, grow up in the care and under the responsibility of his parents, and, in any case, in an atmosphere of affection and of moral and material security; a child of tender years shall not, save in exceptional circumstances, be separated from his mother. Society and the public authorities shall have the duty to extend particular care to children without a family and to those without adequate means of support. Payment of State and other assistance towards the maintenance of children of large families is desirable.

Principle 7

The child is entitled to receive education, which shall be free and compulsory, at least in the elementary stages. He shall be given an education which will promote his general culture and enable him, on a basis of equal opportunity, to develop his abilities, his individual judgment, and his sense of moral and social responsibility, and to become a useful member of society.

The best interests of the child shall be the guiding principle of those responsible for his education and guidance; that responsibility lies in the first place with his parents.

The child shall have full opportunity for play and recreation, which should be directed to the same purposes as education; society and the public authorities shall endeavor to promote the enjoyment of this right.

Principle 8

The child shall in all circumstances be among the first to receive protection and relief.

Principle 9

The child shall be protected against all forms of neglect, cruelty and exploitation. He shall not be the subject of traffic, in any form.

The child shall not be admitted to employment before an appropriate minimum age; he shall in no case be caused or permitted to engage in any occupation or employment which would prejudice his health or education, or interfere with his physical, mental or moral development.

Principle 10

The child shall be protected from practices which may foster racial, religious and any other form of discrimination. He shall be brought up in a spirit of understanding, tolerance, friendship among peoples, peace and universal brotherhood, and in full consciousness that his energy and talents should be devoted to the service of his fellow men.

ILO Convention Concerning Minimum Age for Admission to Employment (1973)

International Labour Conference, Convention 138 (1973)

The General Conference of the International Labour Organisation, having been convened at Geneva by the Governing Body of the International Labour Office, and having met in its Fifty-eighth Session on 6 June 1973, and having decided upon the adoption of certain proposals with regard to minimum age of admission to employment, which is the fourth item on the agenda of the session, and noting the terms of the Minimum Age (Industry) Convention, 1919, the Minimum Age (Sea) Convention, 1920, the Minimum Age (Agriculture) Convention, 1921, the Minimum Age (Trimmers and Stokers) Convention, 1921, the Minimum Age (Non-Industrial Employment) Convention, 1932, the Minimum Age (Sea) Convention (Revised), 1936, the Minimum Age (Industry) Convention (Revised), 1937, the Minimum Age (Fisherman) Convention, 1959, and the Minimum Age (Underground Work) Convention, 1965 and considering that the time has come to establish a general instrument on the subject, which would gradually replace the existing ones applicable to limited economic sectors, with a view to achieving the total abolition of child labour, and having determined that this instrument shall take the form of an international Convention, adopts this twenty-sixth day of June of the year one thousand nine hundred and seventy-three the following Convention, which may be cited as the Minimum Age Convention, 1973:

Article 1

Each member for which this Convention is in force undertakes to pursue a national policy designed to ensure the effective abolition of child labour and to raise progressively the minimum age for admission to employment or work to a level consistent with the fullest physical and mental development of young persons.

Article 2

1. Each member which ratifies this Convention shall specify, in a declaration appended to its ratification, a minimum age for admission to employment or work within its territory and on means of transport registered in its territory; subject to Article 4 to 8 of this Convention, no one under that age shall be admitted to employment or work in any occupation.
2. Each Member which has ratified this Convention may subsequently notify the Director-General of the International Labour Office, by further declarations, that it specifies a minimum age higher than that previously specified.
3. The minimum age specified in pursuance of paragraph 1 of this Article shall not be less than the age of completion of compulsory schooling and, in any case, shall not be less than 15 years.
4. Notwithstanding the provisions of paragraph 3 of this Article, a Member whose economy and educational facilities are insufficiently developed may, after consultation with the organisations of employers and workers concerned, where such exist, initially specify a minimum age of 14 years.
5. Each member which has specified a minimum age of 14 years in pursuance of the provisions of the preceding paragraph shall include in its reports on the application of this Convention submitted under Article 22 of the Constitution of the International Labour Organization a statement—
   (a) that its reason for doing so subsist; or
   (b) that it renounces its right to avail itself of the provisions in question as from a stated date.

Article 3

1. The minimum age for admission to any type of employment or work which by its nature or the circumstances in which it is carried out is likely to jeopardise the health, safety or morals of young persons shall not be less than 18 years.

2. The types of employment or work to which paragraph 1 of this Article applies shall be determined by national laws or regulations or by the competent authority, after consultation with the organisations of employers and workers concerned, where such exist.
3. Notwithstanding the provisions of paragraph 1 of this Article, national laws or regulations or the competent authority may, after consultation with the organisations of employers and workers concerned, where such exist, authorise employment or work as from the age of 16 years on condition that the health, safety and morals of the young persons concerned are fully protected and that the young persons have received adequate specific instruction or vocational training in the relevant branch of activity.

Article 4

1. In so far as necessary, the competent authority, after consultation with the organisations of employers and workers concerned, where such exist, may exclude from the application of this Convention limited categories of employment or work in respect of which special and substantial problems of application arise.
2. Each Member which ratifies this Convention shall list in its first report on the application of the Convention submitted under Article 22 of the Constitution of the International Labour Organisation any categories which may have been excluded in pursuance of paragraph 1 of this Article, giving the reasons for such exclusion, and shall state in subsequent reports the position of its law and practice in respect of the categories excluded and the extent to which effect has been given or is proposed to be given to the Convention in respect of such categories.
3. Employment or work covered by Article 3 of the Convention shall not be excluded from the application of the Convention in pursuance of this Article.

Article 5

1. A Member whose economy and administrative facilities are insufficiently developed may, after consultation with the organisations of employers and workers concerned, where such exist, initially limit the scope of application of this Convention.

2. Each Member which avails itself of the provisions of paragraph 1 of this Article shall specify, in a declaration appended to its ratification, the branches of economic activity or types of undertakings to which it will apply the provisions of the Convention.
3. The provisions of the Convention shall be applicable as a minimum to the following: mining and quarrying; manufacturing; construction; electricity, gas and water; sanitary services; transport, storage and communication; and plantations and other agricultural undertakings mainly producing for commercial purposes, but excluding family and small-scale holdings producing for local consumption and not regularly employing hired workers.
4. Any Member which has limited the scope of application of this Convention in pursuance of this Article—
   (a) shall indicate in its reports under Article 22 of the Constitution of the International Labour Organisation the general position as regards the employment or work of young persons and children in the branches of activity which are excluded from the scope of application of this Convention and any progress which may have been made towards wider application of the provisions of the Convention;
   (b) may at any time formally extend the scope of application by a declaration addressed to the Director-General of the International Labour Office.

Article 6

This Convention does not apply to work done by children and young persons in schools for general, vocational or technical education or in other training institutions, or to work done by persons at least 14 years of age in undertakings, where such work is carried out in accordance with conditions prescribed by the competent authority, after consultation with the organisations of employers and workers concerned, where such exist, and is an integral part of—

(a) a course of education or training for which a school or training institution is primarily responsible;

(b) a programme of training mainly or entirely in an undertaking, which programme has been approved by the competent authority; or

(c) a programme of guidance or orientation designed to facilitate the choice of an occupation or of a line of training.

Article 7

1. National laws or regulations may permit the employment or work of persons 13 to 15 years of age on light work which is—
   (a) not likely to be harmful to their health or development; and
   (b) not such as to prejudice their attendance at school, their participation in vocational orientation or training programmes approved by the competent authority or their capacity to benefit from the instruction received.
2. National laws or regulations may also permit the employment or work of persons who are at least 15 years of age but have not yet completed their compulsory schooling on work which meets the requirements set forth in sub-paragraphs (a) and (b) of paragraph 1 of this Article.
3. The competent authority shall determine the activities in which employment or work may be permitted under paragraphs 1 and 2 of this Article and shall prescribe the number of hours during which and the conditions in which such employment or work may be undertaken.
4. Notwithstanding the provisions of paragraphs 1 and 2 of this Article, a Member which has availed itself of the provisions of paragraph 4 of Article 2 may, for as long as it continues to do so, substitute the ages 12 and 14 for the ages 13 and 15 in paragraph 1 and the age 14 for the age 15 in paragraph 2 of this Article.

Article 8

1. After consultation with the organisations of employers and workers concerned, where such exist, the competent authority may, by permits granted in individual cases, allow exceptions to the prohibition of employment or work provided for in Article 2 of this Convention, for such purposes as participation in artistic performances.
2. Permits so granted shall limit the number of hours during which and prescribe the conditions in which employment or work is allowed.

Article 9

1. All necessary measures, including the provision of appropriate penalties, shall be taken by the competent authority to ensure the effective enforcement of this Convention.

2. National laws or regulations or the competent authority shall define the persons responsible for compliance with the provisions giving effect to the Convention.
3. National laws or regulations or the competent authority shall prescribe the registers or other documents which shall be kept and made available by the employer; such documents which shall be kept and made available by the employer; such registers or documents shall contain the names and ages or dates of birth, duly certified wherever possible, of persons whom he employs or who work for him and who are less than 18 years of age.

Article 10

1. This Convention revises, on the terms set forth in this Article, the Minimum Age (Industry) Convention, 1919, the Minimum Age (Sea) Convention, 1920, the Minimum Age (Agriculture) Convention, 1921, the Minimum Age (Trimmers and Stokers) Convention, 1921, the Minimum Age (Non-Industrial Employment) Convention, 1921, the Minimum Age (Sea) Convention (Revised), 1936, the Minimum Age (Industry) Convention (Revised), 1937, the Minimum Age (Fishermen) Convention, 1959, and the Minimum Age (Underground Work) Convention, 1965.
2. The coming into force of this Convention shall not close the Minimum Age (Sea) Convention (Revised), 1936, the Minimum Age (Non-Industrial Employment) Convention (Revised), 1937, the Minimum Age (Fishermen) Convention, 1959, or the Minimum Age (Underground Work) Convention, 1965, to further ratification.
3. The Minimum Age (Industry) Convention, 1919, the Minimum Age (Sea) Convention, 1920, the Minimum Age (Agriculture) Convention, 1921, and the Minimum Age (Trimmers and Stokers) Convention, 1921, shall be closed to further ratification when all the parties thereto have consented to such closing by ratification of this Convention or by a declaration communicated to the Director-General of the International Labour Office.
4. When the obligations of this Convention are accepted—
   (a) by a Member which is a party to the Minimum Age (Industry) Convention (Revised), 1937, and a minimum age of not less than 15 years is specified in pursuance of Arti-

cle 2 of this Convention, this shall *ipso jure* involve the immediate denunciation of that Convention,

(b) in respect of non-industrial employment as defined in the Minimum Age (Non-Industrial Employment) Convention, 1932, by a Member which is a party to that Convention, this shall *ipso jure* involve the immediate denunciation of that Convention,

(c) in respect of non-industrial employment as defined in the Minimum Age (Non-Industrial Employment) Convention, 1932, by a Member which is a party to that Convention, this shall *ipso jure* involve the immediate denunciation of that Convention,

(d) in respect of maritime employment, by a Member which is a party to the Minimum Age (Sea) Convention (Revised), 1936, and a minimum age of not less than 15 years is specified in pursuance of Article 2 of this Convention or the Member specifies that Article 3 of this Convention applies to maritime employment, this shall *ipso jure* involve the immediate denunciation of that Convention,

(e) in respect of employment in maritime fishing, by a Member which is a party to the Minimum Age (Fishermen) Convention, 1959, and a minimum age of not less than 15 years is specified in pursuance of Article 2 of this Convention or the Member specifies that Article 3 of this Convention applies to employment in maritime fishing, this shall *ipso jure* involve the immediate denunciation of that Convention,

(f) by a Member which is a party to the Minimum Age (Underground Work) Convention, 1965, and a minimum age of not less than the age specified in pursuance of that Convention is specified in pursuance of Article 2 of this Convention or the Member specifies that such an age applies to employment underground in mines in virtue of Article 3 of this Convention, this shall *ipso jure* involve the immediate denunciation of that Convention, if and when this Convention shall have come into force.

5. Acceptance of the obligations of this Convention—

   (a) shall involve the denunciation of the Minimum Age (Industry) Convention, 1919, in accordance with Article 12 thereof,

   (b) in respect of agriculture shall involve the denunciation of the Minimum Age (Agriculture) Convention, 1921, in accordance with Article 9 thereof,

(c) in respect of maritime employment shall involve the denunciation of the Minimum Age (Sea) Convention, 1920, in accordance with Article 10 thereof, and of the Minimum Age (Trimmers and Stokers) Convention, 1921, in accordance with Article 12 thereof, if and when this Convention shall have come into force.

Article 11

The formal ratifications of this Convention shall be communicated to the Director-General of the International Labour Office for registration.

Article 12

1. This Convention shall be binding only upon those Members of the International Labour Organisation whose ratifications have been registered with the Director-General.
2. It shall come into force twelve months after the date on which the ratifications of two Members have been registered with the Director-General.
3. Thereafter, this Convention shall come into force for any Member twelve months after the date on which its ratification has been registered.

Article 13

1. A Member which has ratified this Convention may denounce it after the expiration of ten years from the date on which the Convention first comes into force, by an act communicated to the Director-General of the International Labour Office for registration. Such denunciation shall not take effect until one year after the date on which it is registered.
2. Each Member which has ratified this Convention and which does not, within the year following the expiration of the period of ten years mentioned in the preceding paragraph, exercise the right of denunciation provided for in this Article, will be bound for another period of ten years and, thereafter, may denounce this Convention at the expiration of each period of ten years under the terms provided for in this Article.

Article 14

1. The Director-General of the International Labour Office shall notify all Members of the International Labour Office of the registration of all ratifications and denunciations communicated to him; the Director-General shall draw the attention of

the Members of the Organisation to the date upon which the Convention will come into force.

Article 15

The Director-General of the International Labour Office shall communicate to the Secretary-General of the United Nations for registration in accordance with Article 102 of the Charter of the United Nations full particulars of all ratifications and acts of denunciation registered by him in accordance with the provisions of the preceding Articles.

Article 16

At such times as it may consider necessary the Governing Body of the International Labour Office shall present to the General Conference a report on the working of this Convention and shall examine the desirability of placing on the agenda of the Convention the question of its revision in whole or in part.

Article 17

1. Should the Conference adopt a new Convention revising this Convention in whole or in part, then unless the new Convention otherwise provides—
   (a) the ratification by a Member of the new revising Convention shall *ipso jure* involve the immediate denunciation of this Convention, notwithstanding the provisions of Article 13 above, if and when the new revising Convention shall have come into force;
   (b) as from the date when the new revising Convention comes into force this Convention shall cease to be open to ratification by the Members.
2. This Convention shall in any case remain in force in its actual form and content for those Members which have ratified it but have not ratified the revising Convention.

Article 18

The English and French versions of the text of this Convention are equally authoritative.

Convention on the Rights of the Child (1989)

Adopted by the General Assembly of the United Nations on 20 November 1989.

Preamble

The States Parties to the present Convention,

Considering that, in accordance with the principles proclaimed in the Charter of the United Nations, recognition of the inherent dignity and of the equal and inalienable rights of all members of the human family is the foundation of freedom, justice and peace in the world,

Bearing in mind that the peoples of the United Nations have, in the Charter, reaffirmed their faith in fundamental human rights and in the dignity and worth of the human person, and have determined to promote social progress and better standards of life in larger freedom,

Recognizing that the United Nations has, in the Universal Declaration of Human Rights and in the International Covenants on Human Rights, proclaimed and agreed that everyone is entitled to all the rights and freedoms set forth therein, without distinction of any kind, such as race, colour, sex, language, religion, political or other opinion, national or social origin, property, birth or other status,

Recalling that, in the Universal Declaration of Human Rights, the United Nations has proclaimed that childhood is entitled to special care and assistance,

Convinced that the family, as the fundamental group of society and the natural environment for the growth and well-being of all its members and particularly children, should be afforded the necessary protection and assistance so that it can fully assume its responsibilities within the community,

Recognizing that the child, for the full and harmonious development of his or her personality, should grow up in a family environment, in an atmosphere of happiness, love and understanding,

Considering that the child should be fully prepared to live an individual life in society, and brought up in the spirit of the ideals proclaimed in the Charter of the United Nations, and in particular in the spirit of peace, dignity, tolerance, freedom, equality and solidarity,

Bearing in mind that the need to extend particular care to the child has been stated in the Geneva Declaration of the Rights of the Child of 1924 and in the Declaration of the Rights of the Child adopted by the United Nations on 20 November 1959 and recognized in the Universal Declaration of Human Rights, in the International Covenant on Civil and Political Rights (in particular in articles 23 and 24), in the International Covenant on Economic, Social and Cultural Rights (in particular in article 10) and in the statutes and relevant instruments of specialized agencies and international organizations concerned with the welfare of children,

Bearing in mind that, as indicated in the Declaration of the Rights of the Child, "the child, by reason of his physical and mental immaturity, needs special safeguards and care, including appropriate legal protection, before as well as after birth,"

Recalling the provisions of the Declaration on Social and Legal Principles relating to the Protection and Welfare of Children, with Special Reference to Foster Placement and Adoption Nationally and Internationally; the United Nations Standard Minimum Rules for the Administration of Juvenile Justice ("The Beijing Rules"); and the Declaration on the Protection of Women and Children in Emergency and Armed Conflict,

Recognizing that, in all countries in the world, there are children living in exceptionally difficult conditions, and that such children need special consideration,

Taking due account of the importance of the traditions and cultural values of each people for the protection and harmonious development of the child,

Recognizing the importance of international co-operation for improving the living conditions of children in every country, in particular in the developing countries,

Have agreed as follows:

PART I

Article 1

For the purposes of the present Convention, a child means every human being below the age of 18 years unless, under the law applicable to the child, majority is attained earlier.

Article 2

1. States Parties shall respect and ensure the rights set forth in the present Convention to each child within their jurisdiction

without discrimination of any kind, irrespective of the child's or his or her parent's or legal guardian's race, colour, sex, language, religion, political or other opinion, national, ethnic or social origin, property, disability, birth or other status.

2. States Parties shall take all appropriate measures to ensure that the child is protected against all forms of discrimination or punishment on the basis of the status, activities, expressed opinions, or beliefs of the child's parents, legal guardians, or family members.

Article 3

1. In all actions concerning children, whether undertaken by public or private social welfare institutions, courts of law, administrative authorities or legislative bodies, the best interests of the child shall be a primary consideration.
2. States Parties undertake to ensure the child such protection and care as is necessary for his or her well-being, taking into account the rights and duties of his or her parents, legal guardians, or other individuals legally responsible for him or her, and, to this end, shall take all appropriate legislative and administrative measures.
3. States Parties shall ensure that the institutions, services and facilities responsible for the care or protection of children shall conform with the standards established by competent authorities, particularly in the areas of safety, health, in the number and suitability of their staff, as well as competent supervision.

Article 4

States Parties shall undertake all appropriate legislative, administrative, and other measures for the implementation of the rights recognized in the present Convention. With regard to economic, social and cultural rights, States Parties shall undertake such measures to the maximum extent of their available resources and, where needed, within the framework of international co-operation.

Article 5

States Parties shall respect the responsibilities, rights and duties of parents or, where applicable, the members of the extended family or community as provided for by local custom, legal guardians or other persons legally responsible for the child, to provide, in a manner consistent with the evolving capacities of the child, appropriate direction and guidance in the exercise by the child of the rights recognized in the present Convention.

Article 6

1. States Parties recognize that every child has the inherent right to life.
2. States Parties shall ensure to the maximum extent possible the survival and development of the child.

Article 7

1. The child shall be registered immediately after birth and shall have the right from birth to a name, the right to acquire a nationality and, as far as possible, the right to know and be cared for by his or her parents.
2. States Parties shall ensure the implementation of these rights in accordance with their national law and their obligations under the relevant international instruments in this field, in particular where the child would otherwise be stateless.

Article 8

1. States Parties undertake to respect the right of the child to preserve his or her identity, including nationality, name and family relations as recognized by law without unlawful interference.
2. Where a child is illegally deprived of some or all of the elements of his or her identity, States Parties shall provide appropriate assistance and protection, with a view to speedily re-establishing his or her identity.

Article 9

1. States Parties shall ensure that a child shall not be separated from his or her parents against their will, except when competent authorities subject to judicial review determine, in accordance with applicable law and procedures, that such separation is necessary for the best interests of the child. Such determination may be necessary in a particular case such as one involving abuse or neglect of the child by the parents, or one where the parents are living separately and a decision must be made as to the child's place of residence.
2. In any proceedings pursuant to paragraph 1 of the present article, all interested parties shall be given an opportunity to participate in the proceedings and make their views known.
3. States Parties shall respect the right of the child who is separated from one or both parents to maintain personal relations

and direct contact with both parents on a regular basis, except if it is contrary to the child's best interests.

4. Where such separation results from any action initiated by a State Party, such as the detention, imprisonment, exile, deportation or death (including death arising from any cause while the person is in the custody of the State) of one or both parents or of the child, that State Party shall, upon request, provide the parents, the child or, if appropriate, another member of the family with the essential information concerning the whereabouts of the absent member(s) of the family unless the provision of the information would be detrimental to the well-being of the child. States Parties shall further ensure that the submission of such a request shall of itself entail no adverse consequences for the person(s) concerned.

Article 10

1. In accordance with the obligation of States Parties under article 9, paragraph 1, applications by a child or his or her parents to enter or leave a State Party for the purpose of family reunification shall be dealt with by States Parties in a positive, humane and expeditious manner. States Parties shall further ensure that the submission of such a request shall entail no adverse consequences for the applicants and for the members of their family.
2. A child whose parents reside in different States shall have the right to maintain on a regular basis, save in exceptional circumstances, personal relations and direct contacts with both parents. Towards that end and in accordance with the obligation of States Parties under article 9, paragraph 1, States Parties shall respect the right of the child and his or her parents to leave any country, including their own, and to enter their own country. The right to leave any country shall be subject only to such restrictions as are prescribed by law and which are necessary to protect the national security, public order *(ordre public)*, public health or morals or the rights and freedoms of others and are consistent with the other rights recognized in the present Convention.

Article 11

1. States Parties shall take measures to combat the illicit transfer and non-return of children abroad.

2. To this end, States Parties shall promote the conclusion of bilateral or multilateral agreements or accession to existing agreements.

Article 12

1. States Parties shall assure to the child who is capable of forming his or her own views the right to express those views freely in all matters affecting the child, the views of the child being given due weight in accordance with the age and maturity of the child.
2. For this purpose, the child shall in particular be provided the opportunity to be heard in any judicial and administrative proceedings affecting the child, either directly, or through a representative or an appropriate body, in a manner consistent with the procedural rules of national law.

Article 13

1. The child shall have the right to freedom of expression; this right shall include freedom to seek, receive and impart information and ideas of all kinds, regardless of frontiers, either orally, in writing or in print, in the form of art, or through any other media of the child's choice.
2. The exercise of this right may be subject to certain restrictions, but these shall only be such as are provided by law and are necessary:
   (a) For respect of the rights or reputations of others; or
   (b) For the protection of national security or of public order *(ordre public)*, or of public health or morals.

Article 14

1. States Parties shall respect the right of the child to freedom of thought, conscience and religion.
2. States Parties shall respect the rights and duties of the parents and, when applicable, legal guardians, to provide direction to the child in the exercise of his or her right in a manner consistent with the evolving capacities of the child.
3. Freedom to manifest one's religion or beliefs may be subject only to such limitations as are prescribed by law and are necessary to protect public safety, order, health or morals, or the fundamental rights and freedoms of others.

Article 15

1. States Parties recognize the rights of the child to freedom of association and to freedom of peaceful assembly.
2. No restrictions may be placed on the exercise of these rights other than those imposed in conformity with the law and which are necessary in a democratic society in the interests of national security or public safety, public order *(ordre public)*, the protection of public health or morals or the protection of the rights and freedoms of others.

Article 16

1. No child shall be subjected to arbitrary or unlawful interference with his or her privacy, family, home or correspondence, nor to unlawful attacks on his or her honour and reputation.
2. The child has the right to the protection of the law against such interference or attacks.

Article 17

States Parties recognize the important function performed by the mass media and shall ensure that the child has access to information and material from a diversity of national and international sources, especially those aimed at the promotion of his or her social, spiritual and moral well-being and physical and mental health. To this end, States Parties shall:

(a) Encourage the mass media to disseminate information and material of social and cultural benefit to the child and in accordance with the spirit of article 29;

(b) Encourage international co-operation in the production, exchange and dissemination of such information and material from a diversity of cultural, national and international sources;

(c) Encourage the production and dissemination of children's books;

(d) Encourage the mass media to have particular regard to the linguistic needs of the child who belongs to a minority group or who is indigenous;

(e) Encourage the development of appropriate guidelines for the protection of the child from information and material injurious to his or her well-being, bearing in mind the provisions of articles 13 and 18.

Article 18

1. States Parties shall use their best efforts to ensure recognition of the principle that both parents have common responsibilities for the upbringing and development of the child. Parents or, as the case may be, legal guardians, have the primary responsibility for the upbringing and development of the child. The best interests of the child will be their basic concern.
2. For the purpose of guaranteeing and promoting the rights set forth in the present Convention, States Parties shall render appropriate assistance to parents and legal guardians in the performance of their child-rearing responsibilities and shall ensure the development of institutions, facilities and services for the care of children.
3. States Parties shall take all appropriate measures to ensure that children of working parents have the right to benefit from child-care services and facilities for which they are eligible.

Article 19

1. States Parties shall take all appropriate legislative, administrative, social and educational measures to protect the child from all forms of physical or mental violence, injury or abuse, neglect or negligent treatment, maltreatment or exploitation, including sexual abuse, while in the care of parent(s), legal guardian(s) or any other person who has the care of the child.
2. Such protective measures should, as appropriate, include effective procedures for the establishment of social programmes to provide necessary support for the child and for those who have the care of the child, as well as for other forms of prevention and for identification, reporting, referral, investigation, treatment and follow-up of instances of child maltreatment described heretofore, and, as appropriate, for judicial involvement.

Article 20

1. A child temporarily or permanently deprived of his or her family environment, or in whose own best interests cannot be allowed to remain in that environment, shall be entitled to special protection and assistance provided by the State.
2. States Parties shall in accordance with their national laws ensure alternative care for such a child.
3. Such care could include, *inter alia,* foster placement, Kafala of Islamic law, adoption, or if necessary placement in suitable

institutions for the care of children. When considering solutions, due regard shall be paid to the desirability of continuity in a child's upbringing and to the child's ethnic, religious, cultural and linguistic background.

Article 21

States Parties that recognize and/or permit the system of adoption shall ensure that the best interests of the child shall be the paramount consideration and they shall:

(a) Ensure that the adoption of a child is authorized only by competent authorities who determine, in accordance with applicable law and procedures and on the basis of all pertinent and reliable information, that the adoption is permissible in view of the child's status concerning parents, relatives and legal guardians and that, if required, the persons concerned have given their informed consent to the adoption on the basis of such counselling as may be necessary;
(b) Recognize that intercountry adoption may be considered as an alternative means of child's care, if the child cannot be placed in a foster or an adoptive family or cannot in any suitable manner be cared for in the child's country of origin;
(c) Ensure that the child concerned by intercountry adoption enjoys safeguards and standards equivalent to those existing in the case of national adoption;
(d) Take all appropriate measures to ensure that, in intercountry adoption, the placement does not result in improper financial gain for those involved in it;
(e) Promote, where appropriate, the objectives of the present article by concluding bilateral or multilateral arrangements or agreements, and endeavour, within this framework, to ensure that the placement of the child in another country is carried out by competent authorities or organs.

Article 22

1. States Parties shall take appropriate measures to ensure that a child who is seeking refugee status or who is considered a refugee in accordance with applicable international or domestic law and procedures shall, whether unaccompanied or accompanied by his or her parents or by any other person, receive appropriate protection and humanitarian assistance in the enjoyment of applicable rights set forth in the present Convention and in other international human rights

or humanitarian instruments to which the said States are Parties.

2. For this purpose, States Parties shall provide, as they consider appropriate, co-operation in any efforts by the United Nations and other competent intergovernmental organizations or non-governmental organizations co-operating with the United Nations to protect and assist such a child and to trace the parents or other members of the family of any refugee child in order to obtain information necessary for reunification with his or her family. In cases where no parents or other members of the family can be found, the child shall be accorded the same protection as any other child permanently or temporarily deprived of his or her family environment for any reason, as set forth in the present Convention.

Article 23

1. States Parties recognize that a mentally or physically disabled child should enjoy a full and decent life, in conditions which ensure dignity, promote self-reliance, and facilitate the child's active participation in the community.
2. States Parties recognize the right of the disabled child to special care and shall encourage and ensure the extension, subject to available resources, to the eligible child and those responsible for his or her care, of assistance for which application is made and which is appropriate to the child's condition and to the circumstances of the parents or others caring for the child.
3. Recognizing the special needs of a disabled child, assistance extended in accordance with paragraph 2 of the present article shall be provided free of charge, whenever possible, taking into account the financial resources of the parents or others caring for the child, and shall be designed to ensure that the disabled child has effective access to and receives education, training, health care services, rehabilitation services, preparation for employment and recreation opportunities in a manner conducive to the child's achieving the fullest possible social integration and individual development, including his or her cultural and spiritual development.
4. States Parties shall promote, in the spirit of international cooperation, the exchange of appropriate information in the field of preventive health care and of medical, psychological and functional treatment of disabled children, including dis-

semination of and access to information concerning methods of rehabilitation, education and vocational services, with the aim of enabling States Parties to improve their capabilities and skills and to widen their experience in these areas. In this regard, particular account shall be taken of the needs of developing countries.

Article 24

1. States Parties recognize the right of the child to the enjoyment of the highest attainable standard of health and to facilities for the treatment of illness and rehabilitation of health. States Parties shall strive to ensure that no child is deprived of his or her right of access to such health care services.
2. States Parties shall pursue full implementation of this right and, in particular, shall take appropriate measures:
   (a) To diminish infant and child mortality;
   (b) To ensure the provision of necessary medical assistance and health care to all children with emphasis on the development of primary health care;
   (c) To combat disease and malnutrition including within the framework of primary health care, through *inter alia* the application of readily available technology and through the provision of adequate nutritious foods and clean drinking water, taking into consideration the dangers and risks of environmental pollution;
   (d) To ensure appropriate pre-natal and post-natal health care for mothers;
   (e) To ensure that all segments of society, in particular parents and children, are informed, have access to education and are supported in the use of basic knowledge of child health and nutrition, the advantages of breast-feeding, hygiene and environmental sanitation and the prevention of accidents;
   (f) To develop preventive health care, guidance for parents and family planning education and services.
3. States Parties shall take all effective and appropriate measures with a view to abolishing traditional practices prejudicial to the health of children.
4. States Parties undertake to promote and encourage international co-operation with a view to achieving progressively the full realization of the right recognized in the present article. In this regard, particular account shall be taken of the needs of developing countries.

Article 25

States Parties recognize the right of a child who has been placed by the competent authorities for the purposes of care, protection or treatment of his or her physical or mental health, to a periodic review of the treatment provided to the child and all other circumstances relevant to his or her placement.

Article 26

1. States Parties shall recognize for every child the right to benefit from social security, including social insurance, and shall take the necessary measures to achieve the full realization of this right in accordance with their national law.
2. The benefits should, where appropriate, be granted, taking into account the resources and the circumstances of the child and persons having responsibility for the maintenance of the child, as well as any other consideration relevant to an application for benefits made by or on behalf of the child.

Article 27

1. States Parties recognize the right of every child to a standard of living adequate for the child's physical, mental, spiritual, moral and social development.
2. The parent(s) or others responsible for the child have the primary responsibility to secure, within their abilities and financial capacities, the conditions of living necessary for the child's development.
3. States Parties, in accordance with national conditions and within their means, shall take appropriate measures to assist parents and others responsible for the child to implement this right and shall in case of need provide material assistance and support programmes, particularly with regard to nutrition, clothing and housing.
4. States Parties shall take all appropriate measures to secure the recovery of maintenance for the child from the parents or other persons having financial responsibility for the child, both within the State Party and from abroad. In particular, where the person having financial responsibility for the child lives in a State different from that of the child, States Parties shall promote the accession to international agreements or the conclusion of such agreements, as well as the making of other appropriate arrangements.

Article 28

1. States Parties recognize the right of the child to education, and with a view to achieving this right progressively and on the basis of equal opportunity, they shall, in particular:
   (a) Make primary education compulsory and available free to all;
   (b) Encourage the development of different forms of secondary education, including general and vocational education, make them available and accessible to every child, and take appropriate measures such as the introduction of free education and offering financial assistance in case of need;
   (c) Make higher education accessible to all on the basis of capacity by every appropriate means;
   (d) Make educational and vocational information and guidance available and accessible to all children;
   (e) Take measures to encourage regular attendance at schools and the reduction of drop-out rates.
2. States Parties shall take all appropriate measures to ensure that school discipline is administered in a manner consistent with the child's human dignity and in conformity with the present Convention.
3. States Parties shall promote and encourage international co-operation in matters relating to education, in particular with a view to contributing to the elimination of ignorance and illiteracy throughout the world and facilitating access to scientific and technical knowledge and modern teaching methods. In this regard, particular account shall be taken of the needs of developing countries.

Article 29

1. States Parties agree that the education of the child shall be directed to:
   (a) The development of the child's personality, talents and mental and physical abilities to their fullest potential;
   (b) The development of respect for human rights and fundamental freedoms, and for the principles enshrined in the Charter of the United Nations;
   (c) The development of respect for the child's parents, his or her own cultural identity, language and values, for the national values of the country in which the child is living,

the country from which he or she may originate, and for civilizations different from his or her own;

(d) The preparation of the child for responsible life in a free society, in the spirit of understanding, peace, tolerance, equality of sexes, and friendship among all peoples, ethnic, national and religious groups and persons of indigenous origin;

(e) The development of respect for the natural environment.

2. No part of the present article or article 28 shall be construed so as to interfere with the liberty of individuals and bodies to establish and direct educational institutions, subject always to the observance of the principles set forth in paragraph 1 of the present article and to the requirements that the education given in such institutions shall conform to such minimum standards as may be laid down by the State.

Article 30

In those States in which ethnic, religious or linguistic minorities or persons of indigenous origin exist, a child belonging to such a minority or who is indigenous shall not be denied the right, in community with other members of his or her group, to enjoy his or her own culture, to profess and practise his or her own religion, or to use his or her own language.

Article 31

1. States Parties recognize the right of the child to rest and leisure, to engage in play and recreational activities appropriate to the age of the child and to participate freely in cultural life and the arts.
2. States Parties shall respect and promote the right of the child to participate fully in cultural and artistic life and shall encourage the provision of appropriate and equal opportunities for cultural, artistic, recreational and leisure activity.

Article 32

1. States Parties recognize the right of the child to be protected from economic exploitation and from performing any work that is likely to be hazardous or to interfere with the child's education, or to be harmful to the child's health or physical, mental, spiritual, moral or social development.
2. States Parties shall take legislative, administrative, social and educational measures to ensure the implementation of the

present article. To this end, and having regard to the relevant provisions of other international instruments, States Parties shall in particular:

(a) Provide for a minimum age or minimum ages for admissions to employment;
(b) Provide for appropriate regulation of the hours and conditions of employment;
(c) Provide for appropriate penalties or other sanctions to ensure the effective enforcement of the present article.

Article 33

States Parties shall take all appropriate measures, including legislative, administrative, social and educational measures, to protect children from the illicit use of narcotic drugs and psychotropic substances as defined in the relevant international treaties, and to prevent the use of children in the illicit production and trafficking of such substances.

Article 34

States Parties undertake to protect the child from all forms of sexual exploitation and sexual abuse. For these purposes, States Parties shall in particular take all appropriate national, bilateral and multilateral measures to prevent:

(a) The inducement or coercion of a child to engage in any unlawful sexual activity;
(b) The exploitative use of children in prostitution or other unlawful sexual practices;
(c) The exploitative use of children in pornographic performances and materials.

Article 35

States Parties shall take all appropriate national, bilateral and multilateral measures to prevent the abduction of, the sale of or traffic in children for any purpose or in any form.

Article 36

States Parties shall protect the child against all other forms of exploitation prejudicial to any aspects of the child's welfare.

Article 37

States Parties shall ensure that:

(a) No child shall be subjected to torture or other cruel, inhuman or degrading treatment or punishment. Neither capital punishment nor life imprisonment without possibility of release shall be imposed for offences committed by persons below 18 years of age;

(b) No child shall be deprived of his or her liberty unlawfully or arbitrarily. The arrest, detention or imprisonment of a child shall be in conformity with the law and shall be used only as a measure of last resort and for the shortest appropriate period of time;

(c) Every child deprived of liberty shall be treated with humanity and respect for the inherent dignity of the human person, and in a manner which takes into account the needs of persons of his or her age. In particular every child deprived of liberty shall be separated from adults unless it is considered in the child's best interest not to do so and shall have the right to maintain contact with his or her family through correspondence and visits, save in exceptional circumstances;

(d) Every child deprived of his or her liberty shall have the right to prompt access to legal and other appropriate assistance, as well as the right to challenge the legality of the deprivation of his or her liberty before a court or other competent, independent and impartial authority, and to a prompt decision on any such action.

Article 38

1. States Parties undertake to respect and to ensure respect for rules of international humanitarian law applicable to them in armed conflicts which are relevant to the child.
2. States Parties shall take all feasible measures to ensure that persons who have not attained the age of 15 years do not take a direct part in hostilities.
3. States Parties shall refrain from recruiting any person who has not attained the age of 15 years into their armed forces. In recruiting among those persons who have attained the age of 15 years but who have not attained the age of 18 years, States Parties shall endeavour to give priority to those who are oldest.
4. In accordance with their obligations under international humanitarian law to protect the civilian population in armed conflicts, States Parties shall take all feasible measures to ensure protection and care of children who are affected by an armed conflict.

Article 39

States Parties shall take all appropriate measures to promote physical and psychological recovery and social reintegration of a child victim of: any form of neglect, exploitation, or abuse; torture or any other form of cruel, inhuman or degrading treatment or punishment; or armed conflicts. Such recovery and reintegration shall take place in an environment which fosters the health, self-respect and dignity of the child.

Article 40

1. States Parties recognize the right of every child alleged as, accused of, or recognized as having infringed the penal law to be treated in a manner consistent with the promotion of the child's sense of dignity and worth, which reinforces the child's respect for the human rights and fundamental freedoms of others and which takes into account the child's age and the desirability of promoting the child's reintegration and the child's assuming a constructive role in society.
2. To this end, and having regard to the relevant provisions of international instruments, States Parties shall, in particular, ensure that:
   - (a) No child shall be alleged as, be accused of, or recognized as having infringed the penal law by reason of acts or omissions that were not prohibited by national or international law at the time they were committed;
   - (b) Every child alleged as or accused of having infringed the penal law has at least the following guarantees:
     - (i) To be presumed innocent until proven guilty according to law;
     - (ii) To be informed promptly and directly of the charges against him or her, and, if appropriate, through his or her parents or legal guardians, and to have legal or other appropriate assistance in the preparation and presentation of his or her defence;
     - (iii) To have the matter determined without delay by a competent, independent and impartial authority or judicial body in a fair hearing according to law, in the presence of legal or other appropriate assistance and, unless it is considered not to be in the best interest of the child, in particular, taking into account his or her

age or situation, his or her parents or legal guardians;
- (iv) Not to be compelled to give testimony or to confess guilt; to examine or have examined adverse witnesses and to obtain the participation and examination of witnesses on his or her behalf under conditions of equality;
- (v) If considered to have infringed the penal law, to have this decision and any measures imposed in consequence thereof reviewed by a higher competent, independent and impartial authority or judicial body according to law;
- (vi) To have the free assistance of an interpreter if the child cannot understand or speak the language used;
- (vii) To have his or her privacy fully respected at all stages of the proceedings.

3. States Parties shall seek to promote the establishment of laws, procedures, authorities and institutions specifically applicable to children alleged as, accused of, or recognized as having infringed the penal law, and, in particular:
   - (a) the establishment of a minimum age below which children shall be presumed not to have the capacity to infringe the penal law;
   - (b) whenever appropriate and desirable, measures for dealing with such children without resorting to judicial proceedings, providing that human rights and legal safeguards are fully respected.
4. A variety of dispositions, such as care, guidance and supervision orders; counselling; probation; foster care; education and vocational training programmes and other alternatives to institutional care shall be available to ensure that children are dealt with in a manner appropriate to their well-being and proportionate both to their circumstances and the offence.

Article 41

Nothing in the present Convention shall affect any provisions which are more conducive to the realization of the rights of the child and which may be contained in:

(a) The law of a State Party; or
(b) International law in force for that State.

PART II

Article 42

States Parties undertake to make the principles and provisions of the Convention widely known, by appropriate and active means, to adults and children alike.

Article 43

1. For the purpose of examining the progress made by States Parties in achieving the realization of the obligations undertaken in the present Convention, there shall be established a Committee on the Rights of the Child, which shall carry out the functions hereinafter provided.
2. The Committee shall consist of ten experts of high moral standing and recognized competence in the field covered by this Convention. The members of the Committee shall be elected by States Parties from among their nationals and shall serve in their personal capacity, consideration being given to equitable geographical distribution, as well as to the principal legal systems.
3. The members of the Committee shall be elected by secret ballot from a list of persons nominated by States Parties. Each State Party may nominate one person from among its own nationals.
4. The initial election to the Committee shall be held no later than six months after the date of the entry into force of the present Convention and thereafter every second year. At least four months before the date of each election, the Secretary-General of the United Nations shall address a letter to States Parties inviting them to submit their nominations within two months. The Secretary-General shall subsequently prepare a list in alphabetical order of all persons thus nominated, indicating States Parties which have nominated them, and shall submit it to the States Parties to the present Convention.
5. The elections shall be held at meetings of States Parties convened by the Secretary-General at United Nations Headquarters. At those meetings, for which two thirds of States Parties shall constitute a quorum, the persons elected to the Committee shall be those who obtain the largest number of votes and an absolute majority of the votes of the representatives of States Parties present and voting.

6. The members of the Committee shall be elected for a term of four years. They shall be eligible for re-election if renominated. The term of five of the members elected at the first election shall expire at the end of two years; immediately after the first election, the names of these five members shall be chosen by lot by the Chairman of the meeting.
7. If a member of the Committee dies or resigns or declares that for any other cause he or she can no longer perform the duties of the Committee, the State Party which nominated the member shall appoint another expert from among its nationals to serve for the remainder of the term, subject to the approval of the Committee.
8. The Committee shall establish its own rules of procedure.
9. The Committee shall elect its officers for a period of two years.
10. The meetings of the Committee shall normally be held at United Nations Headquarters or at any other convenient place as determined by the Committee. The Committee shall normally meet annually. The duration of the meetings of the Committee shall be determined, and reviewed, if necessary, by a meeting of the States Parties to the present Convention, subject to the approval of the General Assembly.
11. The Secretary-General of the United Nations shall provide the necessary staff and facilities for the effective performance of the functions of the Committee under the present Convention.
12. With the approval of the General Assembly, the members of the Committee established under the present Convention shall receive emoluments from the United Nations resources on such terms and conditions as the Assembly may decide.

Article 44

1. States Parties undertake to submit to the Committee, through the Secretary-General of the United Nations, reports on the measures they have adopted which give effect to the rights recognized herein and on the progress made on the enjoyment of those rights:
   (a) Within two years of the entry into force of the Convention for the State Party concerned,
   (b) Thereafter every five years.
2. Reports made under the present article shall indicate factors and difficulties, if any, affecting the degree of fulfillment of

the obligations under the present Convention. Reports shall also contain sufficient information to provide the Committee with a comprehensive understanding of the implementation of the Convention in the country concerned.

3. A State Party which has submitted a comprehensive initial report to the Committee need not in its subsequent reports submitted in accordance with paragraph 1(b) of the present article repeat basic information previously provided.
4. The Committee may request from States Parties further information relevant to the implementation of the Convention.
5. The Committee shall submit to the General Assembly, through the Economic and Social Council, every two years, reports on its activities.
6. States Parties shall make their reports widely available to the public in their own countries.

Article 45

In order to foster the effective implementation of the Convention and to encourage international co-operation in the field covered by the Convention:

(a) The specialized agencies, the United Nations Children's Fund and other United Nations organs shall be entitled to be represented at the consideration of the implementation of such provisions of the present Convention as fall within the scope of their mandate. The Committee may invite the specialized agencies, the United Nations Children's Fund and other competent bodies as it may consider appropriate to provide expert advice on the implementation of the Convention in areas falling within the scope of their respective mandates. The Committee may invite the specialized agencies, the United Nations Children's Fund and other United Nations organs to submit reports on the implementation of the Convention in areas falling within the scope of their activities;

(b) The Committee shall transmit, as it may consider appropriate, to the specialized agencies, the United Nations Children's Fund and other competent bodies, any reports from States Parties that contain a request, or indicate a need, for technical advice or assistance, along with the Committee's observations and suggestions, if any, on these requests or indications;

(c) The Committee may recommend to the General Assembly to request the Secretary-General to undertake on its behalf studies on specific issues relating to the rights of the child;

(d) The Committee may make suggestions and general recommendations based on information received pursuant to articles 44 and 45 of the present Convention. Such suggestions and general recommendations shall be transmitted to any State Party concerned and reported to the General Assembly, together with comments, if any, from States Parties.

PART III

Article 46

The present Convention shall be open for signature by all States.

Article 47

The present Convention is subject to ratification. Instruments of ratification shall be deposited with the Secretary-General of the United Nations.

Article 48

The present Convention shall remain open for accession by any State. The instruments of accession shall be deposited with the Secretary-General of the United Nations.

Article 49

1. The present Convention shall enter into force on the thirtieth day following the date of deposit with the Secretary-General of the United Nations of the twentieth instrument of ratification or accession.
2. For each State ratifying or acceding to the Convention after the deposit of the twentieth instrument of ratification or accession, the Convention shall enter into force on the thirtieth day after the deposit by such State of its instrument of ratification or accession.

Article 50

1. Any State Party may propose an amendment and file it with the Secretary-General of the United Nations. The Secretary-General shall thereupon communicate the proposed amendment to States Parties, with a request that they indicate whether they favour a conference of States Parties for the purpose of considering and voting upon the proposals. In the event that, within four months from the date of such communication, at least one-third of the States Parties favour such a

conference, the Secretary-General shall convene the conference under the auspices of the United Nations. Any amendment adopted by a majority of States Parties present and voting at the conference shall be submitted to the General Assembly for approval.

2. An amendment adopted in accordance with paragraph 1 of the present article shall enter into force when it has been approved by the General Assembly of the United Nations and accepted by a two-thirds majority of States Parties.
3. When an amendment enters into force, it shall be binding on those States Parties which have accepted it, other States Parties still being bound by the provisions of the present Convention and any earlier amendments which they have accepted.

Article 51

1. The Secretary-General of the United Nations shall receive and circulate to all States the text of reservations made by States at the time of ratification or accession.
2. A reservation incompatible with the object and purpose of the present Convention shall not be permitted.
3. Reservations may be withdrawn at any time by notification to that effect addressed to the Secretary-General of the United Nations, who shall then inform all States. Such notification shall take effect on the date on which it is received by the Secretary-General.

Article 52

A State Party may denounce the present Convention by written notification to the Secretary-General of the United Nations. Denunciation becomes effective one year after the date of receipt of the notification by the Secretary-General.

Article 53

The Secretary-General of the United Nations is designated as the depository of the present Convention.

Article 54

The original of the present Convention, of which the Arabic, Chinese, English, French, Russian and Spanish texts are equally authentic, shall be deposited with the Secretary-General of the United Nations.

In witness thereof the undersigned plenipotentiaries, being duly authorized thereto by their respective Governments, have signed the present Convention.

Charter on the Rights and Welfare of the African Child (1990)

Preamble

The African States Members of the Organization of African Unity, Parties to the present Convention entitled "African Charter on the Rights and Welfare of the Child"

Recalling that the Assembly of Heads of State and Government of the Organization of African Unity, meeting at its Sixteenth Ordinary Session in Monrovia, Liberia from 17 to 20 July, 1979 recognized the need to take all appropriate measures to promote and protect the rights and welfare of the African child;

Considering that the Charter of the Organization of African Unity recognizes the paramountcy of Human Rights and the African Charter on Human and Peoples' Rights proclaimed and agreed that everyone is entitled to all the rights and freedoms recognized and guaranteed therein, without distinction of any kind such as race, ethnic group, colour, sex, language, religion, political or any other opinion, national and social origin, fortune, birth or status;

Noting with concern that the situation of many African children remains critical as a result of inadequate social conditions, natural disasters, armed conflicts, economic deprivation, exploitation, hunger, disability and that the child, by reason of his physical and mental immaturity, needs special safeguard and care;

Recognizing that the child occupies a unique and privileged position in the African society and that for the full and harmonious development of his personality, the child should grow up in a family environment in an atmosphere of happiness, love and understanding;

Recognizing that the child due to the needs of his physical and mental development requires particular care with regard to health, physical, mental, moral and social development, and requires legal protection in conditions of freedom, dignity and security;

Taking into consideration the virtues of their cultural heritage, historical background and the values of the African civilization which should inspire Geneva and characterize their reflection on the concept of the rights and welfare of the child;

Considering that the promotion and protection of the rights and welfare of the child also implies the performance of duties on the part of everyone;

Reaffirming adherence to the principles of the rights and welfare of the child contained in the declarations, conventions and other instruments of the Organization of African Unity and in the United Nations and in particular the United Nations Convention on the Rights of the Child;

HAVE AGREED AS FOLLOWS:

Rights and Duties

CHAPTER ONE

Rights and Welfare of the Child

ARTICLE 1

1. The Member States of the Organization of African Unity Parties to the present Charter shall recognize the rights, freedoms and duties enshrined in this Charter and shall undertake to take the necessary steps, in accordance with their Constitutional process and with the provisions of the present Charter, to adopt such legislative or other measures as may be necessary to give effect to the provisions of this Charter.
2. Nothing in this Charter shall affect any provisions that are more conducive to the realization of the rights and welfare of the child contained in the law of a State Party or in any other international convention or agreement in force in that State.
3. Any custom, tradition, cultural or religious practice that is inconsistent with the rights, duties and obligations contained in the present Charter shall to the extent to such inconsistency be null and void.

ARTICLE 2

According to the present Charter, a child means every human being up to the age of 18 years whether such a child is born out of wedlock or in wedlock.

ARTICLE 3

Every child shall be entitled to the enjoyment of the rights and freedoms recognized and guaranteed in this Charter irrespective of the child's or his parents or legal guardian's race, ethnic group, colour, sex, language, religion, political or other opinion, national and social origin, fortune, birth or other status.

ARTICLE 4

1. In all actions concerning the child undertaken by any person or authority the best interests of the child shall be the primary consideration.
2. In all judicial or administrative proceedings affecting a child who is capable of forming his own views, an opportunity shall be provided for the views of the child to be heard either directly or through a disinterested representative as a party to the proceedings, and those views shall be taken into consideration by the relevant authority in accordance with the provisions of appropriate laws.

ARTICLE 5

1. Every child has an inherent right to life. This right shall be protected by law. No child shall be arbitrarily deprived of his life.
2. States Parties to the present Charter shall ensure, to the maximum extent possible, the survival and development of the child.
3. Sentence of death shall not be imposed for crimes committed by children.

ARTICLE 6

1. Every child shall have the right from his birth to a name.
2. Every child shall be registered immediately after birth.
3. Every child has the right to acquire a nationality.
4. States Parties to the present Charter shall undertake to ensure that their Constitutional Processes recognize the principles according to which a child shall acquire the nationality of the state in the territory of which he has been born if, at the time of the child's birth, he is not entitled nationality by any other state in accordance with its laws.

ARTICLE 7

Every child who is freely capable of forming his own views shall be assured the right to express his opinions freely in all matters and to disseminate his opinions subject to such restrictions as are prescribed by law.

ARTICLE 8

Every child shall have the right to free association and freedom of peaceful assembly in conformity with the law.

ARTICLE 9

1. Every child shall have the right to freedom of thought, conscience and religion. Parents and where applicable legal guardians have the right to provide guidance and direction in the exercise of these rights to a degree and in a manner consistent with the evolving capacities of the child and a duty to facilitate the enjoyment of these rights subject to national laws and policies.

ARTICLE 10

No child shall be subjected to arbitrary or unlawful interference with his privacy, family, home or correspondence, or to attacks upon his honour or reputation. The child has the right to the protection of the law against such interference or attacks.

ARTICLE 11

1. Every child shall have the right to education.
2. The education of the child shall be directed to:
   a) the promotion and development of the child's personality, talents and mental and physical abilities to their fullest potential;
   b) fostering respect for human rights and fundamental freedoms with particular reference to those set out in the provisions of various African instruments on human and peoples' rights and international human rights declarations and conventions;
   c) the preservation and strengthening of positive African morals, traditional values and cultures;
   d) the preparation of the child for responsible life in a free society, in the spirit of understanding, tolerance, dialogue, mutual respect and friendship among all peoples, ethnic, tribal and religious groups;
   e) the preservation of national independence and territorial integrity;
   f) the promotion and achievements of African unity and solidarity;
   g) the development of respect for the environment and natural resources.

3. States Parties to the present Charter shall take all appropriate measures with a view to achieving the full realization of this right and shall in particular: a) provide free and compulsory basic education; b) encourage the development of secondary education in its different forms and to progressively make it free and accessible to all; c) make higher education accessible to all on the basis of capacity and ability by every appropriate means; d) take measures to encourage regular attendance at schools and the reduction of dropouts; e) take special measures to ensure that children from disadvantaged groups of communities have equal access to education.
4. States Parties to the present Charter shall respect the rights and duties of parents, and where applicable, of legal guardians to choose for their children schools, other than those established by public authorities, which conform to such minimum standards as may be approved by the state, to ensure the religious and moral education of the child in a manner with the evolving capacities of the child.
5. States Parties to the present Charter shall take all appropriate measures to ensure that a child who is subjected to school or parental discipline shall be treated with humanity and with respect for the inherent dignity of the child and in conformity with the present Charter.
6. States Parties to the present Charter shall take all appropriate measures to ensure that children who become mothers before completing their education shall have an opportunity to continue with their education on the basis of their individual ability.
7. No part of this article shall be construed as to interfere with the liberty of individuals and bodies to establish and direct educational institutions subject to the observance of the principles set out in paragraph 1 of this Article and the requirement that the education given in such institutions shall conform to such minimum standards as may be laid down by the State.

ARTICLE 12

1. States Parties recognize the right of the child to rest and leisure, to engage in play and recreational activities appropriate to the age of the child and to participate freely in cultural life and the arts.
2. States Parties shall respect and promote the right of the child to fully participate in cultural and artistic life and shall en-

courage the provision of appropriate and equal opportunities for cultural, artistic, recreational and leisure activity.

ARTICLE 13

1. Every child who is mentally or physically disabled shall have the right to special measures of protection in keeping with his physical and moral needs and under conditions which ensure his dignity, promote his self reliance and active participation in the community.
2. States Parties to the present Charter shall ensure, subject to available resources, to a disabled child and to those responsible for his care, of assistance for which application is made and which is appropriate to the child's condition and in the particular shall ensure that the disabled child has effective access to training, preparation for employment and recreation opportunities in a manner conducive to the child achieving the fullest possible social integration, individual development and his cultural and moral development.
3. The States Parties to the present Charter shall use their available resources with a view to achieving progressively the full convenience of the mentally or physically disabled person to movement and access to public highway buildings and other places to which the disabled may legitimately want to have access to.

ARTICLE 14

1. Every child shall have the right to enjoy the best attainable state of physical, mental and spiritual health.
2. States Parties to the present Charter shall undertake to pursue the full implementation of this right and in particular shall take measures:
   a) to diminish infant and child mortality;
   b) to ensure the provision of necessary medical assistance and health care to all children with emphasis on the development of primary health care;
   c) to ensure the provision of adequate nutrition and safe drinking water;
   d) to combat disease and malnutrition within the framework of primary health care through the application of appropriate technology;
   e) to ensure appropriate health care for expectant and nursing mothers;

f) to develop preventive health care and family planning education;
g) to integrate basic health service programmes in national development plans;
h) to ensure that all sectors of the society, in particular, parents, children community leaders and community workers are informed and supported in the use of basic knowledge of child health and nutrition, the advantages of breastfeeding, hygiene and environmental sanitation and the prevention of domestic and other accidents;
i) to ensure the meaningful participation of non-governmental organizations, local communities and the beneficiary population in the planning and management of basic service programmes for children;
j) to support through technical and financial means the mobilization of local community resources in the development of primary health care for children.

ARTICLE 15

1. Every child shall be protected from all forms of economic exploitation and from performing any work that is likely to be hazardous or to interfere with the child's physical, mental, spiritual, moral, or social development.
2. States Parties to the present Charter shall take all appropriate legislative and administrative measures to ensure the full implementation of the Article which covers both the formal sectors of employment and having regard to the relevant provisions of the International Labour Organisation instrument relating to children, States Parties shall in particular:
   a) provide through legislation, minimum ages for admission to every employment;
   b) provide for appropriate regulation of hours and conditions of employment;
   c) provide for appropriate penalties or other sanctions to ensure the effective enforcement of this Article;
   d) promote the dissemination of information on the hazards of child labour to all sectors of the community.

ARTICLE 16

1. States Parties to the present Charter shall take specific legislative, administrative, social and educational measures to protect the child from all forms of physical or mental injury or

abuse, neglect or maltreatment including sexual abuse, while in the care of a parent, legal guardian or any other person who has the care of the child.

2. Protective measures under this Article shall include effective procedures for the establishment of special monitoring units to provide necessary support for the child and for those who have the care of the child, as well as other forms of prevention and for identification, reporting, referral, investigation, treatment, and follow-up of instances of child abuse and neglect.

ARTICLE 17

1. Every child accused or found guilty of having infringed penal law shall have the right to special treatment in a manner consistent with the child's sense of dignity and worth and which reinforces the child's respect for human rights and fundamental freedoms of others.
2. States Parties to the present Charter shall in particular:
   a) ensure that no child who is detained or imprisoned or otherwise deprived of its liberty is subjected to torture, inhuman, degrading treatment or punishment;
   b) ensure that children are separated from adults in their place of detention or imprisonment;
   c) ensure that every child accused or infringing the penal law:
      i) shall be presumed innocent until proven guilty;
      ii) shall be informed promptly in a language that he understands and in detail of the charge against him;
      iii) shall be afforded legal and other appropriate assistance in the preparation and presentation of his defence;
      iv) shall have the matter determined as speedily as possible by an impartial tribunal and if found guilty be entitled to an appeal by a higher tribunal;
      v) shall prohibit the press and the public from trial;
      vi) shall have the assistance of an interpreter if the child cannot understand the language used;
      vii) shall not be compelled to give testimony or confess guilt.
3. The essential aim of treatment of every child during the trial and also if found guilty of infringing the penal law shall be its reformation, reintegration into its family and social rehabilitation.

4. There shall be a minimum age below which children shall be presumed not to have the capacity to infringe the penal law.

ARTICLE 18

1. The family shall be the natural unit and basis of society. It shall be protected by the state which shall take care of its physical health and morals.
2. States Parties to the present Charter shall take appropriate steps to ensure equality of rights and responsibilities of spouses as to marriage and its dissolution. In case of dissolution, provision shall be made for the necessary protection of the children.
3. No child shall be deprived of maintenance by reference to the parents' marital status.

ARTICLE 19

1. Every child shall be entitled to the enjoyment of parental care and shall, whenever possible, have his place of residence determined by his parents. No child shall be separated from his parents against his will, except when a competent authority subject to judicial review determine in accordance with the appropriate law, that such separation is in the best interest of the child.
2. Every child who is separated from one or both parents shall have the right to maintain personal relations and direct contact with both parents on a regular basis.
3. Where separation results from the action of a State Party, the State Party shall provide the child, or if appropriate, another member of the family with essential information concerning the whereabouts of the absent member or members of the family. State Parties shall ensure that the submission of such a request shall not entail any adverse consequences for the person or persons in whose respect it is made.
4. Where a child is apprehended by a State Party, his parents or guardians shall as soon as reasonably practical be notified of such apprehension by that State Party.

ARTICLE 20

1. Parents or others responsible for the child shall have the primary responsibility for the upbringing and development of the child and shall have the duty:

a) to ensure that the best interest of the child are their basic concern at all times;
b) to secure, within their abilities and financial capacities, conditions of living necessary to the child's development; and
c) to ensure that domestic discipline is administered in moderation and that the child is treated with humanity and with respect for his inherent dignity.

2. States Parties to the present Charter, in accordance with their means and national conditions shall take all appropriate measures:
   a) to assist parents and others responsible for the child and in case of need provide material assistance and support programmes particularly with regard to nutrition, health, education, clothing and housing;
   b) to assist parents and others responsible for the child in the performance of child-rearing and ensure the development of institutions for the care of children; and
   c) to ensure that the children of working parents benefit from child care services and facilities.

ARTICLE 21

1. States Parties to the present Charter shall take all appropriate measures to abolish customs and practices harmful to the welfare, normal growth and development of the child and in particular:
   a) those customs and practices prejudicial to the health or life of the child, and
   b) those customs and practices discriminatory to the child on the grounds of sex or other status.
2. Child marriage and the betrothal of young girls shall be prohibited and effective action, including legislation, shall be taken to specify the minimum age of marriage and make registration of marriage in an official registry compulsory.

ARTICLE 22

1. States Parties to this Chapter shall undertake to respect and ensure respect for rules of international humanitarian law applicable in armed conflicts which are relevant to the child.
2. States Parties to the present Charter shall take all necessary measures to ensure that no child shall take a direct part in hostilities and refrain, in particular, from recruiting any child.

3. States Parties to the present Charter shall, in accordance with their obligations under international humanitarian law, protect the civilian population in armed conflicts and shall take all feasible measures to ensure the protection and care of children who are affected by armed conflict. Such rules shall also apply to children in situations of internal armed conflict, tension or strife.

ARTICLE 23

1. States Parties to the present Charter shall take all appropriate measures to ensure that a child who is seeking refugee status or who is considered a refugee in accordance with applicable international or domestic law shall, whether unaccompanied or accompanied by parents, legal guardians or close relatives, receive appropriate protection and humanitarian assistance in the enjoyment of the rights set out in this Charter and other international human rights and humanitarian instruments to which the States are Parties.
2. States Parties shall undertake to cooperate with existing international organizations which protect and assist refugees in their efforts to protect and assist such a child and to trace the parents or other close relatives of an unaccompanied refugee child in order to obtain information necessary for reunification with the family.
3. Where no parents, legal guardians or close relatives can be found, the child shall be accorded the same protection as any other child permanently or temporarily deprived of his family environment for any reason.
4. The provisions of this Article apply *Mutatis Mutandis* to internally displaced children whether through natural disasters, internal conflicts and strife, breakdown of economic and social order or howsoever caused.

ARTICLE 24

States Parties which recognize the system of adoption shall ensure that the best interest of the child shall be the paramount consideration and they shall:

a) establish competent authorities to determine matters of adoption;
b) such competent authorities shall determine in accordance with applicable law and procedure and on the basis of all relevant and reliable information, that the adoption is permis-

sible in view of the child's status concerning parents, relatives and guardians and that, if required, the appropriate persons concerned have given their informed consent to the adoption on the basis of such counselling as may be necessary;

c) recognize that inter-country adoption may be considered as an alternative means of child's care, if the child cannot be placed in a foster or an adoptive family or cannot in any suitable manner be cared for in the child's country of origin;
d) ensure that the child concerned by inter-country adoption enjoys safeguards and standards equivalent to those existing in the case of national adoption;
e) take all appropriate measures to ensure that, in inter-country adoption, the placement does not result in improper financial gain for those involved in it;
f) promote, where appropriate, the objectives of this Article by concluding bilateral or multilateral arrangements or agreements, and endeavour, within this framework, to ensure that the placement of the child in another country is carried out by competent authorities or organs;
g) establish a machinery to monitor the well-being of the adopted child.

ARTICLE 25

1. Every child who is permanently or temporarily deprived of his family environment for any reason shall be entitled to special protection and assistance.
2. States Parties to the present Charter shall ensure that a child who is parentless, or who is temporarily or permanently deprived of his family environment, or who in his best interest cannot be brought up or allowed to remain in that environment shall be provided with alternative family care, which include, among others, foster placement, or placement in suitable institutions for the care of children.
3. When considering alternative family care of the child and the best interests of the child, due regard shall be paid to the desirability of continuity in a child's upbringing and to the child's ethnic, religious or linguistic background.

ARTICLE 26

States Parties to the present Charter shall individually and collectively undertake to accord the highest priority to the special needs of children living under *Apartheid* and in states subject to military destabilization by the *Apartheid* regime. States Parties shall also undertake to provide, whenever possible, material assistance to such children and to direct their efforts towards the elimination of racial discrimination and *Apartheid* on the African continent.

ARTICLE 27

1. States Parties to the present Charter shall undertake to protect the Child from all forms of sexual exploitation and sexual abuse and shall in particular take measures to prevent:
   a) the inducement or coercion of a child to engage in any sexual activity;
   b) the use of children in prostitution or other sexual practices;
   c) the use of children in pornographic performances and material.

ARTICLE 28

States Parties to the present Charter shall take all appropriate measures to protect the child from illegal use of narcotic and psychotropic substances as defined in the relevant international treaties, and to prevent the use of children in the illegal production and trafficking of such substances.

ARTICLE 29

States Parties to the present Charter shall take appropriate measures to prevent the abduction, the sale of, or traffic in children for any purpose or in any form, by any person including parents or legal guardians of the child.

ARTICLE 30

States Parties to the present Charter shall undertake to provide special treatment to expectant mothers and to mothers of infants and young children who have been accused or found guilty of infringing the penal law and shall in particular:

a) establish special alternative institutions for holding such mothers; and
b) establish and promote measures alternative to institutional confinement for the treatment of such mothers;
c) a non-custodial sentence will always be first considered when sentencing such mothers;
d) a child shall not be imprisoned with its mother;
e) a death sentence shall not be imposed on such mothers;

f) the essential aim of the penitentiary system will be the reformation, the integration of the mother to the family and social rehabilitation.

ARTICLE 31

Every child shall have duties towards his family and society, the State and other legally recognized communities and the international community. The child, subject to his age and ability, and such limitations as may be contained in the present Charter, shall have the duty:

1. To work for the cohesion of the family, to respect his parents at all times and to maintain them in case of needs.
2. To serve his national community by placing his physical and intellectual abilities at its service.
3. To preserve and strengthen social and national solidarity.
4. To preserve and strengthen African Cultural values in his relations with other members of the society, in the spirit of tolerance, dialogue and consultation and to contribute to the moral well-being of society.
5. To preserve and strengthen the independence and the integrity of his country.
6. To contribute to the best of his abilities, at all times and at all levels to the promotion and achievement of African Unity.

CHAPTER TWO

Establishment and Organization of the Committee on the Rights and Welfare of the Child

ARTICLE 32

An African Committee of Experts on the rights and welfare of the child hereinafter called "the Committee" shall be established within the Organization of African Unity to promote and protect the rights and welfare of the Child.

ARTICLE 33

1. The Committee shall consist of 11 members of high moral standing, integrity, impartiality and competence in matters of rights and welfare of the child.
2. The members of the Committee shall serve in their personal capacity.
3. The Committee shall not include more than one national of the same State.

ARTICLE 34

The members of the Committee shall be elected by secret ballot by the Assembly of Heads of State and Government from a list of persons nominated by the States Parties to the present Charter.

ARTICLE 35

Each State Party to the present Charter may not nominate more than two candidates. The candidates must have one of the nationalities of the States Parties to the present Charter. When two candidates are nominated by a state one of them may not be a national of that state.

ARTICLE 36

1. The Secretary-General of the Organization of African Unity shall invite State Parties to the present Charter at least six months before the elections to nominate candidates.
2. The Secretary-General of the Organization of African Unity shall make a list of persons nominated and communicate it to the Heads of State and Government at least two months before the elections.

ARTICLE 37

1. The members of the Committee shall be elected for a term of five years and may be re-elected only once, but the term of four of the members elected at the first election shall expire after two years and the terms of six others, after four years.
2. Immediately after the first election, the Chairman of the Assembly of Heads of State and Government of the Organization of African Unity shall draw lots to determine the names of those members referred to in Paragraph 1 of this Article.
3. The Secretary-General of the Organization of African Unity shall convene the first meeting of the Committee at the Headquarters of the Organization within six months of the Constitution of the Committee, and thereafter the Committee shall be convened by its Chairman whenever necessary but at least once a year.

ARTICLE 38

If a member of the Committee vacates his office for any reason other than the normal expiration of a term, the state which nominated that member shall appoint another member from among its nationals to serve for the remainder of the term—subject to the approval of the Committee.

ARTICLE 39

1. The Committee shall elect its officers for a period of two years.
2. The Committee shall establish its own Rules of Procedure.
3. Seven Committee members shall form the quorum.
4. In case of an equality of votes, the Chairman shall have a casting vote.
5. The working languages of the Committee shall be the official languages of the OAU.

ARTICLE 41

In discharging their duties, members of the Committee shall enjoy privileges and immunities provided for in the General Convention on the Privileges and Immunities of the Organization of African Unity.

CHAPTER THREE

Mandate and Procedure of the Committee

ARTICLE 42

The functions of the Committee shall be:

a) To promote the rights enshrined in this Charter and in particular:
   i) collect document, commission inter-disciplinary assessment of situations on African problems in the fields of the rights and welfare of the child, organize meetings, encourage national and local institutions concerned with the rights and welfare of the child, and where necessary give its views and make recommendations to Governments;
   ii) to formulate and lay down principles and rules aiming at solving problems relating to the rights and welfare of children in Africa;
   iii) cooperate with other African and International Institutions and Organizations concerned with the promotion and protection of the rights and welfare of the child.
b) To monitor the implementation and ensure protection of the rights enshrined in this Charter.

c) Interpret the provisions of the present Charter at the request of a State Party, an Institution of the Organization of African Unity or any other Institution recognized by the Organization of African Unity.

d) Perform such other tasks as may be entrusted to it by the Assembly of Heads of State and Government, Secretary-General of the OAU and any other Organs of the OAU.

ARTICLE 43

1. Every State Party to the present Charter shall undertake to submit to the Committee through the Secretary-General of the Organization of African Unity reports on the measures they have adopted which give effect to the provisions of this Charter and on the progress made in the enjoyment of these rights:
   a) within two years of the entry into force of the Charter for the State Party concerned, and
   b) thereafter, every four years.
2. Every report made under this Article shall
   a) contain sufficient information on the law and practice of each of the rights, duties and obligations contained in the present Charter to provide the Committee with comprehensive understanding of the implementation of the Charter in the relevant country; and
   b) shall indicate factors and difficulties, if any, affecting the fulfillment of the obligations imposed under the Charter.
3. A State Party which has submitted a comprehensive first report to the Committee need not, in its subsequent reports submitted in accordance with paragraph 1(a) of this Article, repeat the basic information previously provided.

ARTICLE 44

The Committee may receive communication, from any group or non-government organization recognized by the Organization of African Unity or the United Nations relating to any matter covered by this Charter.

ARTICLE 45

1. The Committee may resort to any appropriate method of investigating any matter falling within the ambit of the present Charter, request from the States Parties any information relevant to the implementation of the Charter and may

also resort to any appropriate method of investigating the measures a State Party has adopted to implement the Charter.

2. The Committee shall submit to the Ordinary Session of the Assembly of Heads of State and Government through the Economic and Social Commission of the Organization of African Unity, every two years, reports on its activities and on any communication made under Article 46 of this Charter.
3. The Committee shall publish its Report after it has been considered by the Assembly of Heads of State and Government.

CHAPTER FOUR

Miscellaneous Provisions

ARTICLE 46

The Committee shall draw inspiration from International Law on Human Rights, particularly from the provisions of the African Charter on Human and People's Rights, the Charter of the Organization of African Unity, the Universal Declaration of Human Rights, the United Nations Convention on the Rights of the Child and other instruments adopted by the United Nations and by African Countries in the field of human rights.

ARTICLE 47

1. The present Charter shall be open for signature, ratification or adherence of the Member States of the Organization of African Unity.
2. The instruments of ratification or adherence to the present Charter shall be deposited with the Secretary-General of the Organization of African Unity.
3. The present Charter shall come into force 30 days after the reception by the Secretary-General of the Organization of African Unity of the instruments of ratification of adherence of 15 Member States of the Organization of African Unity.

ARTICLE 48

1. The present Charter may be amended or revised if any State Party makes a written request to that effect to the Secretary-General of the Organization of African Unity, provided that the proposed amendment is not submitted to the Assembly of Heads of State and Government for consideration until all the

States Parties have been duly notified of it and the Committee has given its opinion on the amendment.

2. An amendment shall be approved by a simple majority of the States Parties.

Reprinted from Philip E. Veerman, *The Rights of the Child and the Changing Image of Childhood* (Dordrecht, the Netherlands: Martinus Nijhoff, 1992), pp. 579–597. Reprinted by permission of Kluwer Academic Publishers.

World Summit for Children: Year 2000 Goals (1990)

The world's political leaders met in New York City at the World Summit for Children in September 1990 and prepared this list of goals related to the global welfare of children. All the goals listed were deemed both technically and financially feasible by the assembled leadership.

Overall Goals 1990–2000

- A one-third reduction in under-five death rates (or a reduction to 70 per 1,000 live births—whichever is lower).
- A halving of maternal mortality rates.
- A halving of severe and moderate malnutrition among the world's under-fives.
- Safe water and sanitation for all families.
- Basic education for all children and completion of primary education by at least 80%PER.
- A halving of the adult illiteracy rate and the achievement of equal educational opportunity for males and females.
- Protection for the many millions of children in especially difficult circumstances and the acceptance and observance, in all countries, of the recently adopted Convention on the Rights of the Child. In particular, the 1990s should see rapidly growing acceptance of the idea of special protection for children in time of war.

Protection for Girls and Women

- Family planning education and services to be made available to all couples to empower them to prevent unwanted pregnancies and births which are "too many and too close" and to women who are "too young or too old." Such services should be adapted to each country's cultural, religious and social traditions.

- All women to have access to prenatal care, a trained attendant during childbirth and referral facilities for high-risk pregnancies and obstetric emergencies.
- Universal recognition of the special health and nutritional needs of females during early childhood, adolescence, pregnancy, and lactation.

Nutrition

- A reduction in the incidence of low birth weight (under 2.5 kg) to less than 10%PER.
- A one-third reduction in iron deficiency anemia among women.
- Virtual elimination of vitamin A deficiency and iodine deficiency disorders.
- All families to know the importance of supporting women in the task of exclusive breastfeeding for the first four to six months of a child's life.
- Growth monitoring and promotion to be institutionalized in all countries.
- Dissemination of knowledge to enable all families to ensure household food security.

Child Health

- The eradication of polio.
- The elimination of neonatal tetanus (by 1995).
- A 90%PER reduction in measles cases and a 95%PER reduction in measles deaths, compared to pre-immunization levels.
- Achievement and maintenance of at least 90%PER immunization coverage of one-year-old children and universal tetanus immunization for women in the child-bearing years.
- A halving of child deaths caused by diarrhea and a 25%PER reduction in the incidence of diarrhea diseases.
- A one-third reduction in child deaths caused by acute respiratory infections.
- The elimination of guinea worm disease.

Education

- In addition to the expansion of primary school education and its equivalents, today's essential knowledge and life skills could be put at the disposal of all families by mobilizing today's vastly increased communications capacity.

Reprinted from James P. Grant, *The State of the World's Children 1994* (Oxford: Oxford University Press, 1994), p. 56. By permission of Oxford University Press.

The Declaration of Lima and the Narino Accord

The Declaration of Lima and the Narino Accord represent the efforts of Latin American and Caribbean societies to improve the condition of children within the international framework established by the UN Convention on the Rights of the Child. Whereas the Declaration of Lima represents the first statement of Latin American coordinating committees regarding the progress and problems encountered by societies seeking to realize the convention's promise, the Narino Accord constitutes a significant step forward in articulating specific goals linked to the program of the 1990 World Summit for Children, and creating follow-up mechanisms geared to assessing realization of these goals.

Declaration of Lima (1992)

Gathered in the city of Lima, Peru, at the First Latin American meeting to Monitor the Implementation of the Convention on the Rights of the Child, held from 8 to 10 December 1992, we, the representatives of 13 National Coordinating Bodies to Monitor the Implementation of the Convention in Latin America, and the representatives of five regional supporting organizations, aiming to assess the reports submitted to the United Nations Committee and the progress and limitations in the implementation of the Convention on the Rights of the Child in the region, believe it necessary to state to children and adolescents, to the Latin American peoples, to international cooperation and finance organizations, to Governments and to the members of the Committee, the following:

1. That the efforts to implement the Convention in the region are seriously affected by the consequences of the economic adjustment policies implemented by Governments;
2. That, notwithstanding the formal recognition of the Convention, the agreements reached at the World Summit for Children, and the formulation of National Plans of Action for the Child, there is not always a real, concrete political will on the part of Governments to fulfill their commitments;

3. That not all Governments or groups with political and economic power have stated their intention or carried out any actions to reverse the conditions of social injustice and hardship that Latin American children face. This fact, which is serious in itself, becomes even more discouraging in view of the growing poverty and the relegation which affect the most vulnerable sectors of society;
4. That the ratification of the Convention, the formulation of other plans of action and international commitments have in no substantial way solved the age-old exclusion and marginalization of children and adolescents in society;
5. That to be subjects of law, they must be subjects of society and this capacity is denied to most Latin American children and adolescents;
6. That in spite of this situation, there is hope in the potential commitment of civil society as manifested in enormous continent-wide efforts to promote, defend and protect the rights of the child;
7. That the most encouraging element in this popular commitment lies in the signs of organization by children and adolescents who struggle not only to survive but also to develop their own identity.

   Therefore, the undersigned ask:

   1. The United Nations Committee:

      To request Governments to comply with the established deadlines for submitting and circulating official reports on the implementation of the Convention;

      To use all necessary channels to gather information from non-governmental organizations to supplement or correct official reports;

      To make civil organizations, and not only the diplomatic representation of each country, aware of its conclusions and recommendations regarding the reports;

      To recognize, support and grant official consultative status to national and/or regional non-governmental coordination bodies which monitor the implementation of the Convention;

   2. Grass-roots organizations:

      To commit themselves still more actively to implementing the Convention;

      To promote, recognize and strengthen initiatives by children and adolescents to organize themselves;

To participate in national and regional coordination efforts to monitor the implementation of the Convention;

3. Other organized sectors of civil society and the media:
   To promote and comply with the Convention on the Rights of the Child;
   To display solidarity in supporting the initiatives of grass-roots, children's and adolescents' organizations.

Finally, we propose to children and adolescents that they demand from the adult world the legitimate room to organize and mobilize as the only way to guarantee the enforcement, respect and defense of their rights. For our part, we commit ourselves to supporting them in the struggle to achieve conditions for a more dignified life.

Lima, 10 December 1992

Narino Accord

Agenda 2000: Children Now

Second Meeting on Children and Social Policy in the Americas

Preamble

The Ministers and Representatives of the Governments participating in the Second Meeting on Children and Social Policy in the Americas, held in the city of Santa Fe de Bogota, Republic of Colombia, on 5 and 6 April, 1994,
CONSIDERING:

1. That the nature and specificity of the commitments set out in the Declaration of the World Summit for Children, together with the agreements reached during the Tlatlelolco Meeting in Mexico, 1992; the content of Programme 21 of the World Conference on Environment and Development in Brazil, 1992; the provisions of the 111 Conference of Heads of Spanish American States and Governments in Brazil, 1993; the Governmental Preparatory Meeting for the International Year of the Family in Cartagena, 1993; Caricom meetings; the resolutions of the XVII Panamerican Congress for Children in Costa Rica, 1993, which have resulted in increased awareness and articulation in the Americas of the responsibility shared by

the State and society for attending the needs of Children and Youth.

2. That the consolidation of this process will be increased through the integrated action of our Governments in: the preparation of regional strategies for the World Population and Development Conference in Cairo, 1994; the IV Spanish American Conference of Heads of States and Governments in Cartagena, July 1994; the Vl Preparatory Regional Conference for the IV World Conference for Women in Buenos Aires, 1994; the Interamerican Summit Meeting in Miami, 1994; the IV World Conference for Women in Beijing, 1995; the World Summit for Social Development in Copenhagen, 1995, all of which express a continental policy of States.
3. That following the generally adverse economic climate of the decade of the 80s, in the 90s the countries of the region of the Americas are commencing a process of economic reform or adaptation, which is evident in the positive macroeconomic and social indicators of some countries.
4. That one of the points of consensus which is becoming ever clearer in the region is that it is necessary to adopt simultaneous and complementary policies of economic and social development, as the indivisible components of public policy, in which national plans for Children are duly institutionalized.
5. That in this process, human development must form the fulcrum of social policy, whose final objective is to achieve adequate quality of life and the full dignity of the human being, one of the six priorities of the international community being the elimination of the scourges of poverty, hunger, illiteracy, disease, unemployment and violence.
6. That the political will of Governments makes it possible to hope that the region as a whole will achieve the goals and fulfill the commitments for Children by the middle of the final decade of the Century.
7. That this stage of regional political and economic development provides us with a unique opportunity to implement social investments which will result in efficiency, economic productivity and equity.
8. That UNDP, UNICEF, the Government of Norway and various international gatherings have recommended that developing country governments should allocate at least 20%PER of national budgets to priority human development activities

(i.e., primary health care including family planning, basic education, nutrition, low cost water and sanitation); and that likewise, at least 20%PER of donor country assistance should be allocated for the same purposes.

9. That without growth, equity and sustainability there can be no true democracy, so that we can only conclude that investment in children will guarantee the region's access to the XXl Century, within a framework of peace, freedom, solidarity and social progress. This is therefore the moment to assert: CHILDREN NOW.

THE SITUATION

In Latin America and the Caribbean almost all countries have ratified and promulgated the International Convention on the Rights of the Child, and have made good progress in adapting their legal systems to it, as well as taking steps to ensure that it is enforced.

In recent years, the lives of children in the Region have improved in many ways. In 1950, one child in five died before reaching the age of five; today, only one in twenty dies. The causes of death have gradually changed with the notable advances in health service coverage, with the remarkable success of the Extended Programme for Immunization, with the eradication of polio this decade, control of diarrhoeal diseases and the reduction in protein energy malnutrition. Notable advances have been made in access to primary education. Yet 600,000 children under 5 still die every year from preventable causes, and over 21,000 women die from causes related to pregnancy and childbirth. It is estimated that 68%PER of deaths among children under 5 are associated with protein energy malnutrition; nearly half the children entering primary education do not complete the cycle and over 90 million people are struggling to escape from indigence. And there is a growing sense of frustration among young people who cannot find forms of employment to match their educational level.

COMMITMENT

We reaffirm our unconditional commitment to the accords signed during the World Summit for Children within the framework of human development, and declare our commitment to:

- associate economic and social policies, with an integral focus enabling us to overcome the structural factors in poverty, implementing, amongst others, programmes for the generation of employment and income in the poorest rural and urban areas;

- promote the family as the core in which programmes derived from social policy are potentiated and converge.

1. GOALS

To ensure that the commitments of the World Summit for Children are fulfilled, taking the context and peculiarities of each country into consideration for the mid-decade goals for 1995, in the areas of:

A) HEALTH AND NUTRITION

To increase immunization coverage for children under 1 to 85%PER in 1995 and 90%PER in 1996

To eliminate neonatal tetanus as a public health problem

To reduce measles deaths by 95%PER and incidence by 90%PER

To eradicate polio and have eradication certified

To eliminate vitamin A deficiency, considering different alternatives

To iodize salt for consumption

To increase oral rehydration therapy to 80%PER of cases

To reduce acute respiratory infection deaths by one third of 1990 levels among the under 5s

To promote breast feeding and encourage hospitals to join the Mother and Baby Friendly Hospitals Initiative

Following agreements reached at the International Nutrition Conference, to promote action to reduce light, moderate and heavy protein energy malnutrition by 20%PER, principally among children under 5 and pregnant women

To reduce maternal mortality by 25%PER and improve access to family planning information

To strengthen and extend preventive programmes in mother-child areas

To extend coverage of care in pregnancy, childbirth and post-natal health, to be provided by qualified personnel

To give priority to the prevention of pregnancy among adolescent women and provide integral care for them

To develop prevention programmes to reduce the incidence of problems of disability

To implement and/or strengthen programmes to control the growth and development of children aged 0–6 years.

B) DRINKING WATER AND ENVIRONMENTAL SANITATION

To reduce the difference between the population with access to drinking water and the population without it by 25%PER, and to reduce the difference for those with and without basic sanitation by 17%PER; and to treat sewage, ensuring the sustainability of water as a resource.

To encourage action in environmental preservation as set forth in Agenda 21, promoting educational processes throughout society.

C) EDUCATION

To redouble efforts for the universalization of basic schooling, including initial/pre/school education based on the family and the community.

To identify methods and strategies to increase coverage, and to develop alternative models for initial education.

To increase the percentage of children completing primary education to over 50%PER by 1995.

To reduce repetition by 10%PER in Grades 1 and 2 and to ensure that 60%PER complete the early years of schooling.

To raise the quality of primary education, introducing changes to the curriculum, increasing infrastructure investment, obtaining appropriate texts, training teachers, ensuring that school hours are appropriate to the needs of the country and allow effective learning.

To identify strategies to reduce desertion.

To develop options for vocational education and technical training for the young.

D) CIVIC RIGHTS

To encourage action to strengthen or complement National Plans of Action for Children, incorporating specific programmes, projects or actions to foster the observance of civic rights of children contained in the International Convention on the Rights of the Child.

To implement actions designed to eliminate all types of discrimination on grounds of race, culture, social status, nationality or gender.

To promote a culture of respect for human rights, especially the rights of children.

To accelerate the processes of adaptation of internal legislation, and the establishment of judicial procedures for the application of the principles laid down in the Conventions on the Rights of the Child, on the Elimination of All Forms of Discrimination Against Women, and norms on non-discrimination against the disabled.

To promote an improvement in the situation of children at personal and social risk, for example, victims of child abuse, and young offenders, through the introduction of structured programmes targeting these groups.

E) FOLLOW-UP AND EVALUATION

To ensure, before the end of 1994, that systems for the follow-up and evaluation of progress towards goals for 1995 and 2000 are functioning properly, with an emphasis at local level, and in the definition of indicators in the area of protection.

2. INSTITUTIONALIZATION

To institutionalize Plans of Action, incorporating their objectives, strategies and indicators in development plans and policies.

To encourage, within the framework of each country's legal system, the most appropriate means of securing the continuity of National Plans of Action for Children to promote fair fiscal policies and taxation systems to ensure an appropriate distribution of resources'to attend to the social sector, considering the municipalities and regions with the lowest indices of social development as a function of the Plans of Action.

To give priority in National Plans of Action to poor population groups in rural as well as in urban areas.

3. DECENTRALIZATION, STATE ACTION AND SOCIAL PARTICIPATION

To support initiatives and processes in decentralization and deconcentration at regional and municipal levels, so that National, Territorial Plans of Action will become facilitating instruments in the process. This kind of process should go hand in hand with specific policies to promote, organize and guarantee efficient participation and action at all levels.

To promote the creation of room for effective participation by all groups in society such as NGOs, civic groups, religious organizations and other forms of democratic expression, in the actions of National Plans of Action.

To develop social communications policies allowing knowledge and information useful for problem-solving and the satisfaction of needs to be transferred to families and communities. Likewise, to call on the media to take an active part in the transmission of messages and programmes contributing to the goals of the National Plans of Action.

4. FINANCE AND INTERNATIONAL COOPERATION

To continue efforts to increase the level of social investment, efficiency, effectiveness and equity, as a contribution to securing basic rights and needs for the poorest groups, the generation of employment and income.

To provide mechanisms to encourage and/or motivate the private sector to provide financial cooperation for the poorest groups, especially children.

To promote policies which are not restrictive to countries among external financing agencies, taking into consideration the realities and needs of poor sectors, especially children.

To stress among the international community the importance of the goals set at the World Summit to the development of countries in the region, and to recommend that technical and financial cooperation be addressed to complementing government efforts to attain them.

To incorporate the Plans of Action into intra-regional cooperation programmes, creating specific regional and subregional mechanisms for horizontal cooperation for the exchange of experiences, collaboration, technical assistance and advice in all methodologies related to the National Plans of Action which have proved to be effective in the Region.

To ensure that there are appropriate mechanisms for coordination between agencies and governments, and among agencies, in pursuit of the goals of the Plans of Action.

5. REGIONAL FOLLOW-UP

To hold regional follow-up and evaluation meetings annually, involving the organizations and authorities responsible for National Plans of Action, preceded by a technical meeting for the exchange of experiences.

Given the offers made by Guatemala, Chile and Ecuador, the venue of the next meeting will be decided after consultation by the UNICEF Regional Director with the Governments of the Region.

To establish mechanisms at regional and sub-regional levels to exchange experiences and inform and disseminate agreements reached at the various regional or international meetings on the subject of children and national follow-up reports on the Plans of Action.

6. FINAL CONSIDERATIONS

Considering that the IV Ibero-American Summit of Heads of State is to be held shortly, it is agreed that this Declaration be proposed for incorporation at that Meeting, together with the commitments and conclusions adopted. Further, it is proposed that at the Hemisphere Summit shortly to be held, the initiative for the children of the Americas be promoted, in the interests of North-South cooperation.

We express our thanks to the Government of Colombia for its invitation to this Meeting, especially to His Excellency President Cesar Gaviria, and the First Lady, Sra. Ana Milena Munoz de Gaviria. We also thank UNICEF for its support for this initiative, which has made it possible for us to meet here in Bogota to reaffirm the commitment of the Governments of the Americas to the children of all countries in the hemisphere.

In making this Declaration, we are proud to invoke the name of Antonio Narino, protagonist of the Independence of Colombia and champion of the Declaration of the Rights of Man as part of the culture of country.

Santa Fe de Bogota, 6 April 1994

Annex: Narino Accord

PROPOSED MECHANISM FOR REGIONAL FOLLOW-UP

We, the participants in the Second Meeting on Children and Social Policy in the Americas, in view of the successful experience of some sub-regions in the functioning of the coordination and follow-up mechanisms of the National Plans for Children, and having agreed to establish a regional follow-up and information mechanism, propose:

1. That the regional follow-up mechanism have the following functions:
   a) to promote the exchange of successful experiences in social development involving children.

   b) To promote the intra-regional exchange of information on methodologies and social policy instruments.
   c) To implement mass dissemination to the public in general of information relating to social topics especially relevant to children.
2. The Government of the host country of the previous annual American Meeting would be responsible for the regional coordination of the follow-up mechanism until the next Meeting is held.
3. As coordinator, this country would have the following functions and capacities:
   a) To seek the support of international cooperation organizations and institutions to facilitate the functioning of the regional mechanisms.
   b) To establish channels of communication and coordination with intra-regional or international organizations or bodies working in the areas of children's interests and social development.
   c) To support the creation and/or strengthening of national or sub-regional information systems.
4. Levels or organizations of coordination and sub-regional follow-up will be established in order for them to support the functioning of the regional mechanism.

Hon. Winifred Peters Robert
Coordinator of Child Development
Project in the Ministry of Education
ANTIGUA AND BARBUDA

Dr. Alberto Jose Mazza
Minister of Health and Social Action
ARGENTINA

Hon. Theresa Moxey-Ingraham
Minister of Social Development and National Security
BAHAMAS

Hon. Phillip Goldson
Minister of Human Development, Youth and Women's Affairs
BELICE

Dr. Guillermo Seoane
Subsecretary of Health
Ministry of Health
BOLIVIA

Dra. Leonor Franco
Minister of Social Action
BRAZIL

Dr. George Jacobi
Counsellor of Canadian Embassy in Colombia
CANADA

Dr. Luis Maira
Minister of Planning and Cooperation
CHILE

Dr. Juan Luis Londono
Minister of Health
COLOMBIA

Lic. Roxana Viques
Minister Presidential Delegate
COSTA RICA

Dr. Luis Ignacio Gomez
Minister of Education
CUBA

Dr. Patricio Abad
Minister of Health
ECUADOR

Dr. Jesus Kumate Rodriguez
Secretary of Health
MEXICO

Lic. Ximena Barrero Chamorro
Executive Director
Commission for the Promotion and Defense of the Child Rights
NICARAGUA

Dr. Angel Cedeno
Viceminister of Health
PANAMA

Dr. Andres Vidovich Morales
Viceminister of Health
PARAGUAY

Dra. Soledad Ninamango de Yashimoto
President Special Commission of NPA
PERU

Dr. Rolando Reyes
Director ONAPLAN
DOMINICAN REPUBLIC

Hon. Linda Baboolal
Minister of Social Affairs
TRINIDAD AND TOBAGO

Dr. Ricardo Reilly Salaverry
Minister of Labour and Social Security
URUGUAY

Dr. Leonardo Carvajal
Viceminister of the Family
VENEZUELA

Manifesto for Children of the Children's Legal Centre, London (1992)

The first version of this manifesto was published in Great Britain in 1987; the revised version is reprinted here with permission of the Children's Legal Centre, Ltd., London. This manifesto seeks to translate the idea of "children's rights" into specific proposals for action in six areas: participation, independence, adequately resourced services, protection, antidiscrimination, and access to information.

Participation

The right to be involved in decision-making.

Nationally. Young people of 16 and 17, who may work, pay taxes and have children of their own, should be able to vote in elections. A Minister for Children, with Cabinet status, should be appointed to co-ordinate central government policy, currently fragmented between at least five departments. Alongside an independent Commissioner for Children should be appointed under statutory powers to monitor this policy, and conduct investigations into failures of the system to promote children's welfare. Both Minister and Commissioner would actively seek the views of children affected.

Within the family. Parents should be placed under a duty to consult children about major decisions affecting them (following, for example, Finnish law which places parents under such a duty and proposals by the Scottish Law Commission along these lines).

In courts. In civil proceedings there should be a presumption of children's competence to participate in court proceedings unless proved otherwise by the court. Children of sufficient understanding should be able to apply for section 8 orders (matters relating to parental relationships) as of right and to be made parties to those proceedings. Where the court does not consider that the child is of sufficient understanding there should be a right of appeal against that decision.

Clear procedures should be devised to ensure that the wishes and feelings of younger children, of children with disabilities and of children who are not fluent in English are properly conveyed to the court. In all other civil actions, children of sufficient understanding should have the right to initiate and participate in those proceedings without the assistance of a next friend or guardian *ad litem* (as is proposed in relation to family proceedings).

In schools and other institutions. Article 12 of the Convention provides that ". . . in all matters affecting the child, the view of the child [should be] given due weight in accordance with the age and maturity of the child . . . [and] in particular be provided the opportunity to be heard in any judicial and administrative proceedings affecting the child. . . ." The Children Act provides for the child's voice to be heard in most aspects of the care system, but this, despite individual exceptions, is not generally the case in schools, health and other institutions. Education law should provide for mechanisms for individual and collective pupil consultation on all matters affecting them (including the budget) and for their representation at tribunals; section 15 (14) of the Education (No. 2) Act 1986 which bans pupil governors under the age of 18 should be repealed.

In meetings. Children of sufficient understanding should have the statutory right to participate in child protection procedures and to attend child protection conferences where they wish to do so. Children looked after by the local authority should have the statutory right to participate in the whole area of planning and review meetings. Local authorities and Area Child Protection Committees should be required to devise clear procedures so that children can participate in different ways and in a manner meaningful for the child.

Planning. Currently little consideration is taken of children's needs and views in the areas of housing, transport, industrial development, management of green space and play and recreation facilities. Incorporating the perspectives of children would significantly improve their quality of life, health and safety and provide opportunities for learning and exploration.

Independence

The right to self-determination wherever possible.

The Gillick principle. The House of Lords ruling in the Gillick case established the principle, in relation to medical treatment, that parents have "dwindling" powers to control their children and that the child who has "sufficient intelligence and understanding" should be able to control decisions affecting them. This principle should be given statutory force. Additionally, where a professional or institution has decided that the child does not possess sufficient understanding, the child should have the right to judicially appeal that assessment.

Leaving home. Children of sufficient understanding should have the right to make a court application to change their home or to go into care.

Social Security. The social security system should provide children and young people with adequate living standards and promote growing independence rather than perpetuating financial dependence on parents. All unemployed 16 and 17 year-olds should be entitled to income support if they cannot (or need not) find work or a suitable training place, and should receive the full rate of income support (currently paid only to people over 25).

Youth Training. Sufficient and appropriate training places must be available to young people. YT placements must offer attractive, high quality, well paid training which leads young people into employment. The YT allowance should be increased to rates which are up to date with average earnings (if this were so trainees, who are currently earning £29.50 at 16, and £35 at 17 would be earning £66 and £88 respectively). YT trainees must be able to appeal against unfair dismissal and receive state compensation and benefits for industrial injuries.

Adequately resourced services

The right to services which enable children to develop their full potential.

Education. A statutory duty should be placed on the Secretary of State, education authorities, governors and head teachers to give primary consideration to the need to promote the welfare and educational opportunities of all pupils. Resources should be used to entitle children to smaller classes, a wider range of subjects and opportunities (instrument teaching, field trips, sport etc.), more books and equipment and a stimulating environment.

Health. Current geographical inequalities in infant mortality, and identified circumstances giving rise to poor child health (e.g., bed and breakfast accommodation, poor nutirition) should be responsible for ensuring a co-ordinated comprehensive child health service. Parents should be encouraged to accompany or visit children in hospitals and financial assistance for travel be offered if necessary.

Homelessness. The Housing Act 1985 and the Children Act 1989 must be amended to ensure that social services and housing departments cannot disclaim or transfer their responsibilities to provide accommodation to 16 and 17 single homeless people and young people about to leave local authority care. A procedure must be established for the speedy impartial resolution of disputes concerning authorities' powers and duties to provide accommodation. 16 and 17 year-olds who are homeless should be rated as being in priority need under the Housing Act 1985.

Social Security. Child benefit should be increased to reflect the cost of raising a child.

Family Courts. In place of the system of concurrent jurisdiction set up by the Children Act, a properly resourced Family Court should be established to include an independent and fully integrated court welfare and guardian *ad litem* service. Magistrates sitting in Youth Courts should be given training in child welfare and sentencing.

Protection

The right to be adequately safeguarded from injury or abuse.

Environment. Local authorities and central government departments should be required by law to consider the environmental impact of planning decisions on children. An independent body could be established to develop innovative consultative methods, conduct research and advise planning bodies. In the event of a serious threat to children's health by the environment—for example by the depletion of the ozone layer—all children must be entitled to adequate means of protection.

"Legal" abuse. All forms of physical violence towards children should be made illegal—for example corporal punishment by parents—together with a general legal prohibition on humiliating and degrading treatment. Other forms of abuse, for example the use of sedation for control rather than therapeutic purposes, should be banned and the list of prohibited sanctions contained in the Children's Homes Regulations should apply to all institutions for children.

Complaints procedures. Children, wherever they are, should have access to a complaints procedure which contains independent elements and offers if necessary advocacy for the child and some form of final appeal to an uninvolved arbitrator.

Confidential counselling. The work of the charity Childline has shown the enormous need for confidential advice and counselling services for children. Locally based confidential counselling services are needed, employing trained counsellors.

Bullying. Schools and other institutions should give high priority to combatting bullying, for example by having to develop with the students a "school behaviour policy," and by improved protection and facilities in free playtime and other out-of-class activities.

Deprivation of liberty. Young people should not be locked up in prison department accommodation. Other, non-penal, custody for young people should be limited to those for whom containment is proved in court to be necessary to protect themselves or others from serious harm. Any loss of liberty should be authorised by the courts either for a fixed term or automatically reviewed by the court at regular intervals. Resources should be redistributed towards alternatives to custody.

Employment. The 1989 Employment Act, which totally deregulated the employment position of young workers concerning hours of work, nightwork, and holiday entitlement, should be repealed. Full employment protection rights should be acquired at 16. All workers should have access to the protection of industrial tribunals immediately without having to meet employment qualification periods. Under 18's should be entitled to redundancy payments. Minimum wage legislation must be restored and extended to guarantee a minimum rate of pay to young people under 21. It is also important that school aged children should continue to have opportunities for part-time work during term-time and school holidays without being exploited. The Employment of Children Act of 1973 should be implemented and further legislation consolidating locally devised safeguards should be introduced.

Police. The rights of young people under arrest should be protected by giving the Codes of Practice under the 1984 Police and Criminal Evidence Act the force of law. (The Codes of Practice set down police procedures when interviewing arrested young people at police stations but a breach of the Codes can only give rise to disciplinary proceedings against an officer, and courts have the discretion to admit evidence which is obtained in breach.)

Refugee Children. The UK should fulfill its obligations under the 1951 UN Convention on Refugees. The Immigration (Carrier Liability) Act 1987, whereby airlines are fined if they carry people without proper documents, should be repealed, Refugees should have an unconditional right of appeal. Advocates should be appointed for unaccompanied refugee children, to befriend and advise them. Child friendly procedures are needed for entry interviews. Asylum claims should be assessed according to international guidelines from the UN High Commissioner for Refugees.

Witnesses in criminal proceedings. The recommendations of the Pigot Committee (Home Office Advisory Group on Video-Recorded Evidence) as regards pre-trial hearings and other safeguards for child witnesses in criminal proceedings should be implemented in full.

Anti-discrimination

The right to equal access to opportunities and to have special needs met.

Monitoring. Effective monitoring of service provision by central and local government and other service providers should be required to identify any groups of children whose needs are not being met. Monitoring should include statistical data on users and consumers, including their ethnic origin, and any direct or indirect forms of discrimination should be identified. An evaluation should follow to assess the reasons and appropriate remedies.

Immigration. All children whose parents are British citizens or settled in the UK should have equal rights to family life in this country. In line with the Children Act the welfare of children should be made a paramount consideration within immigration law. Immigration rules are implemented in a way which discriminates particularly against children from the Indian subcontinent and the Caribbean, by administrative delays and a negative assumption that children are not related unless this is proven. The rules also discriminate against adopted children and children of single parents. Currently the non-British citizen parents of children who are British (because they were born here before 1983) can be deported. The UK entered a reservation when it ratified the UN Convention on the Rights of the Child which would protect the operation of immigration and nationality law. These should be withdrawn and the Convention should be implemented by amending the Rules and other legislation.

Nationality. Provisions of the British Nationality Act 1981 should be repealed so that all children who are born in the UK should acquire British nationality as of right. Children of unmarried parents should be able to acquire British nationality through their father, where their mother is neither British nor settled in the UK.

European Community. All children residing in the European Community should have equal rights under the Treaty of Rome and EC legislation and to protection for the European Court of justice regardless of nationality. The UK government should press for all EC residents to have equal rights within the Community.

Disability. Legislation should be amended to give children a right not to be segregated unless a particular need can only be met in a segregated setting. Rights for children with disabilities to an advocate under the 1986 Disabled Persons (Services, Consultation and Representation) Act should be introduced. Health and social services duties to meet the identified special needs of individual children should be mandatory not discretionary. Avoidable discrimination on the grounds of disability should be unlawful.

Same race placements. Active recruitment of adoptive and foster parents from different racial origins, religious persuasion and cultural and linguistic backgrounds must be integral to local authority care policies. All children in care should be able to live with a family that reflects their original background. However a child's wishes regarding any proposed placement must be the paramount consideration. Because evidence shows that problems arise from transracial placements, children who are or choose to be placed in this way should be offered counselling and other means of access to their culture of origin.

Access to information

Children's right to information about themselves and matters affecting them.

Files. Children of sufficient understanding should have a statutory right of access to their social work, education and health files. They should have a right of appeal against a determination of lack of understanding to be heard by a committee comprising appropriate professionals and persons experienced in working with young people.

Identity. Article 8 of the UN Convention of Children's Rights states that "State parties undertake to respect the right of the child to preserve his or her identity, including nationality, name and family relations as recognised by law without unlawful interference." This article should be incorporated into adoption practice by statutory requirement on adoption agencies to consider contact (whether by means of information or by face to face contact) before making a placement and on the courts before making an adoption order. The consents of children with sufficient understanding should always be obtained. Children of sufficient understanding should have a right of access to their birth certificate and to the Adoption Contact Register. In future adoptions they should also have access to their adoption agency and court records, including identifiable information about siblings and other family members, unless this would cause harm to others. In addition, they should have the right to trace their birth families where this can be obtained "without undue effort."

Sex education. Children and young people have the right to accurate information about sexuality and relationships, including unbiased information about lesbianism and homosexuality, and information and advice about dealing with abusive sexual behaviour. They also have the right to be informed about the nature of HIV, AIDS and sexually transmitted diseases and to accurate knowledge about how best to prevent infections. Sex education programmes should be introduced in all schools. Legislation which restricts young people's access to information about sexuality, such as section 28 of the Local Government Act 1988 and sections 18 and 46 of the Education (No. 2) Act 1986, should be repealed.

U.S. Policy Recommendations and Supreme Court Rulings

5

This chapter contains policy recommendations and Supreme Court decisions affecting the rights of children in the United States. Consistent with the overall emphasis of the book, only policy recommendations that are national in scope are included. The Supreme Court decisions reflect the increasing emphasis on children's rights evident since the end of World War II in a wide array of concerns ranging from juvenile justice to freedom of expression in the public schools.

Policy Recommendations

Reports of conferences and meetings held in the United States often contain expert testimony and proposals for action that influence policy development. Most notable have been the major conferences and commissions formulated at the federal level, beginning with the first White House Conference on Child Labor (1912) and continuing to the recent National Commission on Children (1991). The proceedings of White House conferences and similar initiatives have frequently informed policy development and the authoring of legislation, while generating new knowledge and stimulating debate and discussion of children's rights issues in the United States and internationally. Nongovernmental organizations such as the Children's Defense Fund (CDF) also make important contributions to the development of increased awareness about the problems of children and families, as documented in the excerpt from a CDF publication on African-American families included here.

The Children's Charter (1930)

Following in the pattern initiated by Presidents Theodore Roosevelt and Woodrow Wilson, Herbert Hoover convened the White House Conference on Child Health and Protection in 1930. Long an advocate of children, particularly through his leadership of relief work in post–World War I Europe, Hoover called together over 3,000 experts to develop reports and recommendations in the fields of education, labor, vocational training, family relations, recreation, health, growth and development, the handicapped child, and related areas. Presented here is the summary of the conference recommendations, developed by President Hoover and his secretary of the interior Ray Wilbur, drawn from the volumes of committee recommendations and supporting evidence generated by the conferees. Although the charter was widely disseminated in the United States at the time, the darkening clouds of the Great Depression made policy implementation of the principles embodied in the charter difficult.

> President Hoover's White House Conference on Child Health and Protection, Recognizing the Rights of the Child as the First Rights of Citizenship, Pledges Itself to these Aims for the Children of America:
>
> I. For every child spiritual and moral training to help him to stand firm under the pressure of life.
>
> II. For every child understanding and the guarding of his personality as his most precious right.
>
> III. For every child a home and that love and security which a home provides; and for that child who must receive foster care, the nearest substitute for his own home.
>
> IV. For every child full preparation for his birth, his mother receiving prenatal, natal and postnatal care; and the establishment of such protective measures as will make childbearing safer.

V. For every child health protection from birth through adolescence, including: periodical health examinations and, where needed, care of specialists and hospital treatment; regular dental examinations and care of the teeth; protective and preventive measures against communicable diseases; the insuring of pure food, pure milk and pure water.

VI. For every child from birth through adolescence, promotion of health, including health instruction and a health program, wholesome physical and mental recreation, with teachers and leaders adequately trained.

VII. For every child a dwelling-place safe, sanitary, and wholesome, with reasonable provisions for privacy; free from conditions which tend to thwart his development; a home environment harmonious and enriching.

VIII. For every child a school which is safe from hazards, sanitary, properly equipped, lighted and ventilated. For younger children nursery schools and kindergartens to supplement home care.

IX. For every child a community which recognizes and plans for his needs, protects him against physical dangers, moral hazards, and disease; provides him with safe and wholesome places for play and recreation; and makes provision for his cultural and social needs.

X. For every child an education which, through the discovery and development of his individual abilities, prepares him for life; and through training and vocational guidance prepares him for a living which will yield him the maximum of satisfaction.

XI. For every child such teaching and training as will prepare him for successful parenthood, home-making, and the rights of citizenship; and for parents, supplementary training to fit them to deal wisely with the problems of parenthood.

XII. For every child education for safety and protection against accidents to which modern conditions subject him—those to which he is directly exposed and those which, through loss of maiming of his parents, affect him directly.

XIII. For every child who is blind, deaf, crippled, or otherwise physically handicapped, and for the child who is mentally handicapped, such measures as will early discover and diagnose his handicap, provide care and treatment and so train him that he may become an asset to society rather than a liability. Expenses of these services should be borne publicly where they cannot be privately met.

XIV. For every child who is in conflict with society, the right to be dealt with intelligently as society's charge, not society's outcast; with the home, the school, the church, the court and the institution when needed, shaped to return him whenever possible to the normal stream of life.

XV. For every child the right to grow up in a family with an adequate standard of living and the security of a stable income as the surest safeguard against social handicaps.

XVI. For every child protection against labor that stunts growth, either physical or mental, that limits education, that deprives children of the right of comradeship, or play and of joy.

XVII. For every rural child as satisfactory schooling and health services as for the city child, and an extension to rural families of social, recreational and cultural facilities.

XVIII. To supplement the home and the school in the training of youth, and to return to them those interests of which modern life tends to cheat children, every stimulation and encouragement should be given to the extension and development of the voluntary youth organization.

XIX. To make everywhere available these minimum protections of the health and welfare of children, there should be a district, county or community organization for health, education, and welfare, with full-time officials, coordinating with a state-wide program which will be responsive to a nationwide service of general information, statistics, and scientific research. This should include:

(a) Trained full-time public health officials with public health nurses, sanitary inspection and laboratory workers

(b) Available hospital beds
(c) Full-time public welfare service for the relief, aid, and guidance of children in special need due to poverty, misfortune, or behavior difficulties, and for the protection of children from abuse, neglect, exploitation, or moral hazard.

FOR EVERY CHILD THESE RIGHTS, REGARDLESS OF RACE, OR COLOR OR SITUATION, WHEREVER HE MAY LIVE UNDER THE PROTECTION OF THE AMERICAN FLAG.

A Bill of Rights for the Handicapped Child (1930)

Developed by the Committee on Physically and Mentally Handicapped Children of the 1930 White House Conference on Child Health and Protection, the Bill of Rights for the Handicapped Child was published as a supplement to the Children's Charter, and consists of five principles.

> If we want civilization to march forward it will march not only on the feet of healthy children, but beside them, shoulder to shoulder, must go those others—those children we have called "handicapped"—the lame ones, the blind, the deaf, and those sick in body and mind. All these children are ready to be enlisted in this moving army, ready to make their contribution to human progress; to bring what they have of intelligence, of capacity, of spiritual beauty. American civilization cannot ignore them.

THE HANDICAPPED CHILD HAS A RIGHT:

1. To as vigorous a body as human skill can give him.
2. To an education so adapted to his handicap that he can be economically independent and have the chance for the fullest life of which he is capable.
3. To be brought up and educated by those who understand the nature of the burden he has to bear and who consider it a privilege to help him bear it.
4. To grow up in a world which does not set him apart, which looks at him, not with scorn or pity or ridicule—but which welcomes him, exactly as it welcomes every child, which offers him identical privileges and identical responsibilities.

5. To a life on which his handicap casts no shadow, but which is full day by day with those things which make it worthwhile, with comradeship, love, work, play, laughter, and tears—a life in which these things bring continually increasing growth, richness, release of energies, joy in achievement.

Declaration of Opportunities for Children (1942)

In 1942 a conference was held in Washington, D.C., to articulate plans for addressing child welfare issues during and after World War II. Representatives from 21 nations in North and South America were joined by experts and representatives of child welfare organizations at this conference, which was convened by the Pan American Union, the forerunner of the Organization of American States. The conference was the seventh children's conference organized by the Pan American Union, and its mandate was to not only develop plans for collaboration throughout the Americas concerning child welfare issues, but to draft a declaration of goals to further such collaboration. The final document, a "Declaration of Opportunities" rather than a charter of rights, was printed in French, Spanish, Portuguese, and English, and signed by the representatives of the 21 nations in attendance, along with the director of the American International Institute for the Protection of Childhood, Dr. Robert Berro from Montevideo, Uruguay.

Adopted by the Eighth Pan American Child Congress

Family Life

Opportunity for every child to grow up within the loving care and affectionate discipline of family life.

To this end the creation of a family atmosphere suitable for the child's development is necessary and the following measures are essential:

(a) Every child should live in a family having an adequate standard of living and a stable economic foundation.
(b) The State should take measures to assure the economic stability of the family.
(c) It should be the concern of the State that homeless children be cared for in a suitable family environment.

(d) Only when the needs of homeless children cannot be met adequately in foster families should such children be placed in an institution.
(e) Poverty of the mother should not be a cause for complete separation from her child; welfare organizations should provide assistance to needy mothers until they can improve their economic circumstances through their own efforts.

Health

Opportunity for every child to obtain the essential elements of wholesome, healthful living—good nutrition, healthful recreation, and sufficient rest—and to learn to give due value to physical, emotional and intellectual development; not only from the point of view of his personal welfare, but of the welfare of those who surround him.

To this end it is necessary to safeguard the physical and mental health of the child from birth until the age at which he becomes a contributing member of the community, for which the following are required:

(a) Adequate diet.
(b) Periodic medical and psychological supervision, and adequate medical care during illness.
(c) Expert guidance in recreation.
(d) Adequate rest.
(e) Guidance in the proper formation of the personality, in all its aspects.
(f) Preparation for life in the community.

Education

Opportunity for every child to discover his special abilities, and to secure education and training to develop those powers—mental, physical, and spiritual—during the years necessary to achieve full development.

To this end, it is necessary to provide appropriate education for each child in accordance with his age and mental capacity, such provision to include especially the following:

(a) Vocational guidance.
(b) Appropriate and adequate organization of intellectual, physical, spiritual and cultural education during the time required for the attainment of maturity, and the full realization of his capacities and natural talents.

Responsibility and Work

Opportunity for every child to develop responsibility and to learn to participate in the life of the community.

To this end it is necessary to provide opportunities for work, and to create a sense of personal responsibility under conditions appropriate to his age and capacity, employing such measures as:

(a) Teaching the child to control himself and to conduct his life in a manner that will enable him to assume appropriate responsibility at each stage of his development.

(b) Promoting child-labor legislation, fixing a minimum age for entrance into gainful employment, limiting the hours of work for children to a maximum of 6 hours a day, and establishing compulsory registration of employed minors under 16.

Leisure Time

Opportunity for every child to use creatively part of his free time in developing skills and practicing activities of his choice, individual as well as social.

To this end it is necessary to foster provisions for suitable recreation and leisure-time activities.

Citizenship

Opportunity for every child as a citizen to take his place in the life of the community.

To this end it is necessary to develop the conscience of the child concerning his obligation to contribute to the progress of the community and to prepare himself for the responsibilities of citizenship, so that he may realize from these early years that the rights he enjoys in a democracy are accompanied by inescapable obligations which require the unselfish and socially desirable use of those privileges.

And, Finally,

Opportunity for every child to take part, creatively, in transforming the raw materials of human life into usefulness or beauty—as artist or craftsman; as worker on the soil or in mine, mill or factory; as a member of organizations for community betterment; or as scholar, scientist, or spiritual leader.

Children's Bill of Rights of the White House Conference on Children and Youth (1970)

The 1970 White House Conference on Children and Youth contained 26 committees called forums. Forum 22 consisted of 15 specialists, and was chaired by the director of the National Commission on Resources for Youth, Mary Conway Kohler. This forum prepared the Children's Bill of Rights, which was heavily influenced by the recommendations of the Joint Commission on Mental Health of Children, whose final report was submitted to the U.S. Congress in 1969. Indeed, some members of Forum 22 had been members of the Joint Commission. Forum 22 viewed the Children's Bill of Rights as a statement of "intrinsic entitlements" for every person born or residing in the United States that were "central to a child's well-being."

I. The right to grow in a society which respects the dignity of life and is free of poverty, discrimination, and other forms of degradation.
II. The right to be born and be healthy and wanted through childhood.
III. The right to grow up nurtured by affectionate parents.
IV. The right to be a child during childhood, to have meaningful choices in the process of maturation and development, and to have a meaningful voice in the community.
V. The right to be educated to the limits of one's capability and through processes designed to elicit one's full potential.
VI. The right to have societal mechanisms to enforce the foregoing rights.

Rights of Youth from the White House Conference on Youth (1971)

In the midst of a society deeply divided by turmoil resulting from the Vietnam War, and grappling with social transformation in the areas of civil rights for women and ethnic, racial, and cultural minorities, and within the family itself, the 1971 White House Conference on Youth reexamined the foundation documents of the U.S. government and developed a statement on the rights of youth. In particular, the 1,500 experts at the conference declared that the Bill of Rights of the U.S. Constitution required reinterpretation in light of historic and contemporary patterns of social change so that it would be "meaningful to all persons in our society."

> To the people:
> We are in the midst of a political, social and cultural revolution. Uncontrolled technology and the exploitation of people by people threaten to dehumanize our society. We must reaffirm the recognition of Life as the Supreme Value which will not bear manipulation for other ends.
>
> The approach of the two hundredth anniversary of the Revolution which gave birth to the United States of America leads us to re-examine the foundations of this country. We find that the high ideals upon which this country was ostensibly founded have never been a reality for all peoples from the beginning to the present day. The Constitution itself was both racist and sexist in its conception. The greatest blemish on the history of the United States of America is slavery and its evil legacy. The annihilation of Indians, genocide, exploitation of labour, and militaristic expansion have been among the important short-comings which have undermined the ideals to which the people of this country have aspired.
>
> It is time now finally to affirm and implement the rights articulated in the Declaration of Independence and the Constitution. Each individual must be given the full rights of life, liberty, and the pursuit of happiness, the Bill of Rights must be reinterpreted so as to be meaningful to all persons in our society. In addition the following rights are crucial:
>
> —The Right to adequate food, clothing and a decent home.
> —The Right of the individual to do her/his own thing, so long as it does not interfere with the rights of another.
> —The Right to preserve and cultivate ethnic and cultural heritages.
> —The Right to do whatever is necessary to preserve these Rights.
>
> Governments and nation-states are created to secure and protect these rights. Through the acquiescence of its citizenry the government and other power structures of this nation have not fulfilled their responsibilities to the people, seeming instead to be concerned primarily with their self-

perpetuation through serving the interests of the powerful at the expense of the people. In so far as any branch, agency, or member of the government or other power structure neglects its responsibility, it forfeits its legitimacy. We proclaim the following grievances:

—Denial of equal opportunity has led to privation in the midst of plenty.
—Repression has denied the free exercise of political rights in a "free society."
—The system of justice lacks legitimacy for vast segments of the people, particularly minority groups and the poor.
—Free cultural expression is discouraged in a supposedly pluralistic society.
—Appeals to chauvinism, nationalism and militarism smother the individual's right to conscientious free choice of action and belief.
—A war which is abhorrent to the majority of Americans and which inflicts inestimable anguish on a foreign people continues.
—The government and the people have allowed economic and political power to be concentrated in institutions which are not responsive or answerable to the people, resulting in the waste and destruction of human and natural resources, and the failure to meet the people's needs.
—The fear of youth identifying with adults and vice-versa, the fear of people identifying with themselves, the fear of people identifying with their race, the fear of people identifying with a country—all create a climate of fear which permeates this nation.
—Internal divisiveness has contributed to a loss of national purpose.

Recommendations of the National Commission on Children (1991)

The National Commission on Children was a bipartisan commission created during the Bush administration and chaired by Senator Jay Rockefeller of West Virginia. Combining an extensive review of the literature with hearings, meetings, site visits, focus groups, and surveys of the public, the Commission's report, *Beyond Rhetoric: A New American Agenda for Children and Families*, contained comprehensive recommendations for improving the condition and potential of children and families. Excerpts from the Executive Summary of *Beyond Rhetoric* are included here, specifically the recommendations for action made by the Commission.

An Agenda for the 1990s

Ensuring Income Security

The National Commission on Children recommends the creation of a $1,000 refundable child tax credit for all children through age 18 and elimination of the personal exemption for dependent children to partially offset the costs.

The National Commission on Children strongly endorses the Earned Income Tax Credit as an incentive for low-income workers with children to enter the paid labor force and to strive for economic independence.

The National Commission on Children recommends that a demonstration of suitable scale be designed and implemented to test an insured child support plan that would combine enhanced child support enforcement with a government-insured benefit. Contingent on positive findings from this demonstration, the Commission recommends the establishment of the insured child support benefit in every state.

The National Commission on Children strongly endorses the JOBS program and the provision of transitional supports and services to low-income parents moving from welfare to work.

For parents who are able and willing to work but cannot find a job, the National Commission on Children recommends that states and localities provide community employment opportunities where feasible and appropriate. We do not recommend the establishment of a major new federal employment program.

The National Commission on Children recommends that welfare be reoriented as short-term relief in periods of unanticipated unemployment, disability, or other economic hardship to provide a safety net to poor families with children who through no fault of their own would otherwise fall through the cracks.

Improving Health

The National Commission on Children recommends that parents protect their children's health by protecting their own health and being role models for healthful behavior, by doing everything in their power to provide a safe home environment, and by seeking and advocating for essential health services for their children.

The National Commission on Children recommends that communities take responsibility for creating safe neighborhoods, supporting the development of community-based health education and health care programs, and sponsoring activities and special projects to help families gain access to needed services.

The National Commission on Children recommends that government and employers together develop a universal system of health insurance coverage for pregnant women and for children through age 18 that includes a basic level of care and provisions to contain costs and improve the quality of care.

The National Commission on Children recommends that the federal and state governments expand effective health care programs that provide services for underserved populations.

The National Commission on Children recommends that health professionals work together with professionals from other disciplines to improve the quality and comprehensiveness of health and social services, participate in publicly funded programs, and serve their communities as volunteers and resource persons.

Increasing Educational Achievement

The National Commission on Children recommends that all children, from the prenatal period through the first years of life, receive the care and support they need to enter school ready to learn—namely, good health care, nurturing environments, and experiences that enhance their development.

To ensure that every child in America receives a quality education, the National Commission on Children recommends a series of fundamental reforms in the academic curriculum, the organization and financing of schools, the training and treatment of teachers, the role and responsibilities of principals, and the nature of the school environment. The specific steps we recommend are:

- a rigorous and challenging academic curriculum for all students, supplemented by improved teaching materials and more effective teaching and learning methods;
- measures to recruit and retain skilled teachers;
- measures to improve the effectiveness of principals;
- school-based management so that principals, teachers and parents have the authority and flexibility to organize schools and learning plans that are appropriate to the needs of their students. This increased authority should be accompanied by increased accountability by schools and school districts for their students' educational attainment;
- greater accountability by schools, parents, students, community, and employers for the quality of education;
- improvements in the school environment to ensure the safety of students and staff and, where possible and appropriate, to use school buildings to meet other needs of students and families; and
- equitable financing across school districts to ensure that every student has access to an excellent education.

The National Commission on Children encourages states to explore school choice policies as part of an overall plan to restructure and improve public schools. School choice should only be implemented where accountability measures are specified and where the special needs of educationally disadvantaged students are addressed.

The National Commission on Children recommends that all schools and communities reevaluate the services they currently offer and design creative, multidisciplinary initiatives to help children with serious and multiple needs reach their academic potential.

The National Commission on Children recommends that parents, communities, employers and the media take mutually reinforcing steps to emphasize to young people the personal rewards and long-term benefits of academic and intellectual achievement, cultural enrichment, hard work and perseverance.

Preparing Adolescents for Adulthood

The National Commission on Children recommends that individual adults, communities, and the public and private sectors take aggressive steps to ensure that all young people have access to a broad array of supports in their communities to promote healthy adolescent development and help them avoid high-risk behaviors—including school dropout, premature sexual activity, juvenile delinquency, crime, violence, and alcohol and drug abuse—that jeopardize their futures.

The National Commission on Children recommends that parents, schools, employers and government initiate or expand efforts to introduce young people to employment and career options; to help them acquire the skills, knowledge, and experience for their chosen fields; and to link more closely the worlds of school and work.

The National Commission on Children recommends that communities create and expand opportunities for community service by young people.

The National Commission on Children urges individuals and society to reaffirm their commitment to forming and supporting strong, stable families as the best environment for raising children.

The National Commission on Children emphasizes the need for parents to share responsibility for planning their families and delaying pregnancy until they are financially and emotionally capable of assuming the obligations of parenthood. Although decisions concerning family planning are and should continue to remain a private matter, public support for family planning services should be sustained to ensure that all families, regardless of income, can plan responsibly for parenthood.

The National Commission on Children recommends that government and all private sector employers establish family-oriented policies and practices—including family and medical leave policies, flexible work scheduling alternatives, and career sequencing—to enable employed mothers and fathers to meet their work and family responsibilities.

The National Commission on Children recommends that government at all levels, communities and employers continue to improve the availability, affordability and quality of child care services for all children and families that need them.

The Commission recommends that federal, state and local governments, in partnership with private community organizations, develop and expand community-based family support programs to provide parents with the knowledge, skills, and support they need to raise their children.

Protecting Vulnerable Children and Their Families

The National Commission on Children recommends a comprehensive community-level approach to strengthen families. We believe that early family support and the availability of preventive services will ultimately lessen the need for children to be removed from their homes. We therefore urge that programs and services for vulnerable children and their families be restructured to include three complementary approaches:

—Promoting child development and healthy family functioning through locally controlled and coordinated community-based family support networks that offer access and referrals to a broad range of services, including health and mental health care, education, recreation, housing, parenting education and support, employment and training, and substance abuse prevention and treatment.

—Assisting families and children in need in order to strengthen and preserve families that voluntarily seek help before their problems become acute. Human service programs—including health and mental health, juvenile services, substance abuse programs, education, and economic and social supports—must collaborate to provide prevention and early intervention services that offer practical solutions to problems faced by families in crisis.

—Protecting abused and neglected children through more comprehensive child protective services, with a strong emphasis on efforts to keep children with their families or to provide permanent placement for those removed from their homes.

Making Policies and Programs Work

The National Commission on Children recommends a series of changes in the organization, administration, implementation and budget of programs at all levels of government to encourage a more collaborative and comprehensive service delivery system, including:

—greater coordination of child and family policies across the executive branch;

—creation of a joint congressional committee on children and families to promote greater coordination and collaboration across the authorizing and appropriating committees with jurisdiction over relevant policies and programs;

—decategorization of selected federal programs to bring greater cohesion and flexibility to programs for children and families;

—uniform eligibility criteria and consolidated, streamlined application processes for the major federal means-tested programs and for other programs that serve the same or overlapping populations;

—incentives to encourage demonstration projects and other experiments in coordination and collaboration of services at the state and local levels;

—new accountability measures that focus on enhanced child and family well-being, rather than solely on administrative procedures.

The National Commission on Children calls upon the nation to increase its investment in the prevention of problems that limit individual potential and drain social resources.

The National Commission on Children recommends that salaries and training opportunities be significantly increased in the early childhood and child welfare fields and that states and school districts with teachers' salaries below the national average bring these salaries up to the average. In every case, pay structures and incentives should be linked to demonstrated competence.

The National Commission on Children recommends that parents be more vigilant and aggressive guardians of their children's moral development, monitoring the values to which their children are exposed, discussing conflicting messages with their children and, if necessary, limiting or precluding their children's exposure to images parents consider offensive.

The National Commission on Children recommends that the recording industry continue and enhance its efforts to avoid the distribution of inappropriate materials to children.

The National Commission on Children recommends that television producers exercise greater restraint in the content of programming for children. We further urge television stations to exercise restraint in the amount and type of advertising aired during children's programs.

The National Commission on Children urges communities to create opportunities for voluntary service by children and adults and to recognize the contributions of volunteers that better the community and assist its members.

The National Commission on Children urges all Americans to renew their personal commitment to the common good and demonstrate this commitment by giving highest priority to personal actions and public policies that promote the health and well-being of the nation's children.

Source: National Commission on Children, *Beyond Rhetoric: A New American Agenda for Children and Families, Executive Summary* (Washington, DC: U.S. Government Printing Office, 1991).

Twelve Key Facts about Black Children and Families (1993)

African-American children in the United States face daunting obstacles in their struggle to achieve adequate standards of living, develop their educational potential, and survive in environments too often characterized by poverty, violence, and neglect. "Twelve Key Facts about Black Children and Families" concisely summarizes these problems in the context of a call to action that seeks to address the crisis within the family structure of African-American life.

1. A Black infant is more than twice as likely as a White infant to die in the first year of life. There has been very little improvement in the infant mortality rate among Black babies since the early 1980s. During this period, the relative gap between Blacks and Whites has increased, and in 1990 was greater than at any time since 1940.
2. A Black woman is more than four times as likely as a White woman to die of complications related to pregnancy and childbirth. In 1990 the Black maternal mortality rate was higher than it was in 1980.
3. Only three in five babies born to Black mothers receive early prenatal care, compared with four out of five babies born to White mothers. Fewer than one in two babies born to Black teen mothers receives early prenatal care.
4. Since the mid-1980s, the proportion of Black babies born at low birthweight has increased, and is now back up to the levels of the early 1970s. A Black baby is more than

twice as likely as a White baby to be born at low birthweight.

5. More than four out of five White children live in two-parent families, compared with less than two out of five Black children. More than one in two Black children live with only one parent, compared with only one in five White children. Black children are about three times as likely as White children to live with neither parent.
6. About one in three Black children lived with a parent who had never married, compared with only one in 25 White children.
7. Starting at age 20, the ration of Black men to Black women declined precipitously, reflecting the steady loss of Black men in communities to violence and early death, incarceration, and homelessness or other marginal living situations that make them difficult to locate. Among Whites, this decline is negligible. A Black 20- to 24-year old is murdered every four hours.
8. Only one in 12 Black children lives in a family headed by a college graduate, compared with one in four White children. More than one in four of all Black children live in families headed by a parent who has not completed high school.
9. The number of Black children living in poverty increased by 717,000 between 1979 and 1990 as a result of falling earning among Black parents, the declining effectiveness of government aid in lifting children out of poverty, and the increasing proportion of Black children living in female-headed families. In 1979, 3.8 million Black children were in poverty; by 1990 the number had risen to 4.6 million. Nearly half (44.8 percent) of all Black children were poor in 1990.
10. The federal government recommends that families spend no more than 30 percent of their income for housing so that they will have enough left for food, transportation, and other necessities. Yet 36 percent of all Black households and 63 percent of all poor Black households spend more. Thirty-nine percent of poor Black households spend more than half of their incomes for housing—leaving them very little for other needs.
11. Since 1967 the high school graduation rate among Black 18- to 24-year olds has increased from 56 percent to over

76 percent. During the same time period, the graduation rate among Whites increased from 78 percent to 82 percent. Black students are twice as likely as their White peers to drop out, although they eventually complete school.

12. White teens accounted for about two-thirds of the total births to teens in the United States in 1989; Black teens accounted for less than one-third of the total births to teens. Black teens, however, accounted for more than half of the births to girls younger than 15. About nine in 10 of the births to Black teens and five in nine of the births to White teens were to unmarried girls. Between 1969 and 1989 the out-of-wedlock birth ration almost tripled. Among Whites, the ratio almost quadrupled; among Blacks, it almost doubled. In 1989 more than one out of four births were to an unmarried woman. A Black infant was more than three times as likely as a White infant to be born to an unmarried woman.

Excerpted and reprinted with permission from Children's Defense Fund, *Progress and Peril: Black Children in America* (Washington, DC: Children's Defense Fund, 1993), pp. 28–29.

Supreme Court Rulings

Landmark U.S. Supreme Court rulings concerning the rights of children illustrate the increased attention devoted to child welfare issues after the end of World War II. U.S. Supreme Court rulings are included to establish the relationship of children's rights concerns to constitutional issues within the United States since 1900. A number of the Supreme Court rulings included in this chapter originated from state-level actions or disputes, a major tradition in the constitutional history of the United States. Rather than seek out all relevant legislative and judicial actions at the state level, the authors chose to identify the most significant Supreme Court decisions that have influenced the continuing concerns about children's rights in the United States.

Central to the evolving conceptions of children's rights has been the federal government's protection of the child's right to equal educational opportunity, heralded in the landmark *Brown v. Board of Education of Topeka, Kansas* (1954) ruling, and reinforced in the 1955 *Brown II* decision, along with the extension of specific First Amendment freedoms to students under the age of 18 (*Tinker v. Des Moines Independent School District*, 1969). Since the mid-1970s, the Supreme Court has become more restrictive in its protection of children's rights in the schools, permitting school authorities greater discretion in defining limitations on freedom of expression, both oral and written (*Bethel School District No. 403 v. Fraser*, 1986; *Hazelwood School District et al. v. Cathy Kuhlmeier et al.*, 1988), and in the areas of privacy and search and seizure (*New Jersey v. T.L.O.*, 1985). Since 1972, however, the Supreme Court has expanded access to education for the children of illegal aliens (*Plyler v. Doe*, 1982) and established that the religious freedom of students is an important consideration when parents seek to retain control over the upbringing of their children, particularly when family cultural traditions clash with compulsory education laws (*Wisconsin v. Yoder*, 1972).

Juvenile justice is the other central concern of recent Supreme Court rulings concerning the rights of children. *In Re Gault* (1967) established the rights of juveniles to due process protections before the law, and its influence remains critical in defining the limits of police powers concerning juvenile justice issues.

Similarly, *Levy v. Louisiana* (1968) established that being born out of wedlock was not a sufficient justification to deny children equal protection of the laws. At the same time, the U.S. Supreme Court has upheld the constitutionality of executions of juveniles, making the United States one of the few societies in the world to employ capital punishment against convicted felons under the age of 18. Currently, 24 of the 37 states with capital punishment statutes permit the execution of defendants under the age of 18. The most significant recent rulings on the juvenile death penalty in the United States (*Thompson v. Oklahoma*, 1988; *Stanford v. Kentucky*, 1989) are included in this section of the chapter.

Brown et al. v. Board of Education of Topeka et al. (1954) (347 U.S. 483)

The Brown case established the unconstitutionality of segregation in the second half of the twentieth century by reversing the legality of "separate but equal" public facilities, the standards that had guided U.S. interpretation of the Fourteenth Amendment since the *Plessy v. Ferguson* (163 U.S. 537) decision of 1896. Holding that it was impossible to know what the authors of the amendment meant by "equal opportunity" and that conditions had changed since it was written in 1868, the court then interpreted that education was of key importance to success in life. As to education, intangible factors as well as tangible measures (number of classrooms and teacher qualifications, among others) needed to be taken into account in determining school composition. Justice Earl Warren wrote: "to separate [children] from others of similar age and qualifications solely because of their race generates a feeling of inferiority as to their status in the community that may affect their hearts and minds in a way unlikely ever to be undone." The court had declared segregation unconstitutional, but not how and when desegregation was to be accomplished. Subsequently, when asked to suggest remedies for segregation, the court issued *Brown II* (349 U.S. 294 [1955]), in which it declined to offer "immediate relief," or overnight desegregation, but required instead that "appropriate relief" should be undertaken with "all deliberate speed." *Brown II* went on to suggest broad permissible guidelines to desegregate, including pupil assignment as an appropriate technique.

In Re Gault (1967)
(387 U.S. 1, 87 S.Ct. 1428)

Addressing a series of violations of a 15-year-old boy's rights to "equal protection of the laws," the Supreme Court established in *In Re Gault* that "whatever be their precise impact, neither the Fourteenth Amendment nor the Bill of Rights is for adults alone." Detailing the events that led to Gault's designation as a delinquent minor by the Arizona courts, the court found six areas in which his rights to due process of law were violated. With this action, the Supreme Court specifically gave minors the civil and political rights contained in the U.S. Constitution.

Levy v. Louisiana (1968)
(391 U.S. 68)

Invoking the Fourteenth Amendment, the Supreme Court affirmed the right of five illegitimate children to sue for damages in the wrongful death of their mother. The court maintained that the children were denied "equal protection of the laws" when a Louisiana court disallowed their suit because the children were born out of wedlock. Justice Douglas found that "it was invidious to discriminate against the children when no action, conduct, or demeanor of theirs was possibly relevant to the harm that was done their mother." The Levy case evoked the first clear Supreme Court statement that illegitimacy is no fault of the child.

Tinker v. Des Moines Independent School District (1969) (393 U.S. 503)

Students were given the right to self-expression in a seminal case regarding the wearing of armbands to protest the Vietnam War. Holding that "In our system, state-operated schools may not be enclaves of totalitarianism . . . [students] may not be regarded as closed-circuit recipients of only that which the State chooses to communicate. They may not be confined to the expression of these sentiments that are officially approved." The court unequivocally affirmed a minor's right to express opinions and engage in conduct to support that self-expression not condoned by their school. The school was prevented from claiming that the wearing of armbands would impinge on the rights of other students to engage in learning by transferring the burden of proof to the complainant as a means of justifying that disruption would occur.

Wisconsin v. Yoder (1972) (406 U.S. 205)

In the absence of expressed desires on the part of the children, Amish parents' rights to the free exercise of their religion were upheld against the state of Wisconsin's law requiring school attendance until the age of 14. The court held that Amish parents could refuse to send their children to secondary schools where ". . . [they would be exposed] to worldly influences in terms of attitudes, goals and values contrary to sincere religious beliefs, and [would] substantially interfere with the religious development of the Amish child and his integration into the way of life of the Amish faith community at the crucial adolescent stage. . . ." The court considered that the "physical or mental health of the child" would not be damaged by this decision, and since the children's opinions were not in the record, the court decided on the side of the parents. Two justices' concurring opinions note that "this case in no way involves any questions regarding the right of the children of Amish parents to attend public high school, or any other institutions of learning, if they wish to do so."

Plyler v. Doe (1982) (457 U.S. 202)

In a landmark case exploring the implication of denying public education to children of illegal aliens, the court decided in *Plyler v. Doe* that it was irrational not to grant access to education to children who found themselves in the state of Texas through no actions of their own. The court declared that public education is not a fundamental right, but "neither is it merely some governmental 'benefit' indistinguishable from other forms of social welfare legislation." The court also considered the "inestimable toll of the deprivation [of basic education] on the social, economic, intellectual and psychological well-being of an individual, and the obstacle it poses to individual achievement." Under the Fourteenth Amendment's "equal protection clauses," and using the "irrationality" standard, the court decided that the state of Texas would be irrational in trying to justify "the creation and perpetuation of a subclass of illiterates within our boundaries."

New Jersey v. T.L.O. (1985) (105 S.Ct. 733)

An assistant vice-principal at a New Jersey public high school searched the purse of a student suspected of smoking in the school lavatory. During the search, the assistant vice-principal found material evidence associated with marijuana use and sales. Delinquency charges were brought against the juvenile, while the juvenile sought to suppress evidence by applying Fourth Amendment prohibitions against unreasonable searches and seizures. Following conflicting rulings at the New Jersey Superior Court appellate level and the New Jersey Supreme Court, the case was appealed to the U.S. Supreme Court. The Supreme Court held, in its majority opinion, that while the Fourth Amendment's prohibition on unreasonable searches and seizures did apply to searches conducted by public school officials, the search in this case was appropriate based on the standard of "reasonable suspicion," rather than probable cause. Simultaneously, the court ruled that school officials who act to enforce disciplinary policies mandated by state statutes do so as representatives of the state and not as surrogates for parents, thus maintaining the applicability of Fourth Amendment guidelines regarding searches on school grounds. As a result of this decision, a less restrictive standard was permitted by the U.S. Supreme Court concerning school officials' authority to search students in order to maintain an environment in which learning can take place. In particular, the removal of the requirement for warrants to engage in searches on school grounds established a clear distinction between the probable cause and reasonable suspicion standards used by the court.

Bethel School District No. 403 v. Fraser (1986) (U.S. 106 S.Ct. 3159)

The U.S. Supreme Court held in a 7–2 ruling that students do not have First Amendment protections when uttering speech that goes beyond the boundaries of socially appropriate behavior. Matthew Fraser, a 17-year-old senior at a Washington high school, had given a nominating speech for a peer at a school assembly. The content of the speech was judged by school officials to be in violation of the school's disruptive conduct rule. Fraser was suspended for three days and had his name removed from the list of candidates for graduation speaker. Fraser appealed the disciplinary action to the school superintendent, who denied his appeal. He then took the case to federal district court, which held that Fraser's First and Fourteenth Amendment rights had been violated, and awarded him a monetary judgment. The school board appealed this decision to the U.S. Court of Appeals, Ninth Circuit, which again upheld Fraser. Upon appeal to the U.S. Supreme Court, the school board succeeded in having the Court of Appeals ruling reversed.

Bethel v. Fraser further elaborated the scope of authority of school officials to restrict the content of student speech, notably when such speech is lewd, vulgar, or indecent. However, the court's decision in *Bethel v. Fraser* did not invalidate the First Amendment protections for student expression put forth in *Tinker v. Des Moines Independent School District* (1969). Indeed, the majority opinion in *Bethel v. Fraser* was joined by one of the court's most vigorous advocates of First Amendment protections, Associate Justice William Brennan, Jr., most likely due to the clear distinctions established between the *Bethel v. Fraser* and *Tinker v. Des Moines Independent School District* cases by Chief Justice Warren Burger, who wrote the majority opinion for the court.

Hazelwood School District et al. v. Cathy Kuhlmeier et al. (1988)
(108 S.Ct. 562)

In a 5–3 decision, the U.S. Supreme Court reversed the finding of the U.S. Court of Appeals and held that reasonable restrictions on the content of school-sponsored publications could be imposed by school officials, and that such restrictions did not violate the First Amendment rights of the authors of the school newspaper articles in question. In this case, the high school principal had acted to remove two pages of an issue of the school newspaper that he felt violated the privacy rights of selected students, and the students who had authored the articles alleged that the principal's actions violated their First Amendment rights. Because the newspaper was published as part of the school's journalism course, the claim that the newspaper constituted a "public forum" for the exchange of ideas was not applicable according to the court, thus giving school officials the right to impose "reasonable restrictions" on student speech in the paper.

This decision narrowed the scope of student First Amendment rights in the schools initially put forth in the *Tinker v. Des Moines Independent School District* decision (1969). While *Hazelwood* did not restrict the expression of students' personal views unless they caused substantial disruption of the educational process or interfered with the rights of others, it did impose a test of "reasonableness" on certain forms of school-sponsored expression, thus sanctioning editorial control over the style and content of "school-sponsored expressive activities" when this control was "reasonably related to legitimate pedagogical concerns."

Thompson v. Oklahoma (1988)
(487 U.S. 815)

This decision established that executions of offenders age 15 or younger at the time of their crimes are unconstitutional. The effect of the Thompson decision has been to limit states from executing offenders below the age of 16, which is consistent with the more recent Supreme Court ruling in *Stanford v. Kentucky*, 492 U.S. 361 (1989), where the court held that the Eighth Amendment does not prohibit the death penalty for crimes committed at ages 16 or 17 regardless of state statutes. In the Thompson case, the petitioner had been given the death sentence for participating in the murder of his former brother-in-law when he was 15. In a 5–4 decision, four justices of the court ruled that imposition of the death penalty in this case would constitute cruel and unusual punishment in all circumstances. Justice Sandra Day O'Connor concurred to vacate Thompson's death sentence on narrower grounds, arguing that the Oklahoma death penalty statute failed to meet the standard for "special care and deliberation" required in capital cases, primarily because the law set no minimum age at which the death penalty could be imposed.

Stanford v. Kentucky (1989) (492 U.S. 361)

In 1989, the U.S. Supreme Court decided two juvenile cases together: *Stanford v. Kentucky* and *Wilkins v. Missouri*. The court held, in a 5–4 decision, that the execution of offenders ages 16 and 17 was permissible under the U.S. Constitution, thus upholding death sentences for Kevin Stanford and Heath Wilkins, who were sentenced to death for murders committed at ages 17 and 16, respectively. Writing for the majority, Justice Antonin Scalia argued that society had not formed a consensus that executions of juveniles constitute "cruel and unusual punishment," and he also rejected arguments that the death penalty was not a deterrent for young people seeking to commit violent crimes. Justice Scalia also argued that "evolving standards of decency" should be based on conceptions of decency in the United States, not on the sentencing policies and practices of the international community.

As of 1995, executions of offenders who have committed capital offenses are permitted by 21 states at age 16, and 4 states at age 17; 12 states, as well as the federal government, set the minimum age at 18.

Statistics 6

The statistics in this chapter represent selections from documents produced by government agencies and international organizations. Statistics are used by many agencies, organizations, and individuals to buttress their arguments about children's rights concerns. Statistics also are employed in the policy development and analysis process, the writing of legislation, and informing the public about the historic and current status of children. These statistics address four critical children's rights concerns: poverty, health, violence, and education. With one exception, the statistics employed have been excerpted from U.S. government and United Nations sources in an effort to provide the most comprehensive and relevant data available. The reader should recognize, however, that both the U.S. government and the United Nations continually update their statistical publications, and the excerpts included in this section represent snapshots and trends at particular points in time that will be revised in light of new data.

Poverty

The five tables in this section demonstrate the increasing problem of children living in poverty throughout the United States. Since the early 1980s, more children have become recipients of federal aid programs, while the number of persons below the poverty level set by the federal government had reached, by 1992, over 36 million persons (tables 1, 2, 5). Of those 36 million plus persons, 21.9 percent were under six years of age, the largest percentage of any age group below the poverty level. More tragic yet is the realization that of every 100 African-Americans living in poverty, 46.6 percent are under 18 years of age, while the rate was 39.9 percent for Hispanics (table 1). Whereas substantial progress had occurred in reducing poverty rates in the population during the Great Society programs of the 1960s, by 1982 the percentage of children below the poverty level had risen to 21.3 percent, varying by less than 2.3 percent over the period 1982–1992 (table 5). The persistence of poverty among children is illustrated graphically in table 4, which displays the marked contrasts evident among the numbers of white, African-American, and Hispanic children living below the poverty line. For every white child living in poverty, there are two Hispanic children and three African-American children living in poverty in the world's wealthiest country (table 3).

Health

Despite enormous difficulties imposed by the physical environment, failed government politics, patterns of war and violence, the persistence of disease and famine, and lack of access to health facilities and basic resources such as food, water, and sanitation, substantial worldwide improvement has been registered in the area of child health since the 1960s. Evidence on reductions in infant mortality rates is striking and demonstrates the progress that can be made when resources and commitment are blended effectively to address a compelling need (table 6).

How widespread such improvements are is addressed in table 8, where the "quality of life for children" is measured utilizing a variety of indicators. Although variations do exist both from one world region to another and within regions themselves, it is clear that the quality of life for children is improving in more world states than not (table 7). At the same time, significant disparities remain in infant mortality rates among racial groups in the United States, where despite a decline in infant mortality for the white and black children between 1980–1990, the rate of black infant mortality remained more than twice that for white children (table 6).

Table 1. Persons below the poverty level in the United States of America: 1993

AGE AND REGION	NUMBER BELOW POVERTY LEVEL (1,000)				PERCENT BELOW POVERTY LEVEL			
	All races[1]	White	Black	Hispanic[2]	All races[1]	White	Black	Hispanic[2]
Total	**36,880**	**24,523**	**10,613**	**6,655**	**14.5**	**11.6**	**33.3**	**29.3**
Under 18 years old	14,617	8,955	4,938	3,116	21.9	16.9	46.6	39.9
18 to 24 years old	4,367	3,023	1,121	844	18.0	15.3	31.7	30.0
25 to 34 years old	5,540	3,749	1,521	1,076	13.2	10.8	28.2	25.2
35 to 44 years old	3,944	2,641	1,077	719	9.8	7.8	23.3	21.6
45 to 54 years old	2,245	1,591	544	349	7.9	6.5	18.7	17.1
55 to 59 years old	1,073	771	262	137	10.0	8.4	22.9	20.2
60 to 64 years old	1,112	800	263	145	10.6	8.7	25.2	26.2
65 yrs. old and over	3,983	2,992	887	269	12.9	10.9	33.3	22.0
Northeast	6,227	4,319	1,663	1,167	12.3	9.9	31.6	34.5
Midwest	7,983	5,389	2,340	452	13.1	10.1	35.7	27.3
South	14,763	8,433	5,976	1,997	16.9	12.4	34.2	28.5
West	7,907	6,381	634	3,038	14.4	13.5	24.4	28.5

Persons as of March 1993. Based on Current Population Survey. [1] Includes other races not shown separately. [2] Persons of Hispanic origin may be of any race.

Source: *The Statistical Abstract of the United States 1994* (Washington, DC: U.S. Government Printing Office, 1994), p. 476.

Table 2. Children below the poverty level in the United States of America: 1970–1992

YEAR	NUMBER BELOW POVERTY LEVEL (1,000)				PERCENT BELOW POVERTY LEVEL			
	All races[1]	White	Black	Hispanic[2]	All races[1]	White	Black	Hispanic[2]
1970	10,235	6,138	3,922	(NA)	14.9	10.5	41.5	(NA)
1975	10,882	6,748	3,884	1,619	16.8	12.5	41.4	33.1
1980	11,114	6,817	3,906	1,718	17.9	13.4	42.1	33.0
1981	12,068	7,429	4,170	1,874	19.5	14.7	44.9	35.4
1982	13,139	8,282	4,388	2,117	21.3	16.5	47.3	38.9
1983[3]	13,427	8,534	4,273	2,251	21.8	17.0	46.2	37.7
1984	12,929	8,086	4,320	2,317	21.0	16.1	46.2	38.7
1985	12,483	7,838	4,057	2,512	20.1	15.6	43.1	39.6
1986	12,257	7,714	4,037	2,413	19.8	15.3	42.7	37.1
1987[4]	12,275	7,398	4,234	2,606	19.7	14.7	44.4	38.9
1988	11,935	7,095	4,148	2,576	19.0	14.0	42.8	37.3
1989	12,001	7,164	4,257	2,496	19.0	14.1	43.2	35.5
1990	12,715	7,606	4,412	2,750	19.9	15.1	44.2	37.7
1991	13,658	8,316	4,637	2,977	21.1	16.1	45.6	39.8
1992	13,876	8,333	4,850	2,946	21.1	16.0	46.3	38.8

Persons as of March of the following year. Covers only related children in families under 18 years old. Based on Current Population Survey.
NA = Not available. [1] Includes other races not shown separately. [2] Persons of Hispanic origin may be of any race. [3] Beginning 1983, data based on revised Hispanic population controls and not directly comparable with prior years. [4] Beginning 1987, data based on revised processing procedures and not directly comparable with prior years.

Source: U.S. Bureau of the Census, *Current Population Reports*, P60–185. From *The Statistical Abstract of the United States 1994* (Washington, DC: U.S. Government Printing Office, 1994), p. 475.

Table 3. Children receiving Aid to Families with Dependent Children program assistance in the United States of America: 1980–1992

PROGRAM	RECIPIENTS (1,000)					AVG. MONTHLY PAYMENTS (DOLLARS)				
	1980	1985	1990	1991	1992	1980	1985	1990	1991	1992
SSI, total	4,142	4,138	4,817	5,118	5,566	168	226	299	321	358
Aged	1,808	1,504	1,454	1,465	1,471	128	164	213	221	227
Blind	78	82	84	85	85	213	274	342	351	362
Disabled	2,256	2,551	3,279	3,569	4,010	198	261	337	361	407
Old-age assistance[1]	19	18	17	17	17	39	36	45	55	40
Aid to the blind[1]	(Z)	(Z)	(Z)	(Z)	(Z)	36	39	42	56	36
Aid to permanently, totally disabled[1]	21	23	26	27	28	35	38	40	58	40
AFDC:[2] Families	3,843	3,721	4,218	4,708	4,936	288	341	392	388	381
Recipients[3]	11,101	10,924	12,159	13,489	14,035	100	118	136	135	134
Children	7,599	7,247	8,208	9,104	9,471	(NA)	(NA)	(NA)	(NA)	(NA)
General assistance cases	796	1,051	1,060	1,078	979	161	(NA)	(NA)	(NA)	(NA)

As of December, except as noted. Public assistance data for all years include Puerto Rico, Guam, and Virgin Islands; SSI data are for federally administered payments only. Excludes payments made directly to suppliers of medical care.

NA = Not available. Z = Fewer than 500. [1] Average monthly recipients and payments for the year. [2] Aid to Families with Dependent Children program. [3] Includes the children and one or both parents, or one caretaker relative other than a parent, in families where the needs of such adults were considered in determining the amount of assistance.

Source: *The Statistical Abstract of the United States 1994* (Washington, DC: U.S. Government Printing Office, 1994), p. 383.

Table 4. Children receiving federal food program assistance: 1980–1993

PROGRAM	Unit	1980	1985	1988	1989	1990	1991	1992	1993, prel.
Food Stamp:									
Participants	Million	21.1	19.9	18.6	18.8	20.1	22.6	25.4	27.0
Federal cost	Mil. dol.	8,721	10,744	11,149	11,676	14,187	17,339	20,906	22,009
Monthly average coupon value per recipient	Dollars	34.47	44.99	49.83	51.85	58.93	63.86	68.57	67.97
Nutrition assistance program for Puerto Rico:[1]									
Federal cost	Mil. dol.	(X)	825	879	908	937	963	1.002	1,040
National school lunch program (NSLP):[2]									
Free lunches served	Million	1,671	1,657	1,651	1,627	1,662	1,749	1,891	1,978
Reduced-price lunches served	Million	308	255	262	263	273	293	285	288
Children participating[3]	Million	26.6	23.6	24.2	24.3	24.1	24.2	24.6	24.8
Federal cost	Mil. dol.	2,279	2,578	2,908	3,006	3,214	3,525	3,856	4,075
School breakfast (SB):									
Children participating[3]	Million	3.6	3.4	3.7	3.8	4.1	4.4	4.9	5.3
Federal cost	Mil. dol.	288	379	482	513	596	685	787	866
Special supplemental food program (WIC):[4]									
Participants	Million	1.9	3.1	3.6	4.1	4.5	4.9	5.4	5.9
Federal cost	Mil. dol.	584	1,193	1,435	1,489	1,637	1,752	1,958	2,118
Commodity supplemental food program:[5]									
Participants	Million	0.1	0.2	0.2	0.2	0.3	0.3	0.3	0.4
Federal cost	Mil. dol.	19	42	52	62	71	76	87	94

PROGRAM	Unit	1980	1985	1988	1989	1990	1991	1992	1993, prel.
Child and adult care (CC):[6]									
Participants[7]	Million	0.7	1.0	1.3	1.4	1.5	1.6	1.8	1.9
Federal cost	Mil. dol.	207	390	538	612	720	834	966	1,076
Summer feeding (SF):[8]									
Children participating[9]	Million	1.9	1.5	1.6	1.7	1.7	1.8	1.9	2.1
Federal cost	Mil. dol.	104	103	113	132	145	160	182	190
Nutrition program for the elderly:									
Meals served	Million	166	225	240	243	246	245	245	243
Federal cost	Mil. dol.	75	134	146	146	142	140	145	139
Federal cost of commodities donated to—[10]									
Child nutrition (NSLP, CC, SF, and SB)	Mil dol.	930	840	853	793	646	701	736	715
Charitable institutions, summer camps	Mil dol.	71	170	158	136	104	93	115	89
Emergency feeding[11]	Mil dol.	(X)	973	593	266	286	252	229	229

X = Not applicable. [1]Puerto Rico was included in the food stamp program until June 30, 1992. [2]See headnote, table 601. [3]Nine month (September through May) average daily meals (lunches or breakfasts) served divided by the ratio of average daily attendance to enrollment. [4]WIC serves women, infants, and children. [5]Program provides commodities to women, infants, children, and the elderly. [6]Program provides year-round subsidies to feed preschool children in child care centers and family day care homes. Certain care centers serving disabled or elderly adults also receive meal subsidies. [7]Quarterly average daily attendance at participating institutions. [8]Program provides free meals to children in poor areas during summer months. [9]Peak month (July) average daily attendance at participating institutions. [10]Includes the Federal cost of commodity entitlements, cash-in-lieu of commodities, and bonus foods. [11]Provides free commodities to needy persons for home consumption through food banks, hunger centers, soup kitchens, and similar nonprofit agencies. Includes the Emergency Food Assistance Program, the commodity purchases for soup kitchens/food banks program, and commodity disaster relief.

Source: U.S. Department of Agriculture, Food and Nutrition Service. In "Annual Historical Review of FNS Programs" and unpublished data. From *The Statistical Abstract of the United States 1994* (Washington, DC: U.S. Government Printing Office, 1994), p. 386.

Table 5. Percentages of children in poverty by race/ethnicity in selected years

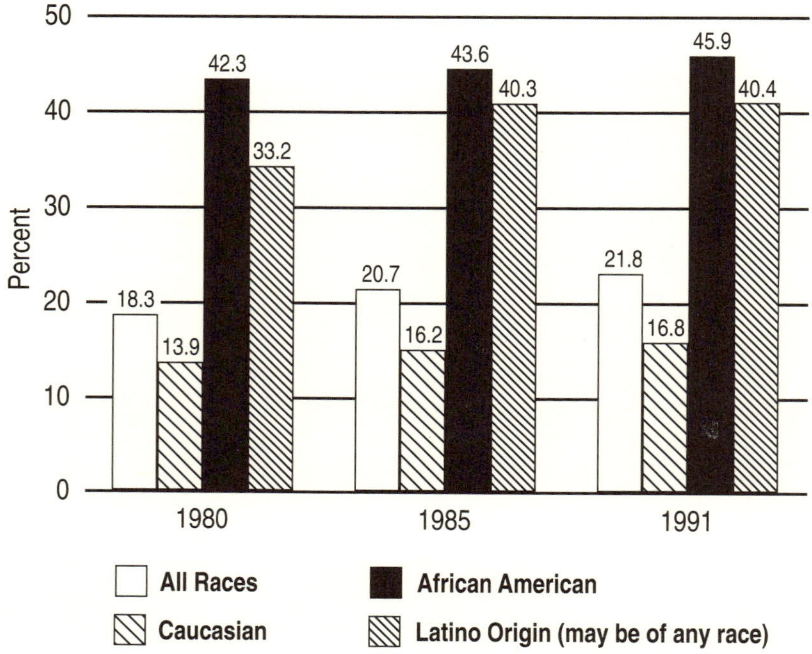

Source: U.S. Bureau of the Census, Current Population Reports, Series P-80, No. 181, *Poverty in the United States: 1991* (Washington, DC: U.S. Government Printing Office, 1992). From Lisa A. Merkel-Holguin with Audrey J. Sobel, *The Child Welfare Stat Book 1993* (Washington, DC: Child Welfare League of America, 1993), p. 153.

Violence

Violence by and against children is a major problem in the United States. Not only are there increasing numbers of people below the age of 18 in public and private juvenile facilities (table 11), but the rate of children and youth (using all categories through the age of 19) dying from the use of firearms is alarming. In particular, the number of African-American males ages 15–19 dying as a result of firearm use is almost five times that of whites in the same age group. When considering only homicides, the ratio increases to over 11 blacks to every white male, while for females the data on deaths due to firearms show that five black females die for every white female ages 15–19 (table 10).

The trend in child abuse and neglect in the United States is also discouraging, with an increase of over 100,000 victims evident in a two-year period from 1990 to 1992 (table 9). With close to 1 million cases being reported of substantiated child maltreatment by 1992, it is no understatement that the difficulties many children encounter in attempting to survive on a daily basis begin in their own homes and neighborhoods.

Education

Substantial imbalances remain in the education of young people around the world, notably in the areas of gender equity and provision of educational services to eligible populations of children and youth. Illiteracy among youth has declined since the early 1970s in many developing world regions, but the percentage of illiterate females remains considerably higher than that of illiterate males in all developing regions with the exception of Latin America and the Caribbean (table 12).

Comparable gender imbalances exist in the ratio of primary-secondary enrollments to eligible populations in selected developing regions. South Asia and both northern and sub-Saharan Africa display the lowest totals of females enrolled in primary-secondary education per 100 eligible population, whereas female enrollments actually surpass male enrollments in Latin America and the Caribbean, and are virtually identical in Eastern Europe and the former Soviet Union (table 13). At the second level (defined by UNESCO as education lasting for seven years, beginning between ages 10 and 12), females fell even farther behind males in Africa and southern Asia, exacerbating difficulties that females encounter in securing expanded work and life opportunities in these societies (table 14).

Children in the Labor Force

Children remain a vital segment of the labor force throughout the world, and in many world regions they encounter hazards and consequences that place their health and welfare in severe jeopardy. Table 15 displays an excerpt from a 1991 International Labour Office publication detailing common occupations in which child laborers regularly encounter workplace hazards to their health and welfare.

Table 6. Infant mortality rates by race in the United States of America: 1980–1991

Deaths per 1,000 live births, by place of residence. Represents deaths of infants under one year old, exclusive of fetal deaths. Excludes deaths of nonresidents of the United States.

DIVISION AND STATE	TOTAL[1]			WHITE		BLACK	
	1980	1990	1991	1980	1990	1980	1990
U.S.	**12.6**	**9.2**	**8.9**	**11.0**	**7.7**	**21.4**	**17.0**
N.E.	**10.5**	**7.2**	**6.8**	**10.1**	**6.8**	**17.7**	**12.3**
ME	9.2	6.2	6.7	9.4	6.2	(NA)	6.1
NH	9.9	7.1	6.1	9.9	7.2	[2]22.5	5.4
VT	10.7	6.4	5.8	10.7	6.5	(NA)	(NA)
MA	10.5	7.0	6.6	10.1	6.7	16.8	10.4
RI	11.0	8.1	8.0	10.9	8.3	[2]17.4	9.7
CT	11.2	7.9	7.4	10.2	6.6	19.1	16.0
M.A.	**12.8**	**9.5**	**9.2**	**11.1**	**7.5**	**21.1**	**17.7**
NY	12.5	9.6	9.4	10.8	7.7	20.0	17.3
NJ	12.5	9.0	8.7	10.3	6.8	21.9	17.3
PA	13.2	9.6	9.1	11.9	7.8	23.1	18.8
E.N.C.	**13.0**	**10.1**	**9.8**	**10.9**	**8.0**	**24.4**	**20.0**
OH	12.8	9.8	9.4	11.2	8.2	23.0	18.3
IN	11.9	9.6	9.1	10.5	8.9	23.4	16.0
IL	14.8	10.7	10.7	11.7	7.7	26.3	21.5
MI	12.8	10.7	10.4	10.6	7.9	24.2	21.0
WI	10.3	8.2	8.3	9.7	7.2	18.5	18.1
W.N.C.	**11.3**	**8.4**	**8.7**	**10.5**	**7.5**	**21.3**	**17.3**
MN	10.0	7.3	7.5	9.6	6.7	20.0	19.7
IA	11.8	8.1	8.0	11.5	7.8	27.2	18.0
MO	12.4	9.4	10.2	11.1	7.8	20.7	17.5
ND	12.1	8.0	8.1	11.7	7.9	[2]27.5	(NA)
SD	10.9	10.1	9.4	9.0	8.6	(NA)	7.4
NE	11.5	8.3	7.6	10.7	7.2	25.2	16.8
KS	10.4	8.4	8.9	9.5	7.7	20.6	15.4
S.A.	**14.5**	**10.7**	**10.2**	**11.6**	**8.0**	**21.6**	**17.4**
DE	13.9	10.1	11.8	9.8	7.3	27.9	19.4
MD	14.0	9.5	9.2	11.6	6.5	20.4	16.3
DC	25.0	20.7	21.0	17.8	12.1	26.7	24.4
VA	13.6	10.2	9.9	11.9	7.5	19.8	18.8
WV	11.8	9.9	8.2	11.4	9.6	21.5	16.6
NC	14.5	10.6	10.8	12.1	8.3	20.0	16.0

Table 6 (continued)

DIVISION AND STATE	TOTAL[1]			WHITE		BLACK	
	1980	1990	1991	1980	1990	1980	1990
SC	15.6	11.7	11.3	10.8	8.3	22.9	17.1
GA	14.5	12.4	11.4	10.8	9.1	21.0	18.0
FL	14.6	9.6	9.0	11.8	7.6	22.8	16.2
E.S.C.	**14.5**	**10.4**	**10.3**	**11.8**	**8.1**	**21.8**	**16.2**
KY	12.9	8.5	8.9	12.0	8.0	22.0	13.6
TN	13.5	10.3	10.0	11.9	8.0	19.3	17.5
AL	15.1	10.8	11.2	11.6	8.3	21.6	15.9
MS	17.0	12.1	11.4	11.1	8.5	23.7	16.1
W.S.C.	**12.7**	**8.7**	**8.5**	**11.1**	**7.4**	**19.8**	**14.7**
AR	12.7	9.2	10.2	10.3	8.0	20.0	13.6
LA.	14.3	11.1	10.5	10.5	7.3	20.6	16.5
OK	12.7	9.2	9.6	12.1	9.4	21.8	13.2
TX	12.2	8.1	7.7	11.2	7.1	18.8	13.9
Mountain	**11.0**	**8.6**	**8.1**	**10.7**	**8.3**	**19.5**	**15.0**
MT	12.4	9.0	7.0	11.8	8.6	(NA)	13.3
ID	10.7	8.7	8.7	10.7	8.7	(NA)	10.9
WY	9.8	8.6	7.9	9.3	8.8	[2]25.9	(NA)
CO	10.1	8.8	8.9	9.8	8.4	19.1	16.5
NM	11.5	9.0	8.1	11.3	9.3	[2]23.1	12.8
AZ	12.4	8.8	8.6	11.8	8.2	18.4	16.7
UT	10.4	7.5	6.1	10.5	7.4	[2]27.3	13.0
NV	10.7	8.4	9.2	10.0	8.1	20.6	12.5
Pacific	**11.2**	**7.9**	**7.6**	**10.9**	**7.6**	**17.8**	**14.1**
WA	11.8	7.8	7.5	11.5	7.6	16.4	14.5
OR	12.2	8.3	7.3	12.2	8.1	[2]15.9	15.1
CA	11.1	7.9	7.6	10.6	7.6	18.0	14.2
AK	12.3	10.5	8.9	9.4	8.5	[2]19.5	11.2
HI	10.3	6.7	7.4	11.6	5.1	[2]11.8	11.5

NA = Not available. [1] Includes other races, not shown separately. [2] Based on a frequency of less than 20 infant deaths.

Source: *The Statistical Abstract of the United States 1994* (Washington, DC: U.S. Government Printing Office, 1994), p. 92.

Table 7. Rate of progress in reducing child mortality, ages 0–5: 1960–1992

		Under-five mortality rate			Average annual rate of reduction (%)		
							required*
	Country	1960	1980	1992	1960 –1980	1980 –1992	1992 –2000
1	Niger	320	320	320	0.0	0.0	19.0
2	Angola	345	261	292	1.4	-0.9	17.9
3	Mozambique	331	269	287	1.0	-0.5	17.6
4	Afghanistan	360	280	257	1.3	0.7	16.3
5	Sierra Leone	385	301	249	1.2	1.6	15.9
6	Guinea-Bissau	336	290	239	0.7	1.6	15.3
7	Guinea	337	276	230	1.0	1.5	14.9
8	Malawi	365	290	226	1.1	2.1	14.6
9	Rwanda	191	222	222	-0.8	0.0	14.4
10	Mali	400	310	220	1.3	2.9	14.3
11	Liberia	288	235	217	1.0	0.7	14.1
12	Somalia	294	246	211	0.9	1.3	13.8
13	Chad	325	254	209	1.2	1.6	13.7
14	Eritrea	294	260	208	0.6	1.9	13.6
15	Ethiopia	294	260	208	0.6	1.9	13.6
16	Mauritania	321	249	206	1.3	1.6	13.5
17	Zambia	220	160	202	1.6	-1.9	13.2
18	Bhutan	324	249	201	1.3	1.8	13.2
19	Nigeria	204	196	191	0.2	0.2	12.5
20	Zaire	286	204	188	1.7	0.7	12.3
21	Uganda	218	181	185	0.9	-0.2	12.1
22	Cambodia	217	330	184	-2.1	4.9	12.1
23	Burundi	255	193	179	1.4	0.6	11.7
24	Central African Rep.	294	202	179	1.9	1.0	11.7
25	Yemen	378	236	177	2.4	2.4	11.6
26	Tanzania, U. Rep. of	249	202	176	1.0	1.2	11.5
27	Ghana	215	157	170	1.6	-0.7	11.1
28	Madagascar	364	216	168	2.6	2.1	11.0
29	Sudan	292	210	166	1.7	2.0	10.8
30	Gabon	287	194	158	2.0	1.7	10.1
31	Lesotho	204	173	156	0.8	0.8	10.0
32	Burkina Faso	318	218	150	1.9	3.1	9.5
33	Benin	310	176	147	2.8	1.5	9.3
34	Senegal	303	221	145	1.6	3.5	9.1
35	Lao Peo. Dem. Rep.	233	190	145	1.0	2.3	9.1

Table 7 (continued)

		Under-five mortality rate			Average annual rate of reduction (%)		
							required*
	Country	1960	1980	1992	1960 –1980	1980 –1992	1992 –2000
36	Pakistan	221	151	137	1.9	0.8	8.4
37	Togo	264	175	137	2.0	2.0	8.4
38	Haiti	270	195	133	1.6	3.2	8.1
39	Nepal	279	177	128	2.3	2.7	7.5
40	Bangladesh	247	211	127	0.8	4.2	7.4
41	Côte d'Ivoire	300	180	124	2.6	3.1	7.1
42	India	236	177	124	1.4	3.0	7.1
43	Bolivia	252	170	118	2.0	3.0	6.5
44	Cameroon	264	173	117	2.1	3.3	6.4
45	Myanmar	237	146	113	2.4	2.1	6.0
46	Indonesia	216	128	111	2.6	1.2	5.8
47	Congo	220	125	110	2.8	1.1	5.6
48	Libyan Arab Jamahiriya	269	150	104	2.9	3.0	4.9
49	Turkmenistan	—	—	91	—	—	—
50	Turkey	217	141	87	2.2	4.0	4.0
51	Zimbabwe	181	125	86	1.8	3.2	4.4
52	Tajikistan	—	—	85	—	—	—
53	Iraq	171	83	80	3.6	0.3	11.5
54	Mongolia	185	112	80	2.5	2.8	4.4
55	Namibia	206	114	79	3.0	3.1	4.4
56	Papua New Guinea	248	95	77	4.8	1.8	4.6
57	Guatemala	205	136	76	2.0	4.8	3.7
58	Nicaragua	209	143	76	1.9	5.3	3.4
59	Kenya	202	112	74	2.9	3.5	4.4
60	Algeria	243	145	72	2.6	5.8	3.9
61	South Africa	126	91	70	1.6	2.2	4.6
62	Uzbekistan	—	—	68	—	—	—
63	Brazil	181	93	65	3.3	2.9	4.3
64	Peru	236	130	65	3.0	5.8	3.5
65	El Salvador	210	120	63	2.8	5.4	3.7
66	Morocco	215	145	61	2.0	7.2	3.0
67	Kyrgyzstan	—	—	60	—	—	—
68	Philippines	102	70	60	1.9	1.2	4.7
69	Ecuador	180	101	59	2.9	4.5	4.2
70	Botswana	170	94	58	3.0	4.0	4.2
71	Honduras	203	100	58	3.6	4.5	4.2
72	Iran, Islamic Rep. of	233	126	58	3.1	6.5	3.3
73	Egypt	258	180	55	1.8	9.9	2.0

Table 7 (continued)

		Under-five mortality rate			Average annual rate of reduction (%)		
							required*
	Country	1960	1980	1992	1960 –1980	1980 –1992	1992 –2000
74	Azerbaijan	—	—	53	—	—	—
75	Dominican Rep.	152	94	50	2.4	5.2	3.6
76	Kazakhstan	—	—	50	—	—	—
77	Viet Nam	219	105	49	3.7	6.3	3.7
78	Lebanon	91	62	44	1.9	2.8	4.2
79	China	209	65	43	5.9	3.4	5.1
80	Saudi Arabia	292	90	40	5.9	6.7	3.7
81	Syrian Arab Rep.	201	73	40	5.1	5.0	3.8
82	Tunisia	244	102	38	4.4	8.2	2.7
83	Moldova	—	—	36	—	—	—
84	Albania	151	57	34	4.9	4.3	5.6
85	Armenia	—	—	34	—	—	—
86	Paraguay	90	61	34	1.9	4.9	4.0
87	Korea, Dem. Peo. Rep.	120	43	33	5.1	2.3	4.4
86	Mexico	141	81	33	2.8	7.5	3.0
89	Thailand	146	61	33	4.4	5.1	3.8
90	Russian Federation	—	—	32	—	—	—
91	Oman	300	95	31	5.7	9.3	3.6
92	Jordan	149	66	30	4.1	6.5	3.3
93	Georgia	—	—	29	—	—	—
94	Romania	82	36	28	4.1	2.0	3.0
95	Latvia	—	—	26	—	—	—
96	Ukraine	—	—	25	—	—	—
97	Argentina	68	41	24	2.5	4.5	4.1
98	Estonia	—	—	24	—	—	—
99	Mauritius	84	42	24	3.4	4.7	4.2
100	Venezuela	70	42	24	2.6	4.6	4.1
101	Belarus	—	—	23	—	—	—
102	Trinidad and Tobago	73	40	22	3.0	5.0	3.9
103	United Arab Emirates	240	64	22	6.6	8.9	4.0
104	Uruguay	47	42	22	0.6	5.3	4.3
105	Yugoslavia (former)	113	37	22	5.6	4.4	4.5
106	Colombia	132	59	20	4.1	8.9	4.4
107	Lithuania	—	—	20	—	—	—
108	Panama	104	31	20	6.0	3.7	4.5
109	Bulgaria	70	25	20	5.1	1.9	6.3
110	Sri Lanka	130	52	19	4.6	8.4	2.7
111	Malaysia	105	42	19	4.6	6.6	4.0
112	Chile	138	35	18	6.9	5.5	3.6

Table 7 (continued)

	Country	Under-five mortality rate 1960	1980	1992	Average annual rate of reduction (%) 1960–1980	1980–1992	required* 1992–2000
113	Kuwait	128	35	17	6.6	6.1	5.2
114	Poland	70	24	16	5.3	3.3	3.8
115	Hungary	57	26	16	3.9	4.0	4.9
116	Costa Rica	112	29	16	6.8	4.9	5.1
117	Jamaica	76	39	14	3.4	8.4	3.5
118	Slovakia	—	—	14	—	—	—
119	Portugal	112	31	13	6.4	7.1	2.6
120	Czech Republic	—	—	12	—	—	—
121	Cuba	50	26	11	3.3	6.9	3.3
122	Israel	39	19	11	3.6	4.6	4.3
123	Belgium	35	15	11	4.3	2.8	6.5
124	USA	30	15	10	3.3	3.3	4.2
125	New Zealand	26	16	10	2.5	3.7	2.3
126	Italy	50	17	10	5.3	4.9	4.9
127	Spain	57	16	9	6.2	4.5	5.0
128	Greece	64	23	9	5.2	7.5	2.9
129	Korea, Rep. of	124	18	9	9.8	5.3	3.7
130	Austria	43	17	9	4.6	5.5	4.2
131	France	34	13	9	4.9	3.0	4.6
132	United Kingdom	27	14	9	3.1	4.1	4.4
133	Australia	24	13	9	3.0	3.8	3.7
134	Switzerland	27	11	9	4.5	2.1	4.1
135	Germany	40	16	8	4.7	5.3	4.3
136	Canada	33	13	8	4.8	3.7	4.5
137	Denmark	25	10	8	4.4	2.3	3.3
138	Norway	23	11	8	3.8	2.8	2.1
139	Netherlands	22	11	7	3.4	3.2	3.3
140	Sweden	20	9	7	4.1	1.6	6.0
141	Hong Kong	52	13	7	6.9	5.2	4.5
142	Singapore	40	13	7	5.6	5.2	3.5
143	Finland	28	9	7	5.9	2.4	4.6
144	Japan	40	11	6	6.6	4.5	5.0
145	Ireland	36	14	6	4.6	7.2	0.0

* The average annual reduction rate required to achieve an under-five mortality rate in all countries of 70 per 1,000 live births or of two-thirds the 1990 rate, whichever is the less. Countries listed in descending order of their 1992 under-five mortality rates.

(—) = Data not available because these were not independent states during the full range of years indicated.

Source: UNICEF, *The State of the World's Children 1994* (Oxford: Oxford University Press, 1994), pp. 80–81. By permission of Oxford University Press.

Table 8. Indicators of the quality of life for children—world regional summaries

	Sub-Saharan Africa	Middle East & North Africa	South Asia	East Asia & Pacific	Latin America & Caribbean	Former USSR	Industrialized countries	Developing countries	Least developed countries
Table 1: Basic indicators									
Under-5 mortality rate 1960	225	240	237	200	157	—	43	216	282
Under-5 mortality rate 1992	181	78	129	56	50	44	11	104	179
Infant mortality rate 1960	152	155	145	132	105	—	36	137	171
Infant mortality rate 1992	111	57	88	42	39	36	9	70	114
Total population (millions)	533	341	1183	1728	451	292	936	4234	537
Annual no. of births (thousands)	24444	12087	37885	39550	11699	4705	12646	125665	23795
Annual no. of under-5 deaths (thousands)	4431	943	4884	2,216	581	205	135	13056	4260
GNP per capita (US$)	505	1944	325	692	2345	2691	18884	843	240
Life expectancy at birth (years)	51	64	58	68	68	69	76	61	50
Total adult literacy rate (%)	51	58	46	76	85	—	95	—	43
% enrolled in primary school	68	95	86	125	107	—	103	100	68
% share of household income, lowest 40%	—	—	21	18	10	—	18	—	—
% share of household income, highest 20%	—	—	41	44	61	—	40	—	—
Table 2: Nutrition									
% with low birth weight	16	10	34	11	11	—	6	19	24
% of children who are exclusively breast-fed, 0–3 months	26	—	—	—	—	—	—	—	—
% of children who are breast-fed with food, 6–9 months	64	—	—	—	—	—	—	—	—
% of children who are still breast-feeding, 20–23 months	—	—	—	—	—	—	—	—	—
% of children suffering from underweight, moderate & severe	31	17	60	26	11	—	—	36	43
% of children suffering from underweight, severe	9	—	25	—	2	—	—	12	—
% of children suffering from wasting, moderate & severe	12	8	19	—	4	—	—	10	17
% of children suffering from stunting, moderate & severe	49	31	64	—	23	—	—	48	56
Total goitre rate (%)	16	23	13	13	15	—	—	15	20
Calorie supply as % of requirements	93	124	99	112	114	—	134	107	90
% share of household consumption, all foods	38	39	51	45	34	—	14	41	—
% share of household consumption, cereals	15	10	19	—	8	—	2	—	—

	Sub-Saharan Africa	Middle East & North Africa	South Asia	East Asia & Pacific	Latin America & Caribbean	Former USSR	Industrialized countries	Developing countries	Least developed countries
Table 3: Health									
% with access to safe water, total	43	77	80	68	78	—	—	70	49
% with access to safe water, urban	75	94	85	83	87	—	—	85	64
% with access to safe water, rural	35	61	78	63	55	—	—	64	46
% with access to adequate sanitation, total	35	68	19	71	66	—	—	51	33
% with access to adequate sanitation, urban	57	93	54	70	80	—	—	70	61
% with access to adequate sanitation, rural	27	46	6	70	33	—	—	41	26
% with access to health services, total	56	78	52	87	74	—	—	77	48
% with access to health services, urban	—	—	—	—	—	—	—	—	—
% with access to health services, rural	—	—	—	—	—	—	—	—	—
% of 1-year-olds immunized against TB	62	85	93	93	87	90	77	86	70
% of 1-year-olds immunized against DPT	45	82	83	91	76	77	80	78	52
% of 1-year-olds immunized against polio	45	82	83	92	76	79	85	78	51
% of 1-year-olds immunized against measles	46	79	79	91	84	84	79	77	51
% of pregnant women immunized against tetanus	27	51	72	19	31	—	—	38	41
ORT use rate (%)	57	50	35	29	57	—	—	40	37
Table 4: Education									
Adult literacy rate 1970, male (%)	34	47	44	76	76	—	97	53	36
Adult literacy rate 1970, female (%)	17	19	19	56	69	—	95	33	18
Adult literacy rate 1990, male (%)	61	70	59	86	87	—	—	75	54
Adult literacy rate 1990, female (%)	41	46	32	67	83	—	—	55	32
No. of radio sets per 1,000 population	147	248	77	197	338	—	1166	177	97
No of television sets per 1,000 population	23	113	27	44	165	—	549	55	9
Primary school enrolment ratio (%) 1960 (gross), male	46	72	77	120	75	—	109	93	48
Primary school enrolment ratio (%) 1960 (gross), female	24	40	39	85	71	—	107	62	23
Primary school enrolment ratio (%) 1986–91 (gross), male	76	103	97	128	105	—	103	107	74
Primary school enrolment ratio (%) 1986–91 (gross), female	60	87	73	120	102	—	103	92	57
Primary school enrolment ratio (%) 1986–91 (net), male	54	90	—	—	74	—	97	87	55
Primary school enrolment ratio (%) 1986–91 (net), female	46	79	—	—	75	—	97	82	45
% reaching final grade, primary school	58	85	53	79	48	—	94	66	54
Secondary school enrolment ratio, male (%)	21	62	47	52	44	—	91	47	21
Secondary school enrolment ratio, female (%)	14	45	28	43	48	—	92	36	12

Table 8 (continued)

	Sub-Saharan Africa	Middle East & North Africa	South Asia	East Asia & Pacific	Latin America & Caribbean	Former USSR	Industrialized countries	Developing countries	Least developed countries
Table 5: Demographic indicators									
Population under 16 (millions)	258	149	464	542	167	80	200	1580	249
Population under 5 (millions)	100	54	161	185	55	26	62	554	95
Population annual growth rate 1965–80 (%)	2.8	2.8	2.3	2.2	2.5	—	0.8	2.4	2.6
Population annual growth rate 1980–92 (%)	3.0	3.0	2.2	1.7	2.1	—	0.6	2.1	2.7
Crude death rate 1960	24	21	21	19	13	—	10	20	25
Crude death rate 1992	15	8	11	7	7	11	9	9	16
Crude birth rate 1960	49	47	44	39	42	—	20	42	48
Crude birth rate 1992	45	35	32	23	26	16	14	30	44
Life expectancy 1960 (years)	40	47	43	47	56	—	69	46	39
Life expectancy 1992 (years)	51	64	58	68	68	69	76	61	50
Total fertility rate	6.4	5.0	4.3	2.5	3.1	2.0	1.8	3.7	6.0
% of population urbanized	30	54	25	30	73	66	75	35	21
Urban population annual growth rate 1965–80 (%)	5.4	4.6	3.8	3.3	3.8	—	1.4	3.9	5.5
Urban population annual growth rate 1980–92 (%)	5.1	4.6	3.5	4.1	3.0	—	0.9	3.9	5.2
Table 6: Economic indicators									
GNP per capita (US$)	505	1944	325	692	2345	2691	18884	843	240
GNP per capita annual growth rate 1965–80 (%)	3.0	3.2	1.5	4.8	4.1	—	2.9	3.7	0.4
GNP per capita annual growth rate 1980–91 (%)	-0.4	-0.7	3.1	6.6	-0.2	1.5	2.2	2.4	0.3
Annual rate of inflation (%)	15	14	8	6	211	—	5	69	16
% below absolute poverty level, urban	—	—	33	—	18	—	—	27	55
% below absolute poverty level, rural	62	—	39	17	49	—	—	31	70
% of government expenditure to health	4	5	2	3	6	—	13	4	5
% of government expenditure to education	12	18	3	16	9	—	4	11	13
% of government expenditure to defence	9	15	18	13	5	—	13	11	13
ODA inflow (US$ millions)	14548	10586	6612	7422	4283	—	—	43451	14263
ODA inflow as % of recipient GNP	10	2	2	1	0	—	—	1	15
Debt service, % of goods & services exports 1970	5	—	21	—	14	—	—	12	7
Debt service, % of goods & services exports 1991	16	28	24	11	22	—	—	18	12

	Sub-Saharan Africa	Middle East & North Africa	South Asia	East Asia & Pacific	Latin America & Caribbean	Former USSR	Industrialized countries	Developing countries	Least developed countries
Table 7: Women									
Life expectancy, females as % of males	107	104	101	106	109	—	109	105	104
Adult literacy, females as % of males	68	66	54	78	96	—	—	74	58
Enrolment, females as % of males, primary school	80	84	75	93	98	—	100	87	78
Enrolment, females as % of males, secondary school	66	72	60	82	109	—	102	77	58
Contraceptive prevalence (%)	12	39	38	73	59	—	71	53	13
Pregnant women immunized against tetanus (%)	27	51	72	19	31	—	—	38	41
% of births attended by trained health personnel	37	56	29	81	81	—	98	55	28
Maternal mortality rate	610	200	490	160	180	—	10	350	590
Table 9 [*sic*]: The rate of progress									
Under-5 mortality rate 1960	255	240	237	200	157	—	43	216	282
Under-5 mortality rate 1980	203	144	179	80	86	—	17	138	222
Under-5 mortality rate 1992	181	78	129	56	50	44	11	104	179
Under-5 mortality annual reduction rate 1960–80 (%)	1.2	2.5	1.4	4.6	3.0	—	4.6	2.2	1.2
Under-5 mortality annual reduction rate 1980–92 (%)	0.9	5.1	2.7	3.0	4.6	—	3.9	2.4	1.8
Under-5 mortality annual reduction rate required 1992–2000 (%)	12.3	5.8	7.7	5.1	4.2	—	4.3	7.9	11.8
GNP per capita annual growth rate 1965–80 (%)	3.0	3.2	1.5	4.8	4.1	—	2.9	3.7	0.4
GNP per capita annual growth rate 1980–91 (%)	-0.4	-0.7	3.1	6.6	-0.2	1.5	2.2	2.4	0.3
Total fertility rate 1960	6.7	7.0	6.1	5.8	6.0	—	2.8	6.0	6.5
Total fertility rate 1980	6.7	5.9	5.2	3.2	4.2	—	1.9	4.4	6.5
Total fertility rate 1992	6.4	5.0	4.3	2.5	3.1	2.0	1.8	3.7	6.0
Total fertility annual reduction rate 1960–80(%)	0.0	0.9	0.8	3.0	1.8	—	1.9	1.6	0.0
Total fertility annual reduction rate 1980–92 (%)	0.4	1.4	1.6	2.1	2.5	—	0.5	1.4	0.7

(Figures in this table are totals or weighted averages.)
(—) = Data unavailable.

Source: UNICEF, *The State of the World's Children 1994* (Oxford: Oxford University Press, 1994), pp. 82–83. By permission of Oxford University Press.

Table 9. Child abuse and neglect cases: 1990–1992

Based on reports alleging child abuse and neglect that were referred for investigation by the respective child protective services agency in each State. The reporting period may be either calendar or fiscal year. The majority of States were unable to provide unduplicated counts. Also, varying number of States reported the various characteristics presented below. Excludes the Armed Forces. A substantiated case represents a type of investigation disposition that determines that there is sufficient evidence under State law to conclude that maltreatment occurred or that the child is at risk of maltreatment.

ITEM	1990		1991		1992	
	Number	%	Number	%	Number	%
TYPES OF SUBSTANTIATED MALTREATMENT						
Victims, total[1]	801,143	(X)	819,922	(X)	918,263	(X)
Neglect	358,846	44.8	366,462	44.7	474,945	51.7
Physical abuse	205,057	25.6	206,235	25.2	212,281	23.1
Sexual abuse	127,853	16.0	129,425	15.8	129,982	14.2
Emotional maltreatment	47,673	6.0	46,334	5.7	48,928	5.3
Other and unknown	61,714	7.7	71,466	8.7	115,848	12.6
SEX OF VICTIM						
Victims, total	775,596	100.0	816,223	100.0	951,312	100.0
Male	360,531	46.5	376,617	46.1	440,493	46.3
Female	409,286	52.8	434,729	53.3	496,952	52.4
Unknown	5,779	0.7	4,877	0.6	11,867	1.2
AGE OF VICTIM						
Victims, total	788,338	100.0	813,057	100.0	950,333	100.0
1 year and younger	107,217	13.6	112,227	13.8	127,487	13.4
2 to 5 years old	194,485	24.7	208,183	25.6	250,780	26.4
6 to 9 years old	177,396	22.5	189,124	23.3	221,625	23.3
10 to 13 years old	151,971	19.3	162,049	19.9	187,202	19.7
14 to 17 years old	117,312	14.9	122,603	15.1	141,169	14.9
18 and over	7,184	0.9	6,327	0.8	8,009	0.8
Unknown	32,773	4.2	12,544	1.5	14,061	1.5
RACE/ETHNIC GROUP OF VICTIM[2]						
Victims, total	775,409	100.0	818,527	99.9	952,620	100.0
White	424,470	54.7	454,059	55.5	525,399	55.2
Black	197,400	25.5	218,044	26.6	245,777	25.8
Asian and Pacific Islander	6,408	0.8	6,585	0.8	8,007	0.8
American Indian, Eskimo & Aleut	10,283	1.3	10,873	1.3	13,067	1.4
Other races	11,749	1.5	12,982	1.6	15,969	1.7
Hispanic origin	73,132	9.4	77,985	9.5	90,840	9.5
Unknown	51,967	6.7	37,999	4.6	53,541	5.6

[Notes appear on facing page]

Table 10. Firearm mortality among children and youth in the United States of America: 1991

[Death rate per 100,000 population. Deaths classified according to the ninth revision of the *International Classification of Diseases*.]

ITEM		Under 5 yrs. old	5 to 9 yrs. old	10 to 14 yrs. old	15 to 19 yrs. old	20 to 24 yrs. old	25 to 29 yrs. old	30 to 34 yrs. old
MALE								
Total:	White	0.5	0.5	4.6	29.1	34.6	29.0	26.0
	Black	1.4	1.5	11.5	140.5	184.3	129.4	94.8
Accidents:	White	0.1	0.3	1.6	2.9	1.6	1.0	0.8
	Black	0.2	0.6	2.0	6.3	4.7	2.2	1.2
Suicide:	White	(X)	(X)	1.5	13.6	17.7	15.3	14.9
	Black	(X)	(X)	1.1	9.0	14.4	13.4	10.5
Homicide:	White	0.3	0.3	1.4	11.8	14.9	12.3	10.1
	Black	1.1	0.9	8.2	123.6	164.4	113.4	82.9
FEMALE								
Total:	White	0.4	0.3	1.0	4.6	5.1	4.9	5.5
	Black	1.5	0.5	3.0	12.7	17.7	16.5	13.9
Accidents:	White	0.1	0.1	0.1	0.2	0.2	0.1	0.1
	Black	0.4	0.1	0.2	0.2	(X)	0.1	0.1
Suicide:	White	(X)	(X)	0.4	2.1	2.0	2.4	2.8
	Black	(X)	(X)	0.1	0.8	0.7	1.9	0.7
Homicide:	White	0.3	0.2	0.5	2.2	2.7	2.3	2.4
	Black	1.1	0.4	2.7	11.2	16.8	14.4	13.1

X = Not applicable.

Source: U.S. National Center for Health Statistics, *Advance Data from Vital and Health Statistics*, No. 231. From *The Statistical Abstract of the United States 1994* (Washington, DC: U.S. Government Printing Office, 1994), p. 101.

Table 9 Notes

X = Not applicable. [1] More than one type of maltreatment may be substantiated per child. [2] Some States were unable to report on the number of Hispanic victims, thus it is probable that nationwide the percentage of Hispanic victims is higher.

Source: U.S. Department of Health and Human Services, National Center on Child Abuse and Neglect, National Child Abuse and Neglect Data System, *Working Paper 2, 1991 Summary Data Component*, May 1993; *Child Maltreatment—1992*, May 1994. From *The Statistical Abstract of the United States 1994* (Washington, DC: U.S. Government Printing Office, 1994), p. 213.

Table 11. Juveniles in public and private juvenile facilities and the confinement rate per 100,000: 1979 and 1987

	1979 Total Number of Juveniles in Confinement	1979 Confinement Rate	1987 Total Number of Juveniles in Confinement	1987 Confinement Rate	Percent Change in Confinement Rate between 1979 and 1987
Alabama	788	143	1,048	205	43.4
Alaska	373	660	384	610	-7.6
Arizona	1,218	333	1,587	421	26.4
Arkansas	901	285	824	279	-2.1
California	12,766	422	19,159	649	53.8
Colorado	1,181	311	1,080	300	-3.5
Connecticut	614	195	1,013	419	114.9
Delaware	206	247	251	359	45.3
District of Columbia	**	**	525	991	(NA)
Florida	2,740	234	3,469	297	26.9
Georgia	1,419	209	1,876	277	32.5
Hawaii	145	116	214	186	60.3
Idaho	307	236	245	191	-19.1
Illinois	1,691	127	2,369	208	63.8
Indiana	2,048	267	2,769	414	55.1
Iowa	821	208	1,324	411	97.6
Kansas	1,425	476	1,522	566	18.9
Kentucky	952	187	1,029	226	20.9
Louisiana	1,424	265	1,339	279	5.3
Maine	463	292	287	209	-28.4
Maryland	1,557	259	1,732	354	36.7
Massachusetts	801	119	1,067	210	76.5
Michigan	2,719	234	3,459	309	32.1
Minnesota	1,428	251	1,569	335	33.5
Mississippi	448	118	381	107	-9.3
Missouri	1,517	271	1,590	323	19.2
Montana	291	271	281	296	9.2
Nebraska	745	361	993	555	53.7
Nevada	461	444	656	631	42.1
New Hampshire	400	314	220	186	-40.8

Table 11 (continued)

	1979 Total Number of Juveniles in Confinement	1979 Confinement Rate	1987 Total Number of Juveniles in Confinement	1987 Confinement Rate	Percent Change in Confinement Rate between 1979 and 1987
New Jersey	1,815	178	2,263	271	52.2
New Mexico	566	293	656	357	21.8
New York	4,714	274	5,693	413	50.7
North Carolina	1,204	205	1,301	240	17.1
North Dakota	193	221	226	297	34.4
Ohio	3,370	253	5,382	423	67.2
Oklahoma	1,264	322	977	256	-20.5
Oregon	1,239	369	1,258	422	14.4
Pennsylvania	3,275	208	5,665	438	110.6
Rhode Island	207	166	252	247	48.8
South Carolina	767	196	836	226	15.3
South Dakota	370	392	446	557	42.1
Tennessee	1,545	248	1,362	236	-4.8
Texas	3,118	184	4,148	228	23.9
Utah	438	214	483	197	-8.0
Vermont	140	269	165	266	-1.1
Virginia	1,613	222	2,112	327	47.3
Washington	1,630	304	1,488	300	-1.3
West Virginia	286	109	316	134	22.9
Wisconsin	1,273	191	1,975	356	86.4
Wyoming	**	**	380	576	(NA)
United Sates Total	**71,922**	**251**	**91,646**	**353**	**40.6**

NA = Information is not available.
**Data not shown to preserve confidentiality

Source: U.S. Department of Justice, Bureau of Justice Statistics, *Sourcebook of Criminal Justice Statistics* (Washington, DC: U.S. Government Printing Office, 1992), p. 598. From Lisa A. Merkel-Holguin with Audrey J. Sobel, *The Child Welfare Stat Book 1993* (Washington, DC: Child Welfare League of America, 1993), pp. 108–109.

Table 12. Youth illiteracy in selected world regions: 1970 and 1990

An illiterate person is one who cannot, with understanding, both read and write a short, simple statement on their everyday life. A person who can only write figures, his or her name or a memorized ritual phrase is not considered literate.

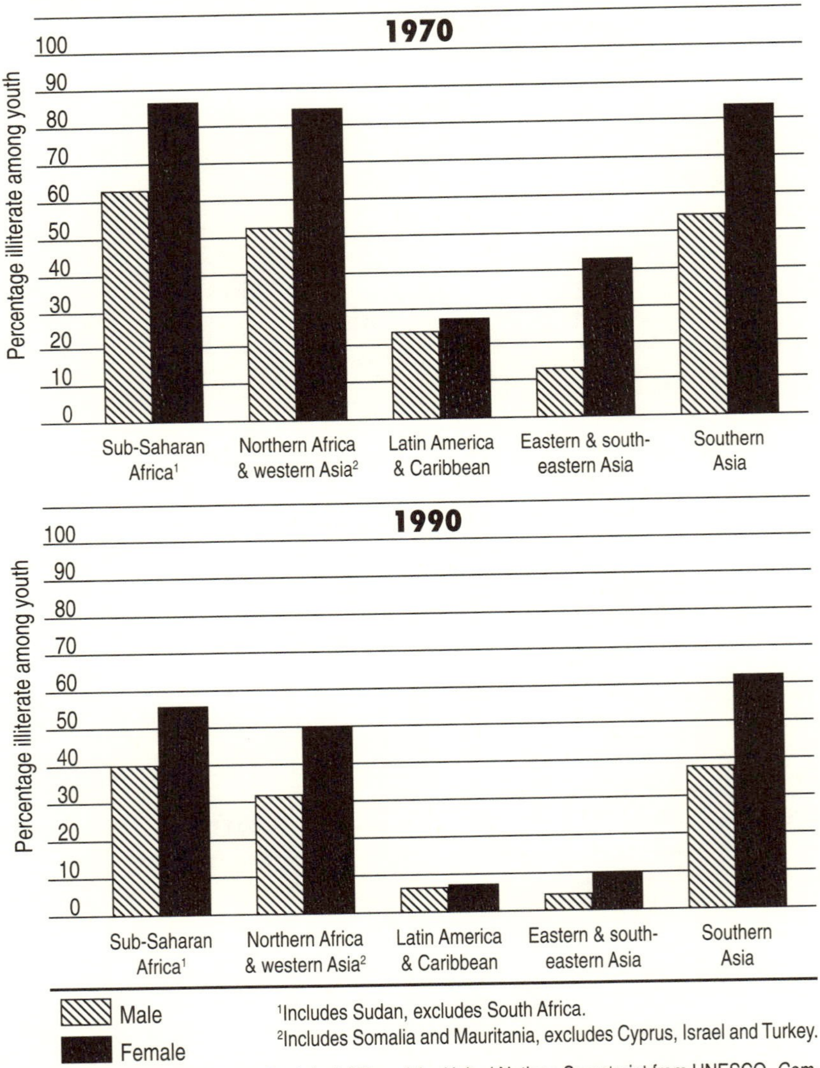

[1]Includes Sudan, excludes South Africa.

[2]Includes Somalia and Mauritania, excludes Cyprus, Israel and Turkey.

Sources: Calculated by the Statistical Office of the United Nations Secretariat from UNESCO, *Compendium of Statistics on Illiteracy—1990 Edition* (Paris 1990) and *Global Estimates and Projections of Population by Sex and Age: The 1988 Revision* (United Nations publication, ST/ESA/SER.R/93).

Source: From United Nations Centre for Social Development and Humanitarian Affairs, *Statistical Charts and Indicators on the Situation of Youth 1970–1990* (New York: United Nations, 1992), p. 13.

Table 13. Gender inequality in schooling, ages 10–17 in world regions during the 1980s

UNESCO defines education at the primary level as usually beginning between the ages of 5 and 7 and lasting for about five years. Education at the second level is defined as beginning at about age 10–12 and lasting for about three years at the first stage, and as beginning at about age 13–15 and lasting for about four years at the second stage. Education at the third level, including universities and colleges, is defined as beginning at about age 17–19 and lasting for at least three or four years.

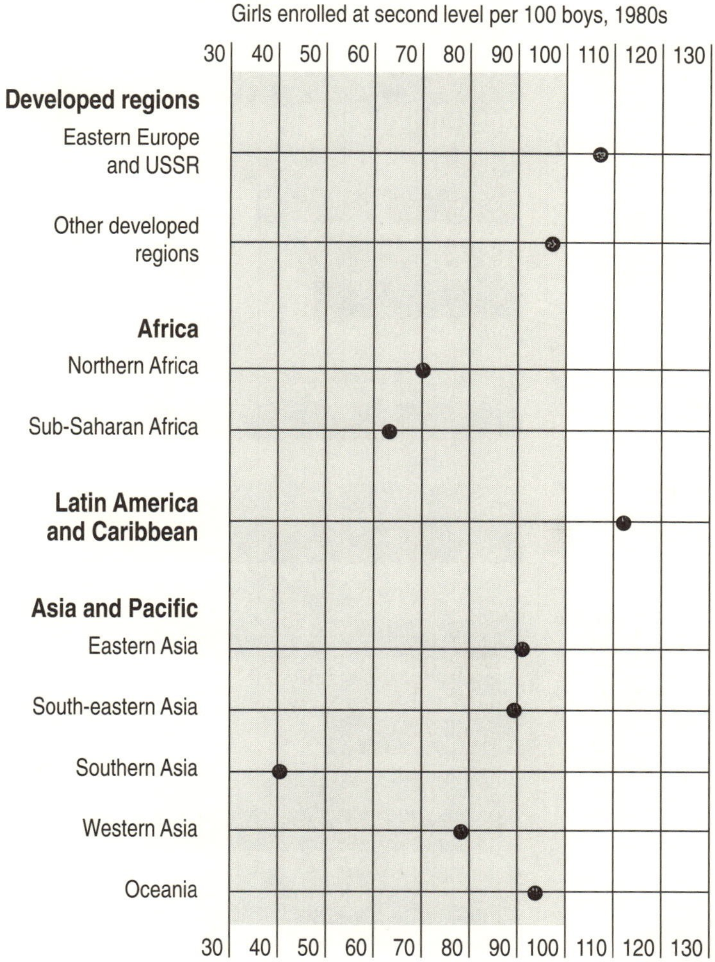

Source: Calculated from United Nations Educational, Scientific and Cultural Organization *Statistical Yearbook* (Paris, various years up to 1989).

From United Nations Centre for Social Development and Humanitarian Affairs, *Statistical Charts and Indicators on the Situation of Youth 1970–1990* (New York: United Nations, 1992), p. 15.

Table 14. Ratio of actual primary-secondary enrollment to eligible population in world regions during the 1980s

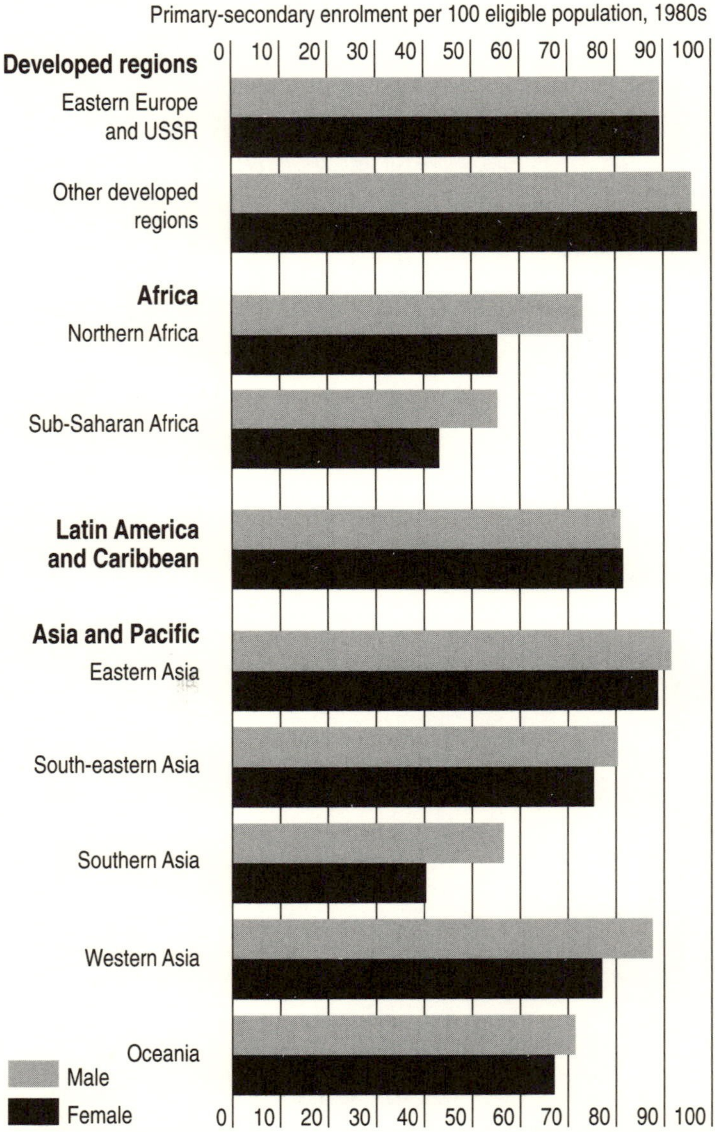

Source: Calculated from United Nations Educational, Scientific and Cultural Organization *Statistical Yearbook* (Paris, various years up to 1989).

From United Nations Centre for Social Development and Humanitarian Affairs, *Statistical Charts and Indicators on the Situation of Youth 1970–1990* (New York: United Nations, 1992), p. 14.

Table 15. Examples of child labor in hazardous occupations and its consequences (in Asia)

Occupation	Tasks	Hazards	Consequences
1. Agriculture	Working with machinery and agrochemicals	Unsafe machinery; hazardous substances	Accidents; chemical poisoning (chronic and acute); chronic cases, often undiagnosed and attributed to nonoccupational causes
2. Carpet weaving	Producing carpets	Inhalation of wool dust contaminated with fungal spores; poor (squatting) work posture; poor lighting	Respiratory diseases
		Hazardous chemicals; poor ventilation, housekeeping and welfare facilities	Musculo-skeletal diseases; eye strain and defective vision at premature age; chemical poisonings; aggravation of nonoccupational diseases
3. Construction work	Digging earth; carrying loads	Being struck by falling objects; stepping on sharp objects; falling from heights	Accidents; musculo-skeletal diseases
	Shovelling sand and cement; metal work	Arduous tasks; exposure to dust; exposure to heat and noise	Respiratory diseases; victims of work-related diseases prematurely
4. Domestic servant	All types of domestic work	At the mercy of the employer; long hours of work; lack of minimum facilities to sleep or rest; abuse of health and morals (sexual abuse, demeaning work, isolation from society)	Malnutrition; health effects of long hours of work, irregular meals, insufficient rest; psychological stress (sexual abuse, confinement, fear of destitution); corporal punishment
5. Deep-sea fishing	Diving to depths of up to 60 meters to attach nets to coral reefs	Exposure to high atmospheric pressure; danger from carnivorous and poisonous fish; congested and insanitary conditions; poor food on board vessels	Decompression illness (rupture of ear drums); death or injury; gastrointestinal diseases; communicable diseases

Table 15 (continued)

Occupation	Tasks	Hazards	Consequences
6. Glass factory work	Drawing molten glass	Radiant heat; thermal stress; stepping on or handling hot broken glass	Eye cataract; heat stress; respiratory diseases; burns and cuts; infection
7. Matches and fireworks	Mixing hot (steaming) chemicals, making matchsticks and boxes, stuffing cracker powder into firecrackers	Exposure to hazardous chemicals, fire, and explosions	Synergistic effects of chemical intoxications; burns and death
8. Scavenging and rag picking	Demeaning, unsanitary work (reclaiming usable material from garbage heaps)	Cuts from glass/metal; exposure to hazardous substances including waste from hospitals; inhaling stench from putrefied matter; infestation by flies; temptation to eat leftover food	Cuts resulting in death from tetanus; chemicals poisoning and risk of contracting or carrying infectious diseases; food poisoning; burns (from buildup of methane gas and explosions)
9. Slate making	Carrying heavy loads; making pencils and slates	Effects of carrying loads; exposure to silicious dust	Musculo-skeletal diseases; lung diseases and premature incapacitation
10. Street trades	Hawking goods; selling; shoe polishing; prostitution	Exposure to drugs, violence, criminal activities; danger to health and morals	Victims of drug addiction; branded as social outcasts (reconvicted criminals); social diseases

Source: International Labour Office, *Report of the Director-General, Eleventh Asian Regional Conference, Bangkok, November–December 1991* (Geneva: International Labour Office, 1991), pp. 90–91.

Organizations, Associations, and Agencies 7

The organizations, associations, and agencies included in this chapter were selected based on these criteria: They were active in addressing children's rights issues encompassed within the framework of the UN Convention on the Rights of the Child; they responded to letters of inquiry and/or had records of service in the literature documenting their activities related to children's rights issues; and accurate, up-to-date information about their activities and services was available for use. No government agencies at the U.S. federal, state, or local levels were included, nor were government agencies of other countries. They were excluded for two reasons: in the case of the United States, the decentralized structure of children's services and programs relating to children's rights issues makes it difficult, if not impossible, to create a central directory of this type; and in the case of other countries, providing listings for some but not others would be inequitable and unfair. Internet addresses, World Wide Web (WWW) and/or Gopher, are listed where available. Descriptions of some World Wide Web sites are provided in chapter 9.

Action Alliance for Children
The Hunt House
1201 Martin Luther King Jr. Way
Oakland, CA 94612-1217
(510) 444-7136
FAX (510) 444-7138

This organization attempts to educate and empower people who work in the state of California on behalf of children and families. The Action Alliance works in collaboration with other local and national child advocacy organizations.

Publications: The Children's Advocate, a bimonthly newspaper-format publication, issued since 1973, has won numerous national awards.

Administrative Committee on Coordination—Subcommittee on Nutrition, World Health Organization (WHO)
20, Avenue Appia
CH-1211 Geneva 27, Switzerland
41-22-791-04-56
FAX 41-22-798-88-91

This WHO subcommittee addresses the relationship of adequate nutrition to child refugees and children in poverty, and the effects of warfare and natural disasters on children. An important measure used by the WHO in the study of childhood nutrition is the indicator of growth failure or underweight in children, which is widely employed as a measure of nutritional status worldwide.

Publications: Extensive publications list, including annual updates on the world nutrition situation, and specialized reports on the nutritional status of refugees, with emphasis on children.

Alliance for Child Survival
315 Dean Drive, Suite 100
Rockville, MD 20851-1144
(301) 738-7122
FAX (301) 738-1196

Founded in 1990, the Alliance for Child Survival works to promote U.S. foreign-aid assistance for development projects that affect the welfare of children worldwide. Efforts since 1990 have focused on improving U.S. foreign aid and World Bank support for the improvement of nutrition, sanitation, education, and health conditions for children worldwide. Working in close coordination with other nongovernmental organizations and selected U.S. congressional representatives, the alliance focuses its efforts on influencing the legislative agenda in the U.S. Congress regarding international children's health issues, notably those identified as goals from the 1990 World Summit for Children in New York City. The alliance also participates in the development of Internet databases on international development issues.

Publications: Periodic newsletters and updates on congressional action.

American Association for Protecting Children (AAPC)
c/o American Humane Association
63 Inverness Drive East
Englewood, CO 80112
(303) 792-9900
FAX (303) 792-5333

This organization is the children's division of the American Humane Association; it seeks to protect children from neglect and abuse through assistance to community child protection services. The AAPC maintains a National Resource Center on Child Abuse and Neglect, along with a database of reports on child neglect and abuse and a speakers bureau.

Publications: The quarterly journal *Protecting Children* and various other reports, books, brochures, and pamphlets.

American Bar Association (ABA) Center on Children and the Law
1800 M Street NW
Washington, DC 20036
(202) 331-2250
FAX (202) 331-2220
WWW: http://www.abanet.org/

Serving as a clearinghouse on the legal rights of children, the ABA Center on Children and the Law distributes information on children's legal issues, provides training to state child-welfare personnel, conducts legal research on the evolution of children's legal rights in the United States, and seeks to influence legislation about children's rights.

Publications: The *ABA Juvenile and Child Welfare Law Reporter,* issued monthly, and the quarterly *Children's Legal Rights Journal.*

American Civil Liberties Union (ACLU) Children's Rights Project
132 West 43rd Street
New York, NY 10036
(212) 944-9800
FAX (212) 921-7916
WWW: http://www.aclu.org/

The Children's Rights Project of the ACLU utilizes litigation, advocacy, and education about children's rights to ensure that government intervention in the lives of troubled families and children is done with appropriate services and treatment, and in a nondiscriminatory manner. The project additionally examines the mechanisms employed by governments to provide placements for children who have been removed by the state from their biological parents. The project is currently involved in litigation in a number of states seeking to force state agencies to improve their child welfare systems and increase protection for children. Inquiries about the history and current activities of the Children's Rights Project should be made in writing c/o the project address.

Publications: Project reports available from the American Civil Liberties Union office.

Amnesty International USA
322 Eighth Avenue
New York, NY 10001
(212) 807-8400
FAX (212) 629-1451
WWW: http://www.amnesty.org/
Gopher: gopher://gopher.igc.apc.org:70/11/

Children's Action Network—Amnesty International USA
53 West Jackson, Room 1162
Chicago, IL 60604
(312) 427-2060
FAX (312) 427-2589

Amnesty International is a worldwide nonpartisan movement dedicated to the defense of international human rights. Formed in 1961, today the organization has over 1.2 million members worldwide. Amnesty International's mandate includes seeking the release of prisoners of conscience, or prisoners who have been detained or imprisoned for their beliefs, and who have neither used nor advocated violence; provision of fair and early trials for all prisoners of conscience; and the abolition of capital punishment and torture in all cases. Amnesty International has implemented international campaigns seeking an end to human rights violations against children, and regularly addresses specific cases involving children in all areas of the world through its many grass-roots networks of educators, legal experts, students, and other human rights activists such as the Children's Action Network. Amnesty International supports adherence to the international covenants and conventions in the field of human rights, including the UN Convention on the Rights of the Child.

Publications: Extensive list of country reports, campaign materials, audiovisual resources, and related human rights publications available, in addition to the annual *Amnesty International Report.*

Anti-slavery International
Unit 4, Stableyard, Broomgrove Road
London, SW9 9TL United Kingdom
(071) 924-9555
FAX (071) 738-4110

The former Anti-slavery Society, founded in the nineteenth century with an abolitionist mandate, has now transformed itself into Anti-slavery International, with an active approach to child labor concerns. The organization's goals include the elimination of slavery in all its forms, with particular emphasis on bonded labor, the plight of indigenous peoples, the oppression of women, and exploitation of child laborers. It also advocates the application of international human rights law at the United Nations and with individual governments.

Publications: Newsletter; issues reports on governmental violations in its mandate areas.

Association of Child Advocates (ACA)
P.O. Box 5873
Cleveland, OH 77107-0873
(216) 881-2225
FAX (216) 391-3522

The ACA is a forum for the exchange of ideas among child advocacy organizations, notably those affecting state and local policies about children. The ACA provides technical assistance about child advocacy concerns and facilitates the dissemination and use of information about children's issues at the state and local levels.

Publications: Bimonthly *Child Advocates' Information Exchange* and a newsletter.

Bal Chetana Samuha (National Coalition for Children)
P. O. Box 1187
Kathmandu Nepal
Phone and FAX not available.

Bal Chetana Samuha is a coalition dedicated to making children aware of their rights; it consists of approximately 80 members from various parts of Nepal representing diverse ethnic groups, communities, and socioeconomic backgrounds. The coalition sponsors workshops for children by children, publishes a newsletter, and arranges events at school fairs and other events. The members' ages range from 8 to 17 years. Children serve on the coalition's executive committee and are facilitated by a secretariat run by adults. The coalition formed after the first Children's National Workshop held in Kathmandu under the auspices of UNICEF-Save the Children (Norway) and the International Institute for Human Rights, Environment and Development (INHURED).

Publications: The newsletter *Bal Aawas* in published in Nepali and is available from the organization's headquarters. Inquire regarding availability of an English-language version.

Big Brothers/Big Sisters of America
230 North 13th Street
Philadelphia, PA 19107-1510
(215) 567-7000
FAX (215) 567-0394

Big Brothers and Big Sisters of America match children from single-parent homes with adult volunteers who serve as mentors and role models. Professional staff work at local agencies administered by volunteer boards of directors. Training, evaluation, consulting, and technical assistance are provided by the headquarters office, along with a wide range of other support services.

Publications: Annual report and agency directory; the *Big Brothers/ Big Sisters of America—Correspondent* three times a year.

Canadian Human Rights Foundation
1425 Boulevard Rene-Levesque Ouest, B 307
Montreal, Quebec
Canada H3G 1T7
(514) 954-0382
FAX (514) 954-0659

This organization develops and publishes curricula and other educational materials for primary and secondary schools and universities in English and French. It convenes conferences to promote human rights and is internationally active in training teachers concerning human and children's rights issues. Its most recent curriculum introduces the Convention on the Rights of the Child into primary school curricula.

Publications: List of curriculum materials and related educational resources available upon request.

Child Welfare League of America (CWLA)
440 First Street NW, Suite 310
Washington, DC 20001-2085
(202) 638-2952
FAX (202) 638-4004
WWW: http://www.handsnet.org/cwla/

Founded in 1920, the CWLA emerged from the heightened concerns about children's rights and welfare embodied in the 1909 White House Conference on Dependent Children called by President Theodore Roosevelt. Today the CWLA is a federation of public and private nonprofit agencies and organizations that advocates children's rights and the provision of the highest quality child welfare services to children in the United States and Canada. CWLA is internationally recognized as a standard-setter in the field of child welfare services, and it monitors the development and implementation of policies concerning children at federal and state levels.

Publications: Broad-based publication program, addressing a wide range of audiences, including child welfare professionals, scholars, legislators, and the general public. Comprehensive catalog of periodicals, books, monographs, videos, and training materials.

Child Workers in Nepal Concerned Center
P.O. Box 4374, Bafal, Kalimati
Kathmandu, Nepal
(977-1) 271658/278064
FAX (977-1) 220483/224466

This social organization for the rights of the child opposes child slavery and child labor exploitation. Beginning as a small team of university graduates, the group has become a national advocacy organization for children's rights in Nepal. It runs welfare and rehabilitation programs for underprivileged children, including street children and child workers. The overall goal of the organization is to empower the rights of the child movement so that social development and social justice can be realized for all.

Publications: The monthly *Action for Children* newsletter and quarterly *Voice of Child Workers* available by subscription.

Childhelp U.S.A., Inc.
6463 Independence Avenue
Woodland Hills, CA 91370
(818) 347-7280
FAX (818) 593-3257

This organization works to research, prevent, and treat child abuse. Childhelp U.S.A. administers a residential center for the treatment and care of abused and neglected children, along with an aftercare program involving professional counseling and home-based intervention. Research, public awareness, and awards programs also are conducted.

Publications: Many publications regularly issued, including the *Child Help Newsletter* and *Child Help Report.*

Childreach
155 Plan Way
Warwick, RI 02886
(800) 556-7918
FAX (401) 738-5608

The U.S. branch of this organization, founded as Foster Parents Plan in 1937, assists over 100,000 needy children throughout the world. It provides an international development education curriculum, an international children's art exhibit, and extensive programs and grass-roots projects in health, education, family issues, and community development.

Publications: Informal Reports (ten times yearly), the quarterly *Journey,* and Kay Castelle's *In the Best Interests of the Child* (published in three languages).

Children of the Americas (COA)
P.O. Box 140165
Dallas, TX 75214-0165
(214) 823-3922
FAX (214) 823-2783

This organization provides information, medical care, counseling, and social services to children between the ages of 6 and 16 who are orphaned or abandoned and live on the streets. The COA also conducts research, holds meetings, and sponsors street health care workers in the Caribbean and Latin America.

Publications: Quarterly *COA Update,* a newsletter, and selected other reports.

Children's Aid International
6270 Melrose Avenue
P.O. Box 480155
Los Angeles, CA 90048-1155
(213) 936-8917
FAX (213) 936-6478

This nondenominational charitable program provides assistance to needy children in Southeast Asia in the areas of nutrition, medical care, and education. The organization operates primary health care clinics; provides educational programs in preventive health care, sanitation, and nutrition; and has a training program for medical students in the treatment of malnourished, ill, and impoverished children.

Publications: Focus on Children and a regular newsletter.

Children's Defense Fund (CDF)
25 E Street NW
Washington, DC 20001
(202) 628-8787
FAX (202) 662-3510
WWW: http://www.tmn.com/cdf/index.html

Founded in 1973, CDF is a nonprofit research and advocacy organization that promotes the interests of all children in the United States who cannot vote, lobby, or speak out on their own behalf. CDF gives particular attention to the concerns and needs of poor, minority, and disabled children, with special emphasis on seeking out root causes of problems, rather than merely the symptoms of child suffering and neglect. Topics addressed by CDF initiatives include family income and child poverty, maternal and child health, child welfare (such as juvenile justice, foster care, and adoption), adolescent pregnancy, early childhood education, violence, and housing and homelessness.

Publications: Reports (especially the annual *Children in the States*), periodicals, and other resources, listed in a comprehensive catalog.

Children's Express
1440 New York Avenue NW, Suite 510
Washington, DC 20005
(202) 737-7377
FAX (202) 737-0193

The Children's Express news bureau was created in 1975 to "give children a significant voice in the world." The bureau produces stories that are researched, reported, and edited by young people; reporters are ages 8–13 and editors are ages 14–18. Children's Express coverage of five presidential elections and many other stories from its five regional news bureaus have appeared in national as well as local newspapers.

Publications: The bureau also publishes full-length books by children such as *Kid's Voices Count: Illuminating the Statistics* and others on topics such as violence in children's lives and school dropouts.

Children's Rights Group
543 Howard Street
San Francisco, CA 94105
(415) 495-7283

Working primarily in the southwestern and western United States, this organization helps communities and parents access existing services for children. It provides training programs and technical assistance to help parents bring federally funded services to their communities, lobbying assistance for fair housing ordinances for children in California, child care services for major San Francisco Bay Area employers, and research services on federal food programs.

Publications: Monthly *Community Services Bulletin* as well as brochures, pamphlets, training guides, and audiovisual materials.

Children's Rights of America (CRA)
8735 Dunwoody Place, Suite 6
Atlanta, GA 30350
(800) 442-4673
WWW: http://home.sprynet.com/sprynet/cra/homepage.htm

This organization provides services to families of missing and exploited children by helping to locate and return missing children to their homes. The CRA provides assistance to the legal community and training seminars for law enforcement personnel, mental health professionals, parents, and family groups, along with outreach programs for street children and child prostitutes.

Publications: Informational brochures available upon request.

Childrights International Research Institute
35 West 83rd Street
New York, NY 10024
(212) 873-7250
FAX (212) 874-2499

This newly established research institute prepares studies and publications about specific children's rights issues and is developing curriculum materials for teachers on the Convention on the Rights of the Child. Other projects under investigation include computerizing children's rights information according to the articles of the CRC.

Publications: A recent publication is *Thirty Questions and Answers about the Convention on the Rights of the Child.* Write for a list of available materials.

Childwatch International
P.O. Box 1132 Blindern
0317 Oslo, Norway
47-22-85-4288
FAX 47-22-85-5028

Childwatch is a network for research on children's issues, currently working on indicators for children's rights. This international network was developed from informal contacts among academics who work in the many disciplines of children's rights, and advocates an interdisciplinary approach to child research. The network is developing the Childwatch TV Global Report, which will disseminate developments in children's rights research; it also sponsors a project to study the positive and negative effects of the electronic media on children.

Publications: Periodic newsletters and reports.

Covenant House Latin America/Casa Alianza
SJO 1039/P.O. Box 025216
Miami, FL 33102-5216
(506) 253-5439 (Costa Rica)
FAX (506) 224-5689 (Costa Rica)
WWW: http://www.magi.com/crica/casa/nza.html

Casa Alianza is the regional office of Covenant House, one of the world's largest privately funded child care agencies, and works on behalf of homeless and runaway children in Latin America. Using outreach programs, crisis centers, and transition and group homes, Casa Alianza staff provide advocacy for children's rights in Latin America through provision of food, shelter, clothing, medical attention, legal assistance, and counseling. Currently operating in Guatemala, Honduras, and Mexico, Casa Alianza's aim is to reintegrate homeless and runaway children into society where they can lead productive lives as part of their families.

Publications: Write to the address provided c/o Bruce Harris, Executive Director for Latin American Programs, for materials about the activities of Casa Alianza and Covenant House.

Defense for Children International (DCI)
Casa Postale 88
CH-1211 Geneva 20, Switzerland
41-22-734-0558
FAX 41-22-740-1145

Defense for Children International—USA (DCI)
30 Irving Place, 9th Floor
New York, NY 10003
(212) 228-4773
FAX (212) 228-4275

DCI is dedicated to the promotion and protection of the rights of the child worldwide. The organization actively works on the international level to advocate children's rights by providing investigations, information, training, technical assistance, and lobbying on behalf of children. DCI sections provide comparable services on the national level, but additionally engage in direct protection work for children such as legal assistance, education, and social assistance programs. DCI is an active consultant to the United Nations and continues to coordinate nongovernmental organization consultation to the Committee on the Rights of the Child. Other areas of concern are children's rights legal issues and training for workers in the areas of juvenile justice and social work.

Publications: The Monitor, a bimonthly children's news and analysis magazine; also research reports on international children's issues.

Food Research and Action Center (FRAC)
1875 Connecticut Avenue NW, Suite 540
Washington, DC 20009
(202) 986-2200
FAX (202) 986-2525

FRAC works on behalf of people in the United States who are least able to provide for themselves in the areas of hunger and undernutrition—most often children, the elderly, the homeless, and the poor. FRAC has engaged in research on the extent of hunger and its impact on low-income families with children, and serves as a support center and coordinating body for a nationwide network of antihunger agencies and advocates. Founded in 1970 as a public-interest law firm, FRAC directs the Community Childhood Hunger Identification Project, a comprehensive study of childhood hunger in the United States, and provides legal and technical assistance to those seeking services from federal food-assistance programs. Additionally, FRAC serves as a clearinghouse for national and local organizations seeking information about hunger and antihunger programs.

Publications: Bimonthly newsletter, fact sheets, reports, surveys, and technical assistance pamphlets, along with policy recommendations for improving federal food-assistance programs.

Holt International Children's Services (HICS)
1195 City View
P.O. Box 2880
Eugene, OR 97402
(541) 687-2202
FAX (541) 683-6175
WWW: http://www.thesphere.com/~holtbear/index.html

HICS helps to rehabilitate biological families with children needing deinstitutionalization, encourage adoption within the developing country, and arrange intercountry adoption, emphasizing the best interest of the child. Educational and nutrition programs are provided, along with special programs to acquire funds for the maintenance and health care of handicapped children.

Publications: Bimonthly *Holt International Families!* and an annual report.

Human Rights Watch—Children's Rights Project
485 Fifth Avenue
New York, NY 10017-6104
(212) 972-8400
FAX (212) 972-0905
Gopher: gopher://gopher.igc.apc.org:5000/11/

The Children's Rights Project of Human Rights Watch, the U.S.-based international human rights organization, works to defend children's rights worldwide through investigations and publication of reports about human rights abuses against children. Created in 1994, the Children's Rights Project has issued reports on child soldiers in Liberia, conditions of detention for children in Jamaica, and abuse of children in Northern Ireland by security forces and paramilitary groups, and children in the Sudan.

Publications: List of publications available upon request.

INHURED International
P. O. Box 2125
Kathmandu Nepal
(977-1) 419610/421727
FAX: (977-1) 412538

INHURED (the International Institute for Human Rights, Environment and Development) International undertakes public advocacy on issues touching upon its mandate to promote human rights, preserve Nepal's environment, and develop its economy and society in a democratic manner. Among its other activities, INHURED provides human rights education and training for law enforcement officials, educators, and community leaders. It is also the host for a number of other advocacy groups in Nepal, including Children's Rights Watch Nepal, a coalition of over 150 children's rights–related groups. Children's Rights Watch Nepal monitors Nepal's compliance with the UN Convention on the Rights of the Child.

Publications: A newsletter is available from the organization's headquarters upon request.

International Association for the Child's Right To Play (U.S. Affiliate) (IPA)
Box 7701
Raleigh, NC 27695-7701
(919) 737-2204
FAX (919) 737-3787

This organization endorses the UN Convention on the Rights of the Child and provides an international forum and advocacy group for the promotion of play opportunities for all children and youth. The organization sponsors research on the importance of play in the training of professionals, seminars and workshops on the need for play, and seeks to end the production and sale of war toys and games emphasizing violence and destruction.

Publications: The *IPA Newsletter,* conference proceedings, books, and audiovisual materials.

International Catholic Child Bureau (ICCB)
63–65 Rue de Lausanne
CH 1202 Geneva, Switzerland
41-22-731-3248
FAX 41-22-731-7793

International Catholic Child Bureau, Inc.—USA
866 United Nations Plaza, Suite 529
New York, NY 10017
(212) 355-3992
FAX (212) 754-4674

The ICCB carries out pilot projects and research on children, provides documentation on matters concerning children, serves

Catholic and other organizations dealing with children internationally, and represents and defends the interests of children on the national and international levels. The bureau is very active regarding street children, refugee children, and the sexual exploitation and sexual abuse of children.

Publications: Newsletter, the journal *Children Worldwide,* and numerous reports advocating children's rights with individual states and international organizations such as the United Nations.

International Child Resource Institute
1810 Hopkins Street
Berkeley, CA 94707
(510) 644-1000
FAX (510) 525-8271

This organization emphasizes the study and advocacy of day care for children, notably the issues of health care, abuse, and neglect, along with legal advocacy. It implements model projects and provides information on various innovations in child care and child health, and serves as a clearinghouse on children's issues.

Publications: The periodic *ICRI World Child Report* and *The Bulletin,* published eight times a year.

International Committee of the Red Cross (ICRC)
19 Avenue de la Paix
CH 1202 Geneva, Switzerland
41-22-734-6001
FAX 41-22-733-2057
WWW: http://www.icrc.org/

Since its origins in 1863 in Geneva, Switzerland, the ICRC has worked as an international movement to protect and help civilian and military victims of armed conflicts and situations or internal disturbances or tensions. The ICRC is a major developer and advocate of international humanitarian law, which protects humans against the consequences of war. Thus, it is concerned with the plight of children who, because of their vulnerability, require special protection where armed conflicts, tensions, or disturbances exist. The ICRC, its International Federation of Red Cross and Red Crescent Societies, and the National Red Cross and Red Crescent Societies are recognized worldwide for their mediation of international conflicts and protection of the rights of prisoners of armed conflict.

Publications: Important research reports on child soldiers as well as other children who are victims of armed conflict; extensive publications catalog available upon request.

International Federation Terre Des Homes (IFTDH)
31 chemin Frank-Thomas
CH-1208 Geneva, Switzerland
41-22-736-33-72
FAX 41-22-736-15-10

The IFTDH is a coordinating structure composed of nine member movements that support development projects in Asia, Africa, Latin America, the Middle East, and Europe dedicated to relief and development for children in need. The projects aim at the improvement of living conditions of underprivileged children, their families, and their whole human environment, with special emphasis on assistance to children in especially difficult circumstances. Each member movement publishes its own materials, as the coordinating structure in Geneva does not have independent publications.

Publications: Write to the Geneva office address to gather further information concerning the publications of individual member movement offices.

International Labour Organization (ILO)
4 Route des Morillons
CH-1211 Geneva 22, Switzerland
22-799-6111
FAX 22-798-8685
WWW: http:/www.unicc.org/ilo/index.html

Founded in 1919, the International Labour Organization has long held the issue of child labor as a major concern. The ILO seeks the elimination of child labor, and as it moves toward this goal, the ILO plans to protect working children by establishing international labor standards and providing governments with assistance in embodying these standards into their own laws and policies. The ILO holds international conferences and publishes journals, studies, and reports on child labor issues from around the world, with particular emphasis on children working under hazardous or forced-labor conditions, street children, and child workers under the age of 12.

Publications: Extensive list of ILO publications available from the ILO office in Geneva c/o ILO Publications.

International Society for Prevention of Child Abuse and Neglect (ISPCAN)
1205 Oneida Street
Denver, CO 80220
(303) 321-3963

ISPCAN serves as a forum for individuals and organizations focused on alleviating problems of child abuse, neglect, and sexual abuse.

Publications: The quarterly *Child Abuse and Neglect: The International Journal.*

International Youth Foundation
34 Market Place, Suite 800
Baltimore, MD 21202
(410) 347-1500
FAX 410-347-1188

International Youth Foundation (IYF) is a nonprofit organization emphasizing the identification, support, and replication of effective programs for children and youth between the ages of 5 and 20. Its primary mission is to assist young people in addressing problems such as alcohol abuse, violence, teenage pregnancy, school truancy, and low self-esteem. Training programs focus on cultural diversity, environmental awareness, AIDS prevention, leadership skills, job training, education, and health promotion. IYF does not raise funds on its own, but rather serves as a networking organization to facilitate program development in countries such as Mexico, Ecuador, Thailand, the Philippines, eastern Germany, and Poland.

Publications: Perspectives newsletter and the IYF Annual Report are available upon request from the Baltimore office.

Minority Rights Group International (MRG)
379/381 Brixton Road
London, SW9 7DE United Kingdom
44-71-978-9498
FAX 44-71-738-6265

Minority Rights Group International—USA
1528 18th Street NW
Washington, DC 20036
(202) 462-5251
FAX (202) 462-4941

MRG is an international human rights organization that has advocated the human rights of minorities since its founding in 1970. Specific minority groups and themes related to minority group concerns such as land rights, constitutional law, international action about genocide, education about prejudice and discrimination, and children's rights constitute the emphases of MRG's advocacy work and publications. MRG's work in the United States has been influential in the documentation of political asylum applications and lobbying for ratification of the UN Convention on the Rights of the Child.

Publications: Publications catalog available upon request from the Washington, D.C., office; includes topical reports about a wide range of minority rights concerns.

National Alliance To End Homelessness, Inc. (NAEH)
1518 K Street NW, Suite 206
Washington, DC 20005
(202) 638-1526
FAX (202) 638-4664

NAEH is a nonprofit organization dedicated to addressing the long-term problems of homelessness in the United States. Focusing on research, advocacy, project development and operation, and education, the NAEH publishes a monthly newsletter, runs national and regional conferences, and lobbies government at the federal and state levels. The NAEH advocates more effective provision of services to meet the housing needs of low-income people, increased job training and financial assistance, enhanced support services for people with disabilities, and preventive programs to limit homelessness arising from unemployment, family problems, and related conditions.

Publications: Monthly newsletter; publication catalog available upon request.

National Center for Youth Law
114 Sansome Street, Suite 900
San Francisco, CA 94104
(415) 956-3307
FAX (415) 956-9024

This child advocacy organization provides legal services to protect children and exercises leadership in training, networking, and publications related to youth law concerns (including foster care, child poverty, adolescent health care, juvenile justice, housing discrimination, and other public benefit programs for children). Founded in 1970, the organization has litigated a number of landmark cases in the area of child advocacy and juvenile justice, and continues to participate in litigation as well as provide support services for other child advocacy groups.

Publications: Youth Law News, bimonthly; selected reports on child advocacy topics prepared by the National Center on Youth Law and other child advocacy organizations. Publications list/bibliography available upon request.

National Committee for the Rights of the Child (NCRC)
125 Cathedral Street
Annapolis, MD 21401
(410) 268-1544
FAX (410) 268-5622

Founded in 1991, NCRC is a coordinating coalition of organizations, individuals, businesses, and other groups committed to promote, advance, and ensure children's rights at all levels of society in the United States, exemplified but not limited to the rights embodied in the UN Convention on the Rights of the Child. NCRC seeks to develop and refine a national agenda to enhance children's rights, facilitate children's rights action by committee members via collaboration and individual efforts, and mobilize other organizations and institutions to support advocacy of children's rights.

Publications: The *Children's Rights Reporter*, published periodically.

National Committee To Prevent Child Abuse (NCPCA)
332 South Michigan Avenue, Suite 1600
Chicago, IL 60604-4357
(312) 663-3520
FAX (312) 939-8962

Since 1972 the NCPCA has served as a coordinating committee for a coalition of state-based chapters and affiliated partners from the public and private sectors whose goal is to prevent child abuse and provide improved lives for children and families. The organization emphasizes four core programs: public education about preventing child abuse, research focused on prevention services and trends in child abuse in the United States, advocacy of prevention initiatives (such as abolition of corporal punishment in schools), and prevention training and technical assistance.

Publications: Comprehensive publications catalog available upon request.

Physicians for Human Rights (PHR)
100 Boylston Street, Suite 702
Boston, MA 02116
(617) 695-0041
FAX (617) 695-0307
Gopher: gopher://gopher.igc.apc.org:5000/11/

This organization of health professionals, scientists, and citizens employs knowledge and skills of the medical and forensic sciences to investigate and work toward prevention of violations of international human rights and humanitarian law. PHR has worked on behalf of both adults and children in a wide variety of countries since 1986, implementing educational and training projects for health profesionals, members of the judiciary, and human rights advocates, particularly concerning the application of medical and forensic skills in the investigation of human rights violations. PHR adheres to a policy of strict impartiality and emphasizes study of the medical consequences of human rights abuses irrespective of the ideology of the perpetrators.

Publications: Physicians for Human Rights RECORD, a newsletter published three times annually.

Rädda Barnen
Box 27320
S—102 54
Stockholm, Sweden
46-8-665-0100
FAX 46-8-661-5326
WWW: http://www.rb.se/raddabarnen/

One of the most active national sections of the Save the Children Alliance, Rädda Barnen sponsors numerous projects on children's rights in Sweden and in Third World countries. Founded in 1919 to work with children in post–World War I Europe, Rädda Barnen expanded its mandate to work on reforming Sweden's laws on capital and physical punishment. By the 1980s and 1990s, its focus had shifted to ending the maltreatment of children in the areas of sexual abuse and the abuse of refugee children. Dedicated to fighting for the rights of the child, Rädda Barnen's first principle is "respect for the child." The organization sponsors pilot projects to generate new understandings of children in vulnerable situations and transform these into model programs, which are then disseminated to influence public opinion.

Publications: Numerous publications available in English and Swedish to educate both children and adults about the Convention on the Rights of the Child. Publications catalog available upon request.

Save the Children
54 Wilton Road
Westport, CT 06880
(800) 728-2445
FAX (203) 227-5667

International Save the Children Secretariat
147 Rue de Lausanne
1202 Geneva, Switzerland
22-731-70-16
FAX 22-738-08-58

The Save the Children Fund
Mary Batchelor House
17 Grove Lane, Camberwell
London, 5E5 8RD United Kingdom
071-703-5400
FAX 071-703-2278
WWW: http://www.oneworld.org/scf/

This nongovernmental organization was founded by Eglantyne Jebb, developer of the first major international children's rights declaration, the Declaration of the Rights of the Child (1924). Since its founding in 1919, Save the Children has served as one of the world's leading child advocacy organizations, providing relief services to child refugees and their families, promoting children's rights, supporting programs dedicated to ending child poverty and discrimination, and protecting children influenced by war and famine in over 130 countries. In 1977 the International Save the Children Alliance (ISCA), a consortium of national Save the Children sections, was established to represent the Save the Children movement internationally, and as of 1988 it consisted of 25 member organizations from around the world.

Publications: Extensive publications program, with materials about children's rights receiving special emphasis given that the historic antecedent of the UN Convention on the Rights of the Child (1989) was Save the Children founder Eglantyne Jebb's 1924 Declaration of the Rights of the Child.

Swedish Association for Sex Education (SASE)
Drottninghomsvagen 37, P.O. Box 12128
S-102 2 Stockholm, Sweden
46-8-692-07-00
FAX 46-8-653-08-23

Founded in 1933, SASE works to foster an impartial and tolerant attitude toward sexuality and intimate relationships. For many years it has advocated the introduction of broadly defined sex education in the schools, informed family planning, abortion on request, and safeguarding of children from pornography and other forms of sexual exploitation.

Publications: List of publications and reports available upon request.

United Nations Children's Fund (UNICEF)
3 United Nations Plaza
New York, NY 10017
(212) 326-7306; (212) 326-7302
FAX (212) 326-7768; (212) 888-7454
WWW: http://www.unicef.org/
Gopher: gopher://hqfaus01.unicef.org:70/11

The major UN organization working on behalf of children worldwide, UNICEF was founded in 1946. With a staff of over 5,100 serving in over 200 offices around the world, UNICEF utilizes its funds (gathered from the United Nations, government donations, and private fund-raising) to address these issues: child health, water supply and sanitation, child nutrition, community/family-based services for children and women, formal and nonformal education, project planning and support, and emergency relief for children. UNICEF is the major UN organization devoted to advocacy of the UN Convention on the Rights of the Child, and it played a key role in developing the 1990 World Summit for Children in New York City.

Publications: Extensive publications program, including print and audiovisual materials, available from UNICEF regional offices and national committees for UNICEF in over 30 countries. Specific UNICEF publications on children's rights include the newsletter *First Call for Children,* issued bimonthly, and the annual *State of the World's Children Report,* published by Oxford University Press.

U.S. Committee for UNICEF
333 East 38th Street
New York, NY 10016
(800) 367-5437
FAX (212) 779-1679

This organization strives to inform the American people about programs of UNICEF and provides opportunities for U.S. citizens to support UNICEF activities and appeals, including U.S. ratification of the Convention on the Rights of the Child. The U.S. Committee for UNICEF also administers annual programs for children and collects funds generated by sales of UNICEF materials, greeting cards, and other resources.

Publications: Annual Report and the *Review of the Year,* along with pamphlets and educational materials.

World Association for the School as an Instrument of Peace (EIP)
5 rue du Simplon
CH-1207 Geneva, Switzerland
41-22-735-242
FAX 41-22-736-4863

U.S. Branch—Peace and Human Rights in Education, Inc.
806 Contra Costa Avenue
Berkeley, CA 94707
(510) 527-7978
FAX (510) 527-6291

This international human rights education organization publishes the newsletter *Ecole et Paix* (Peace and the Schools) in French, and soon in English. It convenes an international human rights course for teachers of primary, secondary, and vocational education—taught in English, French, and Spanish—and conducts human rights courses for teachers in Africa, Europe, and Latin America at the invitation of governments or teaching groups. Also known by its French acronym, EIP, the organization consults with various UN bodies on human rights education and children's rights. National affiliates advocate for children's rights at the national and international levels.

Publications: The newsletter *Ecole et Paix* (Peace and the Schools); classroom materials and professional studies on teaching human rights.

World Movement of Mothers (Mouvement Mondial des Meres) (WMM)
36 rue de Passy, 75016
Paris, France
33-1-45-20-55-80

WMM is a nongovernmental organization advocating the dissemination and support of the Convention on the Rights of the Child in various French and international settings. It participates within UNESCO in activities concerning the protection of children in armed conflicts and the International Year of the Family. WMM conducts international surveys of problems related to children's rights, such as international adoption laws, and is a member of ECPAT, a group of organizations working to end child prostitution and sex tourism in Asia. WMM lobbies on behalf of children in a variety of UN bodies, among them UNESCO, UNICEF, and the Economic and Social Council, and at international conferences such as the Social Summit in Copenhagen (1995) and the Fourth World Women's Conference in Beijing (1995).

Publications: Documents are not published for sale, but results of its surveys and reports on its symposia are made available. Direct inquiries to the organization's Paris address.

Print Resources 8

The books, reports, and other print materials regarding children's rights in this chapter have been selected using one or more of these criteria: The materials are (1) significant in addressing the historic and/or contemporary condition of children's rights, (2) representative of current theory and/or practice regarding the implementation of children's rights worldwide, (3) reflective of diverse perspectives concerning philosophical rationales about children's rights in the contemporary world, and (4) cogent analyses of policy proposals and legislation affecting children's rights around the globe. The educational materials have been chosen because they effectively address the range of children's rights concerns embodied in U.S. and international human rights documents, and present diverse approaches to classroom instruction that can address the varied learning characteristics of student populations.

Books

Abbott, Grace. ***The Child and the State: Select Documents, with Introductory Notes.*** Vol. 1: ***Legal Status in the Family, Apprenticeship and Child Labor.*** Vol. II: ***The Dependent and***

the Delinquent Child and the Child of Unmarried Parents. New York: Greenwood Press, 1968. Reprint of 1938 ed. Vol. I, 678 pp.; Vol. II, 701 pp. No ISBN given.

This two-volume set of documents represents the effort of Grace Abbott, one of the leading children's rights advocates of the twentieth century, to "make available to the student of social service some of the source material which illuminates our present conditions and problems" (preface, Vol. I). As one of her last major projects in a long career of social service on behalf of children, this set remains one of the most comprehensive compilations of documents about the condition of children and the relationship of government policy to children's welfare ever published in the United States. Including both state- and federal-level materials as well as selected sources from other countries such as Great Britain, Grace Abbott created a work in which the development of concern about the welfare of children can easily be traced and the materials readily examined and studied. She provides thorough narrative introductions to all sections in both volumes, as well as a select bibliography, table of cases cited, and a comprehensive index in each.

Alston, Philip, Stephen Parker, and John Seymour, eds. ***Children, Rights and the Law.*** Oxford: Clarendon Press, 1992. 268 pp. ISBN 0-19-825776-7.

The primary editor is the Australian legal scholar and current member of the UN Committee on Economic, Social, and Cultural Rights who analyzed the UN Convention on the Rights of the Child for UNICEF. This collection of essays by international experts tackles issues inherent in the CRC and offers insights into the convention's potential to better the lives of children around the world. Coming from many childhood-related disciplines, the authors look at issues of parents' rights vis-à-vis children's rights, theories of children's rights, privacy, juvenile justice, etc. The book includes thoughtful critiques of most of these original essays. Of interest to scholars, teachers, and professionals.

Archard, David. ***Children: Rights and Childhood.*** London: Routledge, 1993. 188 pp. ISBN 0-415-082510-X.

A philosophical examination of children's rights in which the author explores the history and modern conception of childhood, discusses the ideas and assumptions behind child liberation and child protection, and argues for "a collective responsibility" for children containing four goals: "a 'diffusion of parenting,' a collective valuation of children, and a significant extension of children's rights." Archard also argues that all children have the right to the best possible upbringing, and critiques the traditional roles of the family and the state in rearing children.

Beals, Melba Pattillo. ***Warriors Don't Cry: A Searing Memoir of the Battle To Integrate Little Rock's Central High.*** New York: Pocket Books, 1994. 312 pp. ISBN 0-671-86638-9.

Beals re-creates her early years during which she was one of the "Little Rock Nine" who integrated her high school in 1957. In chronicling the events of the first attempt to desegregate southern schools, Beals introduces her family, to whom she attributes her strength of character, and the historical actors who helped or hindered the courageous young African-Americans. The style is forthright and accessible.

Clinton, Hillary Rodham. ***It Takes a Village and Other Lessons Children Teach Us.*** New York: Simon & Schuster, 1996. 319 pp. ISBN 0-684-81843-4.

Hillary Rodham Clinton's book discusses the problems facing children in the United States within a context framed by the first lady's ongoing efforts to advocate children's rights, both as a lawyer for the Children's Defense Fund and as a public figure working closely with her husband, beginning during his tenure as governor of Arkansas and continuing in the White House. Mrs. Clinton interweaves personal anecdotes with data and case studies drawn from scholarly journals, newspaper articles, government documents, and the studies of international organizations to highlight the precarious condition of children in the United States. Focusing primarily on the collective responsibility of society for engendering the growth and development of children, Mrs. Clinton advocates an emerging partnership between government and other societal institutions who have for generations had the welfare of children as a major priority, particularly the family, religious institutions, schools, and civic organizations. Throughout the text, examples drawn from model programs in other countries are highlighted to demonstrate how the growth and development of children in the United States could be improved with changes in policies and practices. There is no glossary or index provided.

Cohen, Cynthia Price, and Howard A. Davidson, eds. ***Children's Rights in America: U.N. Convention on the Rights of the Child Compared with United States Law.*** Washington DC: American Bar Association, 1990. 344 pp. ISBN 0-89707-641-9.

Defense for Children—USA and the American Bar Association published this early interdisciplinary analysis of the potential impact the ratification of the UN Convention on the Rights of the Child could have on existing U.S. law. The authors of this book, prominent in their field, examine issues in connection with ratification such as the conformity of federal and state laws, as well as possible changes in children's civil rights, health care, and the prevention of abuse.

Cohen, Howard. ***Equal Rights for Children.*** Totowa, NJ: Littlefield, Adams & Co., 1980. 172 pp. ISBN 0-8226-0350-0.

Cohen argues that all adult rights should be extended to children, in the process abolishing what he calls a double standard of one set of rights for adults and a more restricted set of rights for children. Critical of the persistence of the caretaker role that adults have assumed on behalf of children, Cohen believes that adults should act as the agents of children in asserting their rights when children lack the capacity to do so. Indeed, Cohen asserts that granting equal rights to children would serve the interests of social justice, and that, on those grounds alone, adults must help children assert their rights when children lack the capacity to do so themselves. The author also argues that children should have equal rights based upon the application of universal principles of human rights, and that society would be better off when children have such rights. The book's concluding chapters explore the implications of providing equal rights to children in the areas of political participation, due process, and privacy.

Cohn, Ilene, and Guy S. Goodwin-Gill. ***Child Soldiers: A Study for the Henry Dunant Institute.*** Geneva, Switzerland: The Henry Dunant Institute of the International Committee of the Red Cross, August 1993. 178 pp. No ISBN given.

In this comprehensive report, the political and psychological reasons why children participate in armed conflict are examined in addition to the social and economic legal consequences of their participation and ways to implement legal protections.

Coles, Robert. ***The Moral Life of Children.*** Boston: Houghton Mifflin, 1986. 302 pp. ISBN 0-395-59921-0.

The most recent in Robert Coles's series on children's inner lives, this book gives Coles's insights on the psychological and moral development of children in the United States and abroad who tell him their reactions to movies and stories. Coles talks about the effects of social class and the reality of the nuclear bomb on forming children's moral sense and examines their vulnerability as well as their capacity for idealism. One of his sources, children's drawings, are reproduced in color in the book.

———. ***The Political Life of Children.*** Boston: Atlantic Monthly Press, 1986. 341 pp. ISBN 0-87113-035-1.

Published in the same year as *The Moral Life of Children,* this book includes six thematic case studies drawn from Coles's interviews with children in various world societies. Topics include religion and nationalism; ideology and nationalism; language, culture, and nationalism; race and nationalism; class and nationalism; and exile and nationalism. Three other chapters, as well as an introduction, address the relationship of political authority to the young, psychoanalysis and the political thought of children, and children's dreams of survival in politically unstable societies. *The Political Life of Children* seeks to illuminate the forces that shape the political life and experiences of children, and Coles effectively uses the words of his informants to explore how young people's political identities are manifested, with nationalism as the common thread.

———. ***A Robert Coles Omnibus.*** Iowa City: University of Iowa Press, 1993. 278 pp. ISBN 0-87745-411-6.

This collection of essays provides insight into the more recent works of Robert Coles, one of the most eloquent children's advocates of the past 50 years in the United States. Representing his wide-ranging interests, Coles includes essays about children from a variety of perspectives: as museum learners, participants in community service work, subjects in literature, elementary school students, and members of poverty-stricken communities. Also provided in this collection are the complete contents of literary essays published in *That Red Wheelbarrow* and *Times of Surrender.*

Costin, Lela B. ***Two Sisters for Social Justice: A Biography of Grace and Edith Abbott.*** Urbana: University of Illinois Press, 1983. 315 pp. ISBN 0-252-01013-2.

This biography highlights the Abbott sisters' long years of struggle on behalf of social welfare programs dedicated to assisting women, children, and the poor. The influences of their Nebraska upbringing and social work experiences at Hull House under the direction of Jane Addams are detailed, along with their years of dedicated public service in education and government. Special emphasis is given to Grace Abbott's 17 years of leadership at the U.S. Children's Bureau, which was the first major federal agency to address children's issues. Examination of the two sisters' roles in shaping federal legislation on behalf of children, women, and families is provided for the period from World War I until the outbreak of World War II. A comprehensive bibliographic essay is included.

Edelman, Marian Wright. ***The Measure of Our Success: A Letter to My Children and Yours.*** Boston: Beacon Press, 1992. 97 pp. ISBN 0-8070-3102-X.

Written as a personal message to her own family, but focusing on a universal set of themes, the author (director of the Children's Defense Fund) sets out guidelines for the treatment of children and for interpersonal relations that evoke the moral and spiritual values of her upbringing. In five brief chapters, Edelman identifies irreducible minimum standards for moral behavior and provides substantial evidence of the endangered status facing many children in the contemporary United States. Severely critical of government policies concerning children, the author calls for a significantly increased moral, financial, and human resources commitment to improving the quality of life for all children in the United States.

Franklin, Bob, ed. ***The Rights of Children.*** Oxford: Basil Blackwell, 1986. 237 pp. ISBN 0-631-14711-X.

Presenting different perspectives on children's rights in Great Britain, this collection of essays includes selections on children's political rights, their rights at school, the rights of children in care, juvenile justice, children's labor rights, children's sexual rights, and the rights of girls and black children. A separate chapter on children's rights from a Scottish perspective also is provided. The authors all agree on the need to expand the rights of children, although they disagree on the scope of the state's role in either liberating or protecting children. The introduction offers a concise history of the idea of rights for children, placing greater emphasis on the differing historical conceptions of childhood rather than on the twentieth-century emergence of international law addressing children's rights.

Freeman, Michael, and Philip Veerman, eds. ***The Ideologies of Children's Rights.*** Dordrecht, the Netherlands: Martinus Nijhoff Publishers, 1992. 367 pp. ISBN 0-7923-1800-5.

This collection of essays is divided into two areas: theory and application. Contributions by scholars from Europe, North America, and the Middle East provide a wide-ranging consideration of the current status of children's rights, blending theoretical and practical considerations. A major emphasis in the theory section is the UN Convention on the Rights of the Child, with contributions by individuals who helped to draft it and others who have worked to establish policy initiatives to realize its aims. The application section contains chapters on major problems facing children in the contemporary world such as child prostitution, juvenile justice policy, the protection of children in armed conflicts, and infants suffering from parental drug abuse. Two important dimensions provided in this volume are the inclusion of non-Western perspectives on child abuse and the major role of nongovernmental organizations in developing children's rights initiatives around the globe.

Fyfe, Alec. ***Child Labour.*** Cambridge: The Polity Press, 1989. 189 pp. ISBN 0-7456-03998.

The author takes the position that child labor is a serious problem worldwide, arguing that its eradication in industrialized countries such as Great Britain and the United States is a myth, while its growth in the nonindustrialized world is accelerating. He traces the development of the international system of child labor standards, highlighting the role of the International Labour Organization and, in recent years, the United Nations and the working group that wrote the UN Convention on the Rights of the Child. Case studies of how both individuals and groups campaign against child labor in diverse settings are provided, along with a concluding chapter on the debates and dilemmas faced by advocates of "child liberation" and "child protection" in addressing child labor problems. A bibliography is included, along with an appendix containing the conclusions and recommendations of a 1985 UN seminar on child labor.

Grant, James P. ***The State of the World's Children 1995.*** New York: Oxford University Press, 1994. 89 pp. ISBN 0-19-262642-6.

This annual publication provides worldwide statistical data gathered by UNICEF and other UN agencies about the current status of child health, nutrition, education, socioeconomic status, mortality, and other indicators of progress related to human development. Topics of special emphasis related to problems facing children worldwide are included annually, highlighting achievements that improve the daily lives of children, as well as areas of continuing need or decline. Discussions of the current status of major UN initiatives regarding children, such as efforts to realize the goals of the World Summit for Children in 1990, are also provided.

Guggenheim, Martin, and Alan Sussman. ***The Rights of Young People.*** New York: Bantam, 1985, rev. ed. 312 pp. ISBN 0-553-24818-9.

Defining young people as ranging in age from infants to the age of 18, this American Civil Liberties Union handbook addresses many topics under the broad heading of "rights." Noting the distinctions evident in definitions of rights when applied to young people, the authors explain relevant legal decisions and precedents in the areas of juvenile justice, treatment of children by parents and the state, age of majority and emancipation, medical and health care concerns, work and economic status, children in need of supervision, and rights shared with adults, such as First Amendment freedoms. The book is organized in a very legible question-and-answer format, and contains a selected bibliography as well as 11 appendixes supplementing the text with an organizational directory of legal defense groups for young people and tables noting ages at which young people are granted specific legal rights and access to social services.

Hamburg, David A. ***Today's Children: Creating a Future for a Generation in Crisis.*** New York: Times Books, 1994. 376 pp. ISBN 0-8129-2208-5.

Focusing on early childhood and early adolescence, Hamburg examines the emerging problems facing young people in the United

States and offers proposals to stem the tide of child neglect he asserts is pervasive. Placing the problems facing young people in a historical context, Hamburg reviews the role of the family in child-raising and examines the effects on children of changes in family structure and social norms during the last half of the twentieth century. The author includes discussions of recent research on child development and offers proposals based upon careful review of programs and policies dealing with child-rearing, emphasizing that appropriate and thoughtful interventions can make a difference in children's lives. Among the areas suggested for intervention are prenatal care, education for disadvantaged youth, substance abuse, and child care for working parents.

Hatkoff, Amy, and Karen Kelly Klopp. ***How To Save the Children.*** New York: Simon & Schuster, 1992. 224 pp. ISBN 0-671-76997-9.

This is an all-purpose resource guide designed to help readers assist children coping with a diversity of problems ranging from literacy to health care to advocacy on behalf of children's rights and welfare. Organized topically, the book provides brief descriptions of problems followed by recommended actions on behalf of children. The recommended actions are accompanied by quotes from existing children's advocates and illustrative activities currently under way focused on specific problems. The authors include topical chapters on "Youth Reaching Out," "Youth Working with Seniors," "College Programs," and "Holidays and Celebrations," offering an expanded perspective on the contributions of children and youth to U.S. society. A select bibliography includes resources that can be utilized for further exploration of the book's topics.

Hawes, Joseph. ***The Children's Rights Movement: A History of Advocacy and Protection.*** Boston: Twayne Publishers, 1991. 169 pp. ISBN 0-8057-9747-5.

This brief history of the children's rights movement in the United States devotes the bulk of its contents to the effects of children's rights advocacy since 1890. Recognizing the distinction between advocates who are child liberationists and those who are child protectionists, Hawes interprets the development of child advocacy within the context of a historic debate about the nature of children and childhood, as well as the appropriate role of the state in protecting children. Beginning with a brief overview of the book's contents, the author discusses the concept of children's rights in the colonial and federal periods, continues with the development of public education in the nineteenth century, and then places his major emphasis on six chapters dealing with child advocacy in the twentieth century. Major federal legislation and court rulings affecting children's rights are discussed, and the book concludes with a selective chronology and a bibliographic essay that includes major works for further study on the history of child advocacy.

Hawes, Joseph, and N. Ray Hiner, eds. ***American Childhood: A Research Guide and Historical Handbook.*** Westport CT: Greenwood Press, 1985. 711 pp. ISBN 0-313-23337-3.

Serving as a starting point for scholarly research into the history of American childhood, this book provides thorough historiographic surveys of childhood from the colonial period to the recent past. The editors have included essays by expert historians, who survey the major themes in the history of American childhood while reviewing the essential historical literature on their specific chronological period. Each contribution contains a comprehensive bibliography representing the works discussed in that essay. The editors provide an introductory chapter that outlines the research concerns facing the field, and suggest themes and topics for future research and study.

———. ***Children in Historical and Comparative Perspective: An International Handbook and Research Guide.*** Westport CT: Greenwood Press, 1991. 571 pp. ISBN 0-313-25760-4.

Drawing upon contributions by a diverse group of historians worldwide, this book presents an overview of contemporary research on the history of children. Following a brief introduction by the editors, the book is divided into 2 sections: "The Premodern World," which presents 4 chapters on the history of children from ancient times to early modern Europe and pre-modern China, and "The Modern World," which includes 14 chapters, each highlighting the history of children in a different world society or cultural region. Contributors provide comprehensive discussions of major historiographic themes in the history of children for their period, society, or cultural region, along with bibliographies/reference lists representing the works discussed in each chapter.

Houlgate, Laurence D. ***The Child and the State: A Normative Theory of Juvenile Rights.*** Baltimore and London: Johns Hopkins University Press, 1980. 164 pp. ISBN 0-8018-2288-2.

At the time of the writing of this book, the author was associate professor of philosophy at California Polytechnic State University, San Luis Obispo, California. He offers a theory of the foundation of children's rights in the United States by examining U.S. law and relevant Supreme Court decisions. Contrasting the "protectionists" with the "liberationists," he takes a middle ground on such issues as treating juvenile offenders as adults and lowering the age of consent, and offers his own principles for a juvenile justice system.

Human Rights: The New Consensus. London: Regency Press in association with the UN High Commissioner for Refugees, 1994. 304 pp. No ISBN given.

Although this publication is liberally sprinkled with advertisements by private corporations, it provides a basic introduction to and information on the current state of human rights worldwide. It reproduces the texts of basic UN human rights documents and discusses the work of NGOs and UN bodies such as the UNHCR. Children's and adult human rights are not treated separately, but this large paperbound report bears mention because of the significant amount of information and the large number of photographs of children included in it.

Human Rights Watch/Americas. ***Final Justice: Police and Death Squad Homicides of Adolescents in Brazil.*** New York: Human Rights Watch, 1994. 140 pp. ISBN 1-56432-123-1.

This is one of the ongoing series of reports by Human Rights Watch on the violations of human rights and children's rights around the world. Well documented, it covers individual cases of the killing of adolescent boys, some of whom are street children, in Brazil.

Human Rights Watch/Asia Watch. ***A Modern Form of Slavery: Trafficking of Burmese Women and Girls into Brothels in Thailand.*** New York: Human Rights Watch, 1993. 160 pp. ISBN 1-56432-107-X.

This is one of the ongoing series of reports by Human Rights Watch on the violations of human rights and children's rights around the world. Well documented, it contains individual portraits as well as evidence of the trade in women in Southeast Asia.

Jupp, Michael. ***Children under Apartheid: A Report by Michael Jupp.*** New York: Defense for Children International—USA, 1987. 192 pp. No ISBN given.

Now that apartheid is officially ended, this report has become a classic example of the missions undertaken by nongovernmental organizations to expose the conditions in which children in South Africa lived. It includes testimony of individual children and adults as well as statistical evidence of apartheid's effects. Illustrated with photographs, it contains an excellent annotated bibliography and is factually yet movingly presented.

Korczak, Janusz. ***Ghetto Diary.*** New York: Holocaust Library, 1978. Contains Aaron Zeitlin's "The Last Walk of Janusz Korczak." 224 pp. ISBN 0-89604-004-6.

Containing the final literary work of child rights advocate Janusz Korczak and a preface by Igor Newerly, this book describes how the Nazi occupation of Warsaw gradually destroyed the safe haven for children that Korczak had developed in his "children's republic," otherwise known as the Children's House (Korczak's ghetto orphanage). The book includes an introductory prose poem by Israeli poet Aaron Zeitlin, which places the *Ghetto Diary* within the context of Korczak's life and works. The preface details the conditions under which Korczak wrote the diary and how he devised a means to preserve it, knowing full well that he and the orphans he served were targeted for death.

———. ***When I Am Little Again and The Child's Right to Respect,*** trans. E. P. Kulawiec. Lanham, MD: University Press of America, 1992. 186 pp. ISBN 0-8191-8306-7.

This book contains two of the most significant works of Polish children's advocate Janucz Korczak. An introduction by the translator places these two publications in the context of Korczak's lifelong work on behalf of children, noting their importance as attempts to articulate the emotional and moral viewpoints of children in a world dominated by adults. The introduction also discusses how *The Child's Right to Respect* anticipated the realization of rights for children identified in the 1923 Declaration of Geneva, and how Korczak was far ahead of his time in seeking to empower children with decision-making responsibilities through experience with democratic institutions in his children's republic.

Kotlowitz, Alex. ***There Are No Children Here.*** New York: Anchor Books, Doubleday, 1991. 323 pp. ISBN 0-385-26556-5.

The story of two years in the life of African-American brothers, ages ten and seven, who lived in a Chicago housing project, told by the *Wall Street Journal* writer. Echoing the boy's mother, Kotlowitz contends that ". . .there are no children here, they've seen too much to be children," as they survive in the harsh conditions of urban poverty and violence. Using interviews and observation along with newspaper excerpts that set the story in historical context, the author reveals a mother's helplessness to protect her sons from the pitfalls of preteen life in this environment. The book is written for a general audience.

Kozol, Jonathan. ***Amazing Grace: The Lives of Children and the Conscience of a Nation.*** New York: Crown, 1995. 286 pp. ISBN 0-517-79999-5.

Based on both documentary research and firsthand interviews with a wide range of residents, Kozol relates the simultaneously haunting and courageous story of poor children and their parents in one section of the South Bronx, which has the distinction of being the poorest congressional district in the United States. Kozol details the daily struggles to survive of poor people, who face an indifferent bureaucracy, staggering rates of violence, AIDS-related diseases and drug use, and a decaying infrastructure, alternately revealing the inner strengths as well as the doubts and uncertainties of his informants. Included after the final chapter is a section titled "In Memoriam," which lists children and adults whom Kozol discussed, but who had died (often violently) prior to publication. This is an essential book for anyone seeking to understand the condition of children in urban poverty in the contemporary United States.

Lee-Wright, Peter. ***Child Slaves.*** London: Earthscan Publications, 1990. 280 pp. ISBN 1-85383-044-5.

The author provides an overview of child labor exploitation worldwide, using case studies from Asia, Europe, the United States, and Latin America. Emphasis is placed on the failure of both national and international laws to remedy abuses of children in the economy. Linkages between child labor exploitation in the underdeveloped world and the generation of profits for First World economies are ilustrated. A select bibliography is included.

Lifton, Betty Jean. ***The King of Children: A Biography of Janusz Korczak.*** New York: Random House, 1989. 404 pp. ISBN 0-8052-0930-1.

A comprehensive biography of Janusz Korczak, drawing extensively on a broad range of written sources, as well as interviews with surviving alumni of Korczak's Children's Home in Warsaw. The author provides a summary of the rights Korczak advocated for children in an appendix entitled "Janusz Korczak's Declaration of Children's Rights," gleaned from his published works. The book contains photographs of Korczak and his key associates, as well as a number of Korczak alumni interviewed for the book, and is an essential source for understanding the life and achievement of this major children's rights pioneer.

Mason, Mary Ann. ***From Father's Property to Children's Rights: The History of Child Custody in the United States.*** New York: Columbia University Press, 1994. 235 pp. ISBN 0-231-08046-8.

The topic of child custody is explored within the context of the history of the American family, with particular emphasis on the development of legal rules concerning child custody and control. Beginning with the colonial period, the author articulates three key themes: the role of children as an economic asset, the development of differential patterns of treatment for children depending on their socioeconomic status, and the emergence of the emphasis on biological parenthood, a relatively new phenomenon. Also given strong emphasis in the text is the changing relationship between the status of women and custody rules concerning children. Throughout the text, the dynamic relationship among the family, the child, and the state is explored, and in the final chapter questions are raised for future study as the role of the social and behavioral sciences in contributing to custody decisions expands.

Mayotte, Judy. ***Disposable People?: The Plight of Refugees.*** Maryknoll, NY: Orbis Books, 1992. 347 pp. ISBN 0-88344-839-4.

The author lived among refugee people in Africa and Asia in order to record their stories and understand their experience. The book analyzes the definition and status of refugees, the political situations that produced late-twentieth-century mass migrations, and humanely ponders the future for the groups she met. Illustrated and well researched, the book is accessible for general readers, but must be read selectively to find the impact of refugee status on children.

Mnookin, Robert H. ***Child, Family and State: Problems and Materials on Children and the Law.*** Boston: Little, Brown, 1978. 857 pp. No ISBN given.

This law school text contains a comprehensive examination of the relationship of the child to the family and the state in the U.S. legal system. Major topics addressed include the child's economic relationship in the family, the parental right to discipline children, medical treatment of the child, child custody, state-enforced limitations on the liberties of minors, and juvenile delinquency. Discussions of trends and major concepts in each area are provided, along with ample excerpts from court rulings, legal opinions, and publications by experts on each topic. Along with a very comprehensive index, a table of cases cited in the text is provided.

Myers, William E., ed. ***Protecting Working Children.*** London: Zed Books, 1991. 173 pp. ISBN 1-85649-006-8.

Providing an international response to the problem of how to protect working children, this book contains three sections: defining and understanding the problem of working children, planning and implementing effective actions, and evaluating program impact. The introduction to each section describes the context and outlines the competing perspectives on the issue. Contributors are experts in the field of child labor or individuals actively working in seeking to protect working children. Case studies illuminate the problems faced by working children and child protection agencies worldwide, although primarily in the developing world. The concluding chapter provides an agenda for action, with specific recommendations for a comprehensive approach involving the child, family, government, and local communities.

Nasu, Masamoto. ***Children of the Paper Crane: The Story of Sadako Sasaki and Her Struggle with the A-Bomb Disease.*** Armonk, NY: M. E. Sharpe, 1991. 221 pp. ISBN 0-87332-716-0.

This translation of Sadako's story from the Japanese seems to be geared to adults who will tell it to children. Sadako, sometimes called "the Anne Frank of Japan," was the 11-year-old girl who started the paper crane campaign for peace as she was dying of the disease contracted at Hiroshima in the 1945 bombing. The narrative memorializes her while telling the story of her short life and her campaign to launch a thousand cranes. The book deals forthrightly with her death and leaves readers with a chance to celebrate her life when it gives instructions for making paper cranes.

Nazario, Thomas A. ***In Defense of Children: Understanding the Rights, Needs, and Interests of the Child, A Resource Book for Parents and Professionals.*** New York: Charles Scribner's Sons, 1988. 518 pp. ISBN 0-684-18606-3.

Now under revision, this book still provides a comprehensive listing of civil rights, social services, and federal programs available to help children in need. Designed to guide parents or professionals with specific needs from before childbirth through the teenage years, it gives legal parameters for a problem and then walks the reader through the steps necessary when a strategy of intervention is chosen. The book is carefully researched, written by legal professionals, and thoroughly accessible to readers.

Ousseimi, Maria. ***Caught in the Crossfire: Growing Up in a War Zone.*** New York: Walker and Company, 1995. 120 pp. ISBN 0-802-78363-5.

This powerful indictment of the effects of violence and warfare on children combines black-and-white photographs with a textual narrative about five societies: Lebanon, Mozambique, Bosnia-Herzegovina, El Salvador, and the United States (specifically, Washington, D.C.). The author was herself a teenage refugee from Lebanon, returning there to examine the condition of children affected by the ongoing violence in her homeland. Throughout the book, interview excerpts with children who have endured emotional, psychological, and physical suffering are interspersed with a concise narrative explaining the historical and political context within which violence and warfare has taken place in each society. Child soldiers are examined in the chapter on Mozambique, where children were forced into military service and often brutalized through participation in the civil war that raged in that country during the 1980s and early 1990s. The results for children of family disintegration and the difficulties encountered by children seeking to rebuild their lives with positive visions for the future also are explored. The book is indexed, but no glossary is provided.

Platt, Anthony. ***The Child Savers: The Invention of Delinquency.*** Chicago: University of Chicago Press, 1969. 230 pp. ISBN 0-226-67072-4.

Platt's study is central to historical understanding of the late-nineteenth-century movement to reform the treatment of juveniles in the justice system. Focusing on the changing images of delinquency between 1870 and 1900 and the emergence of a new penology in the early twentieth century, Platt also profiles two major advocates of "child-saving": Louise de Koven Bowen and Jane Addams. Platt provides an in-depth case study of the development of the first juvenile court system in the United States, initiated in Illinois at the turn of the century, and then details the problems faced by juvenile courts and their progress through the first three-quarters of the twentieth century. A very comprehensive bibliography is provided, along with a list of cases cited and a thorough index.

Pollock, Linda A. ***Forgotten Children: Parent-Child Relations from 1500–1900.*** Cambridge: Cambridge University Press, 1983. 334 pp. ISBN 0-521-25009-9.

The author provides a careful reexamination of the thesis put forth by Philippe Aries in *Centuries of Childhood* that there was no concept of childhood extant in Western society prior to the Renaissance. She also examines two theories: that there was a formal parent-child relationship, with parents remaining distant and unapproachable from their children, and that, except during the eighteenth century, children were often treated with cruelty and exploited by adults. Following a discussion of the competing views in the historiographical literature about these theories, the author systematically analyzes primary sources to determine their validity. She details the historical debate about the theories in light of the evidence, and determines that each of the theories is flawed, in some cases quite seriously. The flaws have resulted from overgeneralization based on excessive use of secondary sources and a failure to carefully examine primary sources in detail and in sufficient variety to warrant conclusions. The author concludes by demonstrating that the continuity of caring relationships between parents and children, which did not change significantly during the Enlightenment, as some authors have contended, is an enduring phenomenon worthy of more precise study. A comprehensive bibliography is provided.

Price, Janet R., Alan H. Levine, and Eve Cary. ***The Rights of Students.*** Carbondale: Southern Illinois University Press, 1988. 3rd ed. 181 pp. ISBN 0-8093-1423-1.

This American Civil Liberties Union handbook details the rights of students within the context of school authorities' capacity to regulate their behavior and schools' responsibilities to deliver services and guarantee protections to students. The topic of racial segregation is addressed in various chapters that concern discrimination in schools, but the enormous scope of racial segregation and related legal issues requires treatment in a separate volume. Topics included in this handbook encompass access to free public education; First Amendment rights and personal appearance; disciplinary and law enforcement concerns; access to school records; gender discrimnination; students with disabilities; grading, testing, and tracking; and rights of students in private schools. Two landmark Supreme Court opinions are provided in appendixes (*Tinker v. Des Moines Independent School District* and *Goss v. Lopez*), along with a selected bibliography and a set of information sources. An easily accessible question-and-answer text format is employed, with relevant case citations provided in notes at the end of each chapter.

Purdy, Laura M. ***In their Best Interest? The Case against Equal Rights for Children.*** Ithaca, NY: Cornell University Press, 1992. 262 pp. ISBN 0-8014-2662-6.

The author places the arguments on behalf of equal rights for children within a philosophical framework and concludes that a protectionist stance withstands scrutiny more effectively than a liberationist view. The book includes two major sections: the first considering children's rights within a social justice context, and the second examining children's rights on the basis of consequences for children if equal rights are withheld. In both sections, Purdy believes that the liberationist viewpoint is unconvincing when subjected to rigorous analysis on moral and philosophical grounds. A selected bibliography is provided for further research and study of the sources cited in the text.

Ronda, Bruce A. ***Intellect and Spirit: The Life and Work of Robert Coles.*** New York: Continuum Press, 1989. 204 pp. ISBN 0-8264-0436-7.

This analytical study of Robert Coles's work through the mid-1980s examines the major influences on his writing style and philosophical foundations. Beginning with a brief introduction in which the major themes of the book are discussed, the author then outlines how Coles came to develop his unique approach to describing the intersection of personal lives with patterns of social change. In six remaining chapters, Coles's work is discussed thematically, with chapters on the *Children of Crisis* series; literary criticism; psychology, psychiatry, and children; politics and culture; the religious sensibility; and loneliness and community. In these chapters, ample reference is made to Coles's work, along with substantial inclusion of his reflections on his own teaching, writing, and social activism.

Schneider, Dona. ***American Childhood: Risks and Realities.*** New Brunswick, NJ: Rutgers University Press, 1995. 223 pp. ISBN 0-8135-2171-8.

The author, professor of Urban Studies and Community Health at Rutgers University, presents an analysis of the health, educational, economic, and social risks facing children in the contemporary United States. Emphasizing the examination of current and prospective public policy strategies to address these risks to children, Schneider combines a wide-ranging discussion of national and state initiatives with her own research and study of individual children and families. Concluding that the children at highest risk must be targeted for systematic action and that programs with proven track records of effectiveness must be given priority, the author strongly recommends reducing the dangers faced by children at risk as both cost effective and the only truly humane option open to society. A select blbliography is provided, along with a comprehensive index.

Sidel, Ruth. ***Women and Children Last.*** New York: Penguin, 1992. Rev. ed. 250 pp. ISBN 0-14-016766-8.

Sidel analyzes the increasingly difficult plight of women and children in poverty, clearly showcasing the problems facing both groups as the United States heads toward the twenty-first century. With one-fifth of all children under age 18 living in poverty, the United States is failing to provide the basic necessities for a growing number of its young population; as of 1992, over 13 million children lived below the poverty line, and of all children under the age of 6, 22.5 percent, or 5 million, were living in poverty. The author documents comprehensively the worsening status of children in female-headed families, where for every major census group (white, black, Hispanic) poverty is much more prevalent than in families where both parents are present. Sidel examines the failing of the current welfare, child care and health care systems in the United States, and concludes the book by calling for a broad-based family policy emphasizing universal entitlements that will assist in eradicating poverty and will support efforts by women to participate fully in the labor force, while maintaining healthy and nurturing families.

Spiegelmann, Judith, and UNICEF. ***We Are the Children: A Celebration of UNICEF's First 40 Years.*** New York: Atlantic Monthly Press, 1986. 224 pp. ISBN 0-87113-105-6.

This book presents an overview of UNICEF's first 40 years in both text and photographs. Beginning with UNICEF's origins after World War II, the book highlights UNICEF's changing role, initially as a refugee relief agency and later as a broad-based child support agency within the UN system. Many key figures in the development of UNICEF, including Eleanor Roosevelt, Maurice Pate, Ludwik Rajchman, and James Grant, are profiled, along with selected UNICEF volunteers. The numerous black-and-white photographs illustrate the many problems of child survival and development that UNICEF seeks to ameliorate, including inadequate nutrition, lack of child immunization against disease, and children suffering from warfare. UNICEF's programmatic responses to these problems are discussed, with successes and areas for further improvement identified.

Starr, Isidore. ***Justice: Due Process of Law.*** St. Paul, MN: West Publishing, 1981. 274 pp. ISBN 0-8299-1020-4.

Written as part of the series Great Ideas in the Law, Starr's book is designed for secondary and postsecondary students in legal education or civics. The text includes ample reference to actual Supreme Court decisions regarding due process, and provides a wide range of judicial opinions to help the reader reach independent conclusions about the issues. A detailed explanation of the judicial process, emphasizing what takes place in courtrooms, is followed by two lengthy sections dealing with juveniles: justice in the juvenile courts and justice in the schools. Because the book is designed as a text for classroom use, activities and questions for investigation are included throughout and analyzed in conjunction with key Supreme Court decisions. Appendixes include a criminal law case study of *Mapp v. Ohio,* a listing of constitutional amendments cited in the text, a table of cases cited in the text, and a glossary and bibliography.

Taylor, Ronald B. ***Sweatshops in the Sun: Child Labor on the Farm.*** Boston: Beacon Press, 1973. 216 pp. ISBN 0-8070-0516-9.

This study of child agricultural workers in the United States paints a devastating picture of poor and unsafe working conditions, lack of enforcement of existing laws and regulations, poor education, and the effects of pervasive poverty on child development. The book includes photographs taken between 1955 and 1972 that illustrate the working and living conditions of child agricultural workers. Concluding that child farm labor is exploitative and damaging to the future health and well-being of children, the author advocates a comprehensive response by farmers, government, and farm workers to eradicate the structural problems of the farm economy that contribute significantly to the persistence of agricultural child labor.

Trattner, Walter I. ***Crusade for Children: A History of the National Child Labor Committee and Child Labor Reforms in America.*** Chicago: Quadrangle Books, 1970. 319 pp. ISBN 0-812-90141-X.

This classic study of the emergence of the child labor reform movement remains the entry point for serious study of child labor in the United States. More recent books have examined the continuation of child labor problems and attempts at reform since 1970, but Trattner's work places the emergence of child labor reform agitation in the context of the Progressive Era, noting both state- and federal-level activity to redress the appalling conditions under which children worked in both urban and rural settings.

U.S. Department of Labor, Bureau of International Labor Affairs. ***By the Sweat and Toil of Children: The Use of Child Labor in American Imports; A Report to the Committees on Appropriations, United States Congress.*** Washington, DC: U.S. Department of Labor, 15 July 1994. 185 pp. No ISBN given.

After a thorough overview of the forms and nature of child labor in 19 developing countries from which the United States imports products, the report looks at each in terms of compliance with international legal norms. The report names products and the hazards that accompany their manufacture, along with the conditions existing for children in mines and sweatshops. The report is excellent in defining terms associated with child labor.

U.S. Department of Labor, Bureau of International Labor Affairs. ***By the Sweat and Toil of Children.*** Vol. II: ***The Use of Child Labor in U.S. Agricultural Imports and Forced and Bonded Child Labor.*** Washington, DC: U.S. Department of Labor, 1995. 209 pp. No ISBN given.

This clearly stated, valuable U.S. government report documents child labor around the world. Laws, statistics, and descriptions of workplaces make the book useful for teachers as well as people interested in child workers. The chapters on forced and bonded labor are particularly strong, detailing the plight of illegally indentured children of all ages. The book is also available on the World Wide Web at http://www.ilr.cornell.edu/lib/e-archive/ChildLabor/.

Van Bueren, Geraldine. ***The International Law on the Rights of the Child.*** The Hague, the Netherlands: Martinus Nijhoff, 1995. 400 pp. ISBN 0-7923-2687-3.

With a foreword by Hoda Badran, chairperson of the Committee on Human Rights, this book examines international law that has been influenced by the UN Convention on the Rights of the Child from a historical, cross-cultural perspective. Analyzed in the light of economic restructuring, the book presents a comprehensive overview and analysis of international law in regard to children in all countries. Although targeted to lawyers and scholars, this book, the only one of its kind, is accessible to adult readers.

Vardin, Patricia A., and Ilene N. Brody, eds. ***Children's Rights: Contemporary Perspectives.*** New York: Teachers College Press, 1979. 182 pp. ISBN 0-8077-2550-1.

Emerging from the proceedings of a conference on Children's Rights and Child Advocacy in 1979, this volume contains contributions from experts in the fields of juvenile justice, philosophy, educational psychology, legal advocacy for children, and children with disabilities, among others. The primary focus is on children's rights in the United States, but one chapter is included on children's rights from an international perspective, detailing some of the worldwide problems facing children in the areas of nutrition, poverty, and education as of 1979. A concluding chapter presents a discussion about children's rights by ten children, two of whom are editors of the *Children's Express* newspaper, followed by interviews conducted by the *Children's Express* editors with a runaway child, a child in the custody of the state, and child patients in a mental institution. No index is provided.

Veerman, Philip E. ***The Rights of the Child and the Changing Image of Childhood.*** Dordrecht, the Netherlands: Martinus Nijhoff, 1992. 655 pp. ISBN 0-7923-1250-3.

For professionals and teachers, this book examines the phenomenology of the terms *children* and *rights,* and the impact of scholars and international law on creating changing definitions of the image of childhood. After tracing the history and growth of movements formed around children's rights and recounting the biographies of pioneers in the field, Veerman proposes the use of Samuel Shye's applied social science "Systemic Quality of Life Model" as a means of examining the images of children that emerge from a comprehensive selection of children's rights proclamations, charters, declarations, and treaties, all included in the last chapter of the book. In all, 42 twentieth-century documents are reproduced in full and analyzed in the book. The documents alone are worth the purchase of this book by libraries; they are grouped as international declarations and conventions, national and regional declarations, ideological declarations, and specified and sectarian declarations and conventions.

Vittachi, Varinda Tarzie. ***Between the Guns: Children as a Zone of Peace.*** London: Hodder & Stoughton, 1993. 136 pp. ISBN 0-340-60231-7.

Citing the statement by Eglantyne Jebb, founder of Save the Children, when she was accused of treason in a World War I London court: "My Lord, I have no enemies below the age of 7," this illustrated book chronicles UNICEF's work to aid children in situations of armed conflict. Vittachi was a former deputy director of UNICEF and writes movingly about its history. For general readers.

Youcha, Geraldine. ***Minding the Children: Child Care in America from Colonial Times to the Present.*** New York: Charles Scribner's Sons, 1995. 413 pp. ISBN 0-684-19336-1.

The author presents a comprehensive history of child care in the United States, focusing on the roles adults have taken in child-rearing. Organized chronologically, the book presents substantial evidence that the rearing of children has never been the sole province of the full-time mother, and that forms of alternative child-rearing, including communal experiments such as those implemented by the Shakers, settlement house efforts in day care, foster family care, and institutional placements, have regularly been employed throughout American history. The concluding chapter places contemporary policy proposals for child care in a historic context, noting their comparisons and contrasts with earlier efforts, and provides a balanced discussion of competing perspectives on how effective child care in the United States can best be implemented in the last decade of the twentieth century.

Books for Children

Amnesty International Puerto Rico. ***Our Rights!*** Rio Piedras, PR: Amnesty International, Puerto Rican Section, 1993. 100p. No ISBN given. [Obtain from Amnestía Internacional, Seccíon de Puerto Rico, Calle El Roble #54 Altos, Oficina 11, Rio Piedras, PR 00925. Tel & Fax: (809) 767-7095.]

Brilliantly designed and presented, this boxed set of seven large booklets presents the CRC in Spanish, English, French, Portuguese, and Maya, one of the indigenous languages of the Caribbean. Along with an introduction and a "Guide for Grownups," the series contains four other pamphlets on participation, protection, survival, and growth rights. The series is beautifully illustrated and produced by teachers and other members of AI—Puerto Rico; its suggested activities for children make it a fine teaching tool for primary and upper-elementary schools as well as for parents and grandparents to read to the young. Because of the imaginative presentation, children may be able to learn rudiments of the other languages from the booklets.

Bauld, Jane Scoggins. ***Rights for Children.*** Austin, TX: Coming of Age Press, 1994. 40 pp. ISBN 1-885340-00-1.

With text in English, French, and Spanish, this illustrated book contains a Rights Proclamation, divided into 16 rights statements. Following a brief preamble, each rights statement is given in the first person, in three languages, with an accompanying illustration of the underlying concept. Although not directly correlated with the UN Convention on the Rights of the Child, the contents of the book blend effectively with that international convention, and the universal message of the text and pictures communicates well the need for fundamental guarantees of children's rights on a global scale.

Choi, Sook Nyul. ***Year of Impossible Goodbyes.*** New York: Dell, 1991. 169 pp. ISBN 0-395574-19-6.

Describing in rich detail the lives of ten-year-old Sookan and her family in Korea at the end of World War II, this book is a powerful story of how a young girl and her family survive in Korea during the period 1945–1950. The impact of war, displacement, and political conflict on the life of a young girl and her family is vividly rendered by the author, who immigrated to the United States after enduring the turbulence of the postwar period in her native land, North Korea. The book is a good introduction to the history of the post–World War II period from a Korean perspective and highlights the ability of children and their parents to adapt and survive under very difficult circumstances.

Coerr, Eleanor. ***Sadako and the Thousand Paper Cranes.*** New York: Dell, 1977. 64 pp. ISBN 0-440-47465-5.

With illustrations by Ronald Hunter, this story of a young Japanese girl who struggles valiantly against the ravages of leukemia resulting from her exposure to radiation in Hiroshima is a compelling narrative of courage and hope for a peaceful world. The story is based on the real-life experiences of Sadako Sasaki, who at the age of 2 suffered radiation from the atomic bombing of Hiroshima. Sadako's determined efforts to fold 1,000 cranes to forestall her impending physical decline becomes a symbol of courage for other Japanese schoolchildren, who upon her death at age 12 in 1955 complete her task and bury the 1,000 cranes with her. As a heroine to children in Japan and other countries, Sadako's story symbolizes the universal desire to establish peace and goodwill so that future children will not be forced to suffer her fate.

Coles, Robert. ***The Story of Ruby Bridges.*** New York: Scholastic, 1995. 32 pp. ISBN 0-590-43967-7.

Drawn from Robert Coles's research about the effects of desegregation on children in the South during the civil rights movement of the late 1950s and 1960s, this illustrated children's book poignantly relates the story of Ruby Bridges, a six-year-old who confronted the hostility of angry segregationists as the first African-American child to integrate Frantz Elementary School in New Orleans. The text includes excerpts from Coles's interviews with Ruby Bridges and her family, which are interspersed within the narrative portrayal of the integration struggle at Frantz Elementary School. George Ford's powerful illustrations clearly display the tensions evident during this crisis, as well as the courage and inner strength of Ruby Bridges in confronting prejudice and hate. The book's afterword explains how integration prevailed and describes how Ruby Bridges, now a successful businesswoman, established an educational foundation to increase parental involvement in schools.

Colman, Penny. ***Mother Jones and the March of the Mill Children.*** Brookfield, CT: Millbrook, 1995. 48 pp. ISBN 1-56294-402-9.

Written for a young adult audience but equally compelling to adults, this book relates the life story of Mary Harris "Mother" Jones, a leader in the emergent labor movement of the late nineteenth century, who was one of the first and most effective advocates for child labor reform. Blending the story of Jones's professional and private lives throughout the text, the author adds interest by interspersing excerpts from Jones's own publications and speeches, along with period photographs and illustrations from newspapers and periodicals. Emphasizing Jones's most notable project on behalf of child labor, the 1904 March of the Mill Children, the book describes the march in detail. It began in Pennsylvania and concluded in Oyster Bay, New York, at the summer home of President Theodore Roosevelt, where the president sent a representative to meet with Mother Jones and her marchers, but refused to meet with them himself. A brief chronology and select bibliography are provided prior to the book's index.

Gikow, Louise, and Ellen Weiss. ***For Every Child, a Better World.*** New York: United Nations, 1993. 42 pp. ISBN 0-307-15628-1.

Written in cooperation with the United Nations and Jim and Brian Henson, Kermit the Frog narrates a simple story of children's rights, demonstrating an ideal situation of human rights and the frequent reality of their absence. Beautifully illustrated by Brian McNally, the book depicts imaginary cultures in which the people are purple, green, and orange. The simple story is a strong statement of the need for human rights.

Gilliquet, R., D. Casten, and F. Walthery. ***La Convention des Droits de L'Enfant.*** Brussels, Belgium: Reginald, 1993. 64 pp. ISBN 2-80361063-9. [Obtain from the World Association for the School as an Instrument of Peace, 5 rue de Simplon, CH-1207 Geneva, Switzerland. Tel: 41-22-735-242.]

This Belgian children's book includes a simplified version of the CRC in French for children as well as the authorized francophone text. It is an action-filled, 35-page cartoon storzy about children battling the conditions that cause poverty and war and creating a world in which they have their rights of protection. The first in a series on the CRC, the book is aimed at a francophone audience of 8–12 years, but can be used effectively in U.S. French-language and culture classes up to age 15.

Hamanaka, Sheila. ***All the Colors of the Earth.*** New York: Morrow, 1995. 32 pp. ISBN 0-688-11131-9.

The author has written and illustrated a book whose message is simple: Cultural diversity is a positive attribute all over the world because "children come in all the colors of the earth." Highlighting common themes in children's lives around the globe such as play, parental love, relationships with animals, and friendship, the book employs a wide variety of colors throughout the text and illustrations to make its point. To reinforce its universal message, no specific cultural or geographic context is emphasized in either the text or illustrations.

Heide, Florence Parry, and Judith Heide Gilliland. ***Sami and the Time of the Troubles.*** New York: Clarion, 1992. 40 pp. ISBN 0-395559-42-2.

Telling the story of the impact of war on a young Lebanese boy and his family, this book combines a poignant text with compelling watercolor illustrations by Ted Lewin that effectively illustrate the difficulties of living under the threat of war. The daily uncertainty and strife imposed by outside forces on Sami and his family are clearly shown, as are the desires of Sami and other young people for peace in a society where terror is commonplace. The illustrator and authors do a fine job in detailing the competing sentiments of hope and despair in a war-torn society.

Knight, Margy Burns. ***Talking Walls.*** Gardiner, ME: Tilbury House, 1992. 36 pp. ISBN 0-88448-102-6.

Using the theme of walls as its centerpiece, this illustrated book tells the story of walls in diverse world cultures, emphasizing their role as meeting places and communication centers in societies. Ranging across every continent with the exception of the Arctic and Antarctic, the author celebrates the similarities and differences in world cultures by describing the contents and purposes of walls. The text and pictures include both children and adults in active encounters with the messages on the walls, with the universal message of respect for cultural diversity developing through the volume.

Knight, Margy Burns, and Thomas V. Chan. ***Talking Walls: Activity Guide.*** Gardiner, ME: Tilbury House, 1992. 68 pp. ISBN 0-88448-106-9.

This activity book accompanies *Talking Walls* by Margy Burns Knight and is illustrated by Anne Sibley O'Brien. The first chapter offers 32 topics for exploration in classroom activities about walls, using the book's contents as a starting point for more in-depth study. The remaining chapters provide suggested activities for each of the 14 world walls in the *Talking Walls* book. The activities presented in this guide range across the elementary and secondary grades, and are accompanied by suggested teacher's references and audiovisual resources. The activity guide can be used independently of *Talking Walls* to stimulate learning about cultural diversity, respect for human dignity, and related concepts of children's rights.

Moore, Margaret, and John Travers Moore. ***Pepito's Journey.*** New York: United Nations, 1987. 47 pp. ISBN 92-1-100308-3.

———. ***Pepito's Speech at the United Nations.*** New York: United Nations, 1989. 47 pp. ISBN 92-1-100412-8.

———. ***Pepito's World.*** New York: United Nations, 1988. 46 pp. ISBN 92-1-100399-7.

Initially published by the United Nations as a commemoration of the United Nation's fortieth anniversary, the Pepito trilogy presents a young boy seeking to realize his dream of achieving world peace. This universal theme permeates each book; in *Pepito's Speech,* Pepito visits the United Nations and develops his vision of world peace as he dreams of what he would say to the General Assembly; in *Pepito's Journey,* he visits Latin America and becomes friends with other children, while calling attention to the difficulties faced by homeless children; and in *Pepito's World,* Pepito learns the importance of sharing his compassion for other children through letter writing and school projects, which help bring support to a crippled boy, in the spirit of the Children's Year of International Friendship. The trilogy is illustrated with pen-and-ink drawings of universal appeal by the Brazilian illustrators Denise and Fernando. Each book in the trilogy is available separately, and each reinforces key principles evident in the UN Convention on the Rights of the Child, particularly in the area of participation rights.

Rocha, Ruth, and Otavio Roth, eds. ***The Universal Declaration of Human Rights: An Adaptation for Children.*** New York: United Nations, 1989. 45 pp. ISBN 92-1-100423-5.

Illustrated with paintings and linocuts of universal appeal, this simplified version of the Universal Declaration of Human Rights clearly communicates the fundamental human rights included in that landmark document.

United Nations. ***My Wish for Tomorrow: Words and Pictures from Children around the World.*** New York: Tambourine Books, 1995. 48 pp. ISBN 0-688-14451-1.

Completed as a joint project of UNICEF and Jim Henson Productions in celebration of the fiftieth anniversary of the United Nations, this book contains the wishes of children from all continents of the world and several Caribbean islands in response to the question "If you were granted one wish to make the world a better place, what would it be?" Combining the actual wishes of young people aged 4 to 14 with illustrations by 36 young artists worldwide, the result is a vision of the future that correlates well with the ideals evident in the UN Convention on the Rights of the Child.

The foreword, written by Nelson Mandela, and the introduction, authored by Boutros Boutros-Ghali, set the context for the following text and pictures.

Books for Young Adults

Amnesty International United Kingdom. ***Childhood Stolen: Grave Human Rights Violations against Children.*** London: Amnesty International, 1995. 65 pp. ISBN 1-8733-2815-X.

This book briefly explains the UN Convention on the Rights of the Child and then presents examples of human rights violations against chldren in simple, straightforward language. The cases are organized by country and by the principles of Amnesty's mandate to prevent torture and the death penalty, as well as to come to the aid of children who have "disappeared" or who face extrajudical execution. The book is illustrated by the poster series discussed in chapter 9 from the same source.

Bender, David L., and Bruno Leone, eds. ***Opposing Viewpoints: Child Abuse.*** San Diego, CA: Greenhaven Press, 1994. 288 pp. ISBN 1-56510-056-5.

One volume in the ongoing series of "Opposing Viewpoints" issues books, *Child Abuse* contains a wide range of clashing perspectives on various topics related to child abuse. Consistent with other volumes in this series, the contents include a brief introduction to the concept of "Opposing Viewpoints" and their value for classroom instruction; a very brief overview of child abuse as a societal problem; topical introductions to the five major chapters of the volume; focused questions accompanied by two opposing views selected from other published sources; lists of additional periodical sources at the end of each chapter; selected discussion questions for each chapter; and a select list of organizations and books for further study. A broad cross section of perspectives is represented in the five topical chapters, which address the nature of child abuse as a social problem, the causes of child abuse, the scope of the problem, possible repsonses of the legal system to child abuse, and attempts to reduce child abuse. Each chapter title is phrased as a question, which helps the reader approach the issues in an open-ended, flexible manner. The book is thoroughly indexed and contains some graphs and cartoons that illustrate aspects of selected chapter topics. The reading level is appropriate for high school students and adults.

Castelle, Kay. ***In the Child's Best Interest: A Primer on the U.N. Convention on the Rights of the Child.*** 4th ed. East Greenwich, RI: Plan International, 1990. 46 pp. ISBN 0-943965-12-8.

Produced by the former director of Defense for Children International—USA, this now-classic pamphlet was the first created to introduce the Convention on the Rights of the Child to U.S. audiences. It explains and documents 21 areas of rights in simple language and includes an unofficial summary of the articles and an explanation of how the treaty is implemented. Illustrations are by children. Because it also contains the official UN text, it is very much up-to-date.

Filipovic, Zlata. ***Zlata's Diary: A Child's Life in Sarajevo.*** New York: Viking Penguin, 1994. 200 pp. ISBN 0-670-85724-6.

Describing the results of the ongoing siege of Sarajevo by the Bosnian Serbs, this diary presents one child's perspective on the effects of the war not only on her own family, but on many others in her neighborhood and city. Zlata Filipovic's diary provides entries for a two-year period from September 1991 through October 1993, giving a detailed rendering of the daily attempts to survive in a city where for hundreds of years a cosmopolitan culture had thrived, uniquely blending religious and ethnic diversity. Photographs of the author and her family, as well as of her original diary entries, illustrate the book, which has now been translated into many languages around the world.

Freedman, Russell. ***Kids at Work: Lewis Hine and the Crusade against Child Labor.*** New York: Clarion, 1994. 104 pp. ISBN 0-395587-03-4.

Beautifully illustrated with many of Hine's finest and most compelling photographic images, this book combines the story of Hine's life with his commitment to chronicle the problems of children in the labor force from the late nineteenth century to the onset of the Great Depression. Russell Freedman's concise text is interwoven with discussion of Hine's emerging career as a photographer with a social conscience, and covers the development of child labor reform movements during the Progressive Era. The book contains selected photographs from Hine's wide-ranging career, including those portraying skyscraper construction in New York City, as well as the "Declaration of Independence by the Children of America in Mines and Factories and Workshops Assembled" of 1913, originally published by the National Child Labor Committee. A select bibliography of books about Hine and child labor is provided. This book has wide appeal through its blending of an effective text narrative and Hine's unforgettable images of child workers.

Greene, Laura Offenhartz. ***Child Labor Then and Now.*** New York: Franklin Watts, 1992. 144 pp. ISBN 0-531-13008-8.

Focusing on the historic and contemporary status of children in the U.S. labor force, this book provides a general introduction to the major trends and topics associated with child labor and its regulation from the mid-nineteenth century to the present. The text includes many photographs of children at work, and in chapter 4 places special emphasis on Lewis Hine's work as a chronicler of child labor conditions in the early twentieth century. One chapter discusses child labor problems worldwide, and the select bibliography, while predominantly including sources about child labor in the United States, also contains important works on global child labor problems.

Holliday, Laurel. ***Children in the Holocaust and World War II: Their Secret Diaries.*** New York: Pocket Books, 1995. 409 pp. ISBN 0-671-52054-7.

Ranging across the European continent, the 23 diaries in this book offer a glimpse into the child's world during the most devastating global conflict of the twentieth century. With the exception of the Israeli parachutist Hanna Senesh, these diaries remained in obscurity for close to 50 years until their publication in this collection. The diary entries reveal the hopes and fears of young people facing the daily uncertainties of warfare, with most of the authors also enduring the genocidal program of Nazi Germany, experiencing it in ghettos, the Nazi camp system, or both. Thorough introductions including biographical information about the authors are provided for each diary, along with a selected bibliography and a complete listing of the original sources of all diaries in the book.

Jacobs, William Jay. ***Great Lives: Human Rights.*** New York: Atheneum, 1990. 272 pp. ISBN 0-684-19036-2.

Focusing only on the United States, Jacobs provides short biographical sketches of 30 defenders of human rights, beginning with the colonial period and continuing to the present day. Although only a select few such as Jane Addams, Jacob Riis, and Clarence Darrow addressed the violations of children's human rights directly, the book draws from a relatively wide cultural context in its selection of human rights leaders and describes their activities with accuracy and commitment. A select bibliography precedes the index, and the book contains photographs or illustrations of all the leaders discussed in the text.

Kindersley, Barnabas, and Anabel Kindersley. ***Children Just Like Me.*** London: Dorling Kindersley, 1995. 82 pp. No ISBN given.

With a foreword by UNICEF's goodwill ambassador Harry Belafonte, this book represents the results of the authors' expedition to photograph and chronicle the cultural similaries and differences of children in more than 30 countries around the world. Using representative children from every continent, the authors combine text and photographs to describe common elements for each child: their home, clothing, family, places of worship, school, food, neighborhood, and selected activities. Thirty-six children are highlighted, representing all major cultural regions of the world, and the opening section displays their photographs on two facing pages, followed by geographically organized sections. The book also contains a brief selection from the authors' travel diary, and concludes with information and an application blank concerning participation in the Make a Friend—Children Just Like Me Penpal Club. This book is a fine supplement for any individual or group studying world cultures or world geography, either at home or in school settings.

Kronenwetter, Michael. ***Under 18: Knowing Your Rights.*** Hillside, NJ: Enslow, 1993. 112 pp. ISBN 0-89490-434-5.

Written as a primer for students, this book describes the current status of rights for young people in schools, making ample reference to recent court decisions at both the state and federal level. Emphasizing civil and political rights, the author clarifies the relationship of rights for young people in schools to those of adults outside of school settings, and addresses four major student rights topics: the right to privacy, dress and grooming codes, freedom of the press for students, and rights in the classroom. Chapters on how students can defend their rights and the methods they can use to understand the boundaries of their rights also are included. The text is written in a personal, direct manner and photographs are employed selectively to illustrate specific cases or key ideas about student rights in schools. A glossary, select bibliography, and brief organizational directory are provided to encourage readers to continue their investigations of issues raised in the text.

Landau, Elaine. ***Child Abuse: An American Epidemic.*** Englewood Cliffs, NJ: Julian Messner, 1990. 138 pp. ISBN 0-671-68874-X.

This book studies the problem of child abuse by detailing a series of cases that highlight the problem in varying family contexts. Each chapter begins with examination of one child abuse case that illustrates the chapter theme, such as emotional abuse, sexual abuse, or attempts to find a solution. The text is written for young adolescents, but does not refrain from addressing difficult concerns such as incest. Suggestions for further reading and a listing of organizations dedicated to helping stem child abuse and provide support for victims are included.

Layman, Richard. ***Current Issues.*** Vol. I: ***Child Abuse.*** Detroit: Omnigraphics, 1990. 122 pp. ISBN 1-55888-271-5.

One volume in the series Current Issues published by Omnigraphics, this book provides reference material concerning child abuse in the United States. The book includes brief introductory chapters that state the issue and define terms, followed by chapters containing statistics, interviews with spokespersons associated with the topic, lists of resource materials, a select bibliography, and an organizational directory. Also included are chapters detailing characteristics of the abused child, how child protective agencies operate, the role of the court system concerning child maltreatment, and how to report child maltreatment in each state. A unique feature is the inclusion of responses by two readers who were asked by the publisher to vet and react to the manuscript. The volume is useful as a reference book for students in the middle high school years and for the general reader.

Levine, Ellen. ***Freedom's Children: Young Civil Rights Activists Tell Their Own Stories.*** New York: Putnam, 1993. 167 pp. ISBN 0-380-72114-7.

Following a brief introduction describing the genesis of the book, six chapters present the story of the civil rights movement through the words of adults who were children at the time. The personal experiences of the young people very effectively illustrate the challenges they faced in seeking to end segregation and embrace the civil and political rights guaranteed to all citizens of the United States. Beginning with the experience of living in a segregated society and continuing to "Bloody Sunday and the Selma Movement," the author interweaves compelling personal testimonies from informants throughout the Deep South with the broad sweep of change articulated by civil rights leaders such as Dr. Martin Luther King, Jr. Each chapter contains a concise introduction written by the author; following the seven topical chapters is an epilogue, a chronology of major events discussed in the text, a who's who that gives capsule biographies of the informants, a list of acronyms employed in the text, and a select bibliography for further reading. The book is indexed thoroughly. This book can stand alone as a very effective oral history of selected aspects of the civil rights movement or it can serve as an excellent supplement in many social studies classes from the middle grades through high school.

Meltzer, Milton. ***Cheap Raw Material: How Our Youngest Workers Are Exploited and Abused.*** New York: Viking, 1994. 167 pp. ISBN 0-670-83128-X.

Meltzer's historical survey of child labor begins with a brief discussion of the roles children have played in the economy from ancient times to the emergence of the Industrial Revolution. Focusing on child workers in the United States, Meltzer chronicles the work of child slaves, children in the newly industrialized and urbanized North, and the heavy use of children in factories with minimal regulation at the turn of the twentieth century. The author places special emphasis on the workplace hazards and unsafe conditions children have dealt with throughout history, focusing in particular on the problems teenage workers face in contemporary U.S. workplaces today. Drawing heavily upon congressional hearings and proposed legislation in the early 1990s, Meltzer offers a prospective agenda for action on child labor problems and offers specific guidelines for teenagers seeking work, using a helpful question-and-answer format. One chapter is devoted to child labor problems worldwide, and a select bibliography is provided.

The book is liberally illustrated with photographs of children at work in historic and contemporary settings.

Peace Child International. ***Children's State of the Planet Handbook.*** Hilversum, the Netherlands: Peace Child International, 1992. 59 pp. No ISBN given.

This book, produced by and for young people, examines the state of the world's environment and proposes actions to improve it. Filled with the letters, poems, and testimonies of children from around the world, the book also contains experts' recommendations and commentaries on environmental and development issues. Suggestions for action and the activities of selected citizen action groups are provided in a section on "Action." The concluding section emphasizes the choices available to young people, particularly in light of emerging international policy actions about children embodied in the 1990 World Summit for Children and the 1992 Environmental Conference in Rio de Janeiro. Filled with the artwork and words of young people, the book is useful for classroom instruction or as a reference tool for community-based learning.

Siegel, Beatrice. ***Marian Wright Edelman: The Making of a Crusader.*** New York: Simon & Schuster, 1995. 160 pp. ISBN 0-02-782629-5.

This compassionate and up-to-date biography of Marian Wright Edelman is a fine introduction to the life and works of one of the major advocates of children's rights in the contemporary world. Siegel details Edelman's journey from her origins in South Carolina, through her college and law school years, and continuing on as a crusader for civil rights, the rights of poor people, and, most importantly, the rights of children. Edelman's work as founder and director of the Children's Defense Fund is given special attention, and the author has liberally employed photographs throughout the text to illustrate Edelman's life history, social activism, and the social context in which she works. A selected bibliography concerning Edelman's life and career, which includes her own published works, is provided. The book is thoroughly indexed.

Stanley, Jerry. ***Children of the Dust Bowl: The True Story of the School at Weedpatch Camp.*** New York: Crown, 1992. 85 pp. ISBN 0-517-58781-5.

Stanley describes the true story of how migrant children and their families struggled against prejudice, indifference, and intolerance to build their own community and eventually their own school in Kern County, California, during the Great Depression and World War II. Placing his narrative in the context of the migration of worker families from Oklahoma to California, much in the spirit of John Steinbeck's *Grapes of Wrath,* Stanley integrates powerful photographs of the time with the narrative of how "Okie" families struggled to survive in a hostile environment. Gradually, with the support of a few dedicated educators and the solidarity of the Okie community itself, a school is constructed during World War II that becomes a monument to the determination and desire of young people to gain access to education denied them in the mainstream school system. Throughout the text, oral history excerpts are employed from individuals who were children at the time, along with archival photographs of the participants and the migrant worker camp and its surroundings. A selected bibliography about the period and issues addressed in the text and a comprehensive index are provided. The book not only provides stimulating personal reading, it is very useful for language arts and social studies classes.

UNICEF. ***A Children's Chorus: Celebrating the 30th Anniversary of the Universal Declaration of the Rights of the Child.*** New York: E. P. Dutton, 1989. 25 pp. ISBN 0-525-44545-5.

Eleven artists collaborated to provide illustrations coordinated with the ten principles of the 1959 Declaration on the Rights of the Child. Each principle is stated as text, accompanied by an illustration depicting the principle's theme. UNICEF spokesperson Audrey Hepburn's introduction provides a context for the publication of the book (the thirtieth anniversary of the declaration), with the hope that world governments will sign and ratify the Convention on the Rights of the Child. The complete text of the 1959 declaration is included as well.

———. ***I Dream of Peace: Images of War by Children of Former Yugoslavia.*** New York: HarperCollins, 1994. 80 pp. ISBN 0-06-251128-9.

Combining the text of children's testimonies and poems with their artwork and selected photographs of children in the former Yugoslavia, this powerful book depicts the anguish, torment, fears, and hopes of children affected by war. The preface by illustrator Maurice Sendak and the introduction by James Grant, former director of UNICEF, place the text and pictorial images in context and call for action to end the destruction and suffering.

United Nations. ***A Dream for Peace: Human Rights Drawings by Cambodian Children.*** New York: United Nations Transitional Authority in Cambodia, 1993. 52 pp. No ISBN given.

The result of a nationwide campaign designed to raise awareness of fundamental human rights in Cambodia, this book includes selected drawings by children who responded to the campaign theme "What Human Rights Means to Me." Following regional and national judging, the best drawings were selected and organized by the United Nations Transitional Authority in Cambodia (UNTAC) for inclusion in this book. In addition to the drawings, children's quotes concerning human rights and peace are included, along with excerpts from Buddhist philosophy and UN documents on peace and human rights issues. The text is provided in English and Hmong, and concludes with a summary in both languages of the main articles of the UN Convention on the Rights of the Child.

Volavkova, Hana, ed., and the U.S. Holocaust Memorial Museum. ***. . . I Never Saw Another Butterfly . . . : Children's Drawings and Poems from Terezin Concentration Camp, 1942–1944.*** Expanded 2nd ed. New York: Schocken, 1993. 106 pp. ISBN 0-8052-1015-6.

Containing the poems and drawings of children condemned to die in the Terezin ghetto from 1942–1944, this expanded edition of the original published in 1959 by the State Jewish Museum in Prague presents the haunting and profound words and images of children during the Holocaust. The poems and drawings were prepared in violation of camp rules under the direction of dedicated teachers who sought to temper the hardships of the camp experience by having children express their feelings through art. This expanded edition includes a foreword by Chaim Potok, an epilogue by Jiri Weil, and an afterword by the president of the Czech Republic, Vaclav Havel. A chronology of the Terezin camp experience is included, as well as a catalog of the poems and drawings.

Wilkes, Sybella. ***One Day We Had To Run.*** London: Evans Brothers, 1994. 61 pp. ISBN 0-237-51489-3. [Obtain from the UNCHR Information Office in Washington, D.C.]

Illustrated with photographs and the colorful drawings of refugee children, this book for upper-elementary and middle schools pulls no punches about the difficult life refugees face. At the same time it provides rich information on life and culture in Sudan, Somalia, and Ethiopia as it tells the story of the efforts of the UN High Commissioner for Refugees to help children and their families. Young people will be able to empathize with the personal stories of child refugees that alternate with folktales and geographical information to make a well-produced book.

Other Print Resources

Innocenti Publications on Child Rights. Florence, Italy: UNICEF, International Child Development Centre, ongoing. [Obtain from the Information Office, UNICEF International Child Development Centre, Piazza SS. Annunziata 12, 50122 Florence, Italy.]

These publications examine many of the issues raised about children's rights, a relatively new area of study. The Innocenti Centre updates and adds to their list of publications regularly, reflecting emerging trends in the study of child development and children's rights.

Child Rights Series

Boyden, Jo. ***The Relationship between Education and Child Work.*** September 1994. 52 pp. No ISBN given. Order Number CRS 9.

Boyden, Jo and William Myers. ***Exploring Alternative Approaches To Combating Child Labour: Case Studies from Developing Countries.*** September 1994. 45 pp. No ISBN given. Order Number CRS 8.

Cardona, Carlos Castillo, Nelson Ortiz Pinilla, and Alejandra Gonzalez Rossetti. ***Home-Based Community Day Care and Children's Rights: The Colombian Case.*** May 1993. 45 pp. No ISBN given. Order Number CRS 3.

Dall, Frank. ***Education and the United Nations Convention on the Rights of the Child: The Challenge of Implementation.*** November 1993. 48 pp. No ISBN given. Order Number CRS 4.

Goonesekere, Savitri. ***Women's Rights and Children's Rights: The United Nations Conventions as Compatible and Complementary International Treaties.*** September 1992. 43 pp. No ISBN given. Order Number CRS 1.

Himes. James R. ***Implementing the United Nations Convention on the Rights of the Child: Resource Mobilization and the Obligations of the States Parties.*** November 1992. 43 pp. No ISBN given. Order Number CRS 2.

Jonsson, Urban. ***Nutrition and the United Nations Convention on the Rights of the Child.*** November 1993. 44 pp. No ISBN given. Order Number CRS 5.

Parker, David. ***Resources and Child Rights: An Economic Perspective.*** February 1994. 66 pp. No ISBN given. Order Number CRS 6.

Sepulveda, Claudio. ***The Right to Child Health: The Development of Primary Health Services in Chile and Thailand.*** April 1994. No ISBN given. Order Number CRS 7.

Stavenhagen, Rodolfo. ***Double Jeopardy: The Children of Ethnic Minorities.*** November 1994. 29 pp. No ISBN given. Order Number CRS 10.

Innocenti Essays

Flekkoy, Maalfrid Grude. ***Working for the Rights of Children.*** 1990. 24 pp. No ISBN given. Order Number IE 1.

Hart, Roger. ***Children's Participation: From Tokenism to Citizenship.*** 1992. 44 pp. ISBN 88-85401-05-8. Order Number IE 4.

Himes, James R. ***The United Nations Convention on the Rights of the Child: Three Essays on the Challenge of Implementation.*** 1993. 39 pp. ISBN 88-85401-12-0. Order Number IE 5.

Himes, James R., Susi Kessler and Cassie Landers. ***Children in Institutions in Central and Eastern Europe and a First Look at Alternative Approaches.*** 1991. 30 pp. ISBN 88-85401-02-3. Order Number IE 3.

Himes, James R., Vicky Colbert de Arboleda, and Emilio García Mendez. ***Child Labour and Basic Education in Latin America and the Caribbean: A Proposed UNICEF Initiative.*** 1994. 30 pp. ISBN 88-85401-17-1. Order Number IE 6.

Innocenti Studies. Subseries on the Urban Child in Difficult Circumstances

Black, Maggie. ***Children of the Runaway Cities: The Impact of Urban Poverty on Childhood and Family Life in the Philippines.*** 1991. 41 pp. No ISBN given. Order Number ISUC 1.

Chatterjee, Amrita. ***India: The Forgotten Children of the Cities.*** 1992. 44 pp. ISBN 88-85401-08-2. Order Number ISUC 4.

Lorenzo, Ray. ***Italy: Too Little Time and Space for Childhood.*** 1992. 48 pp. ISBN 88-85401-08-2. Order Number ISUC 3.

Munyakho, Dorothy. ***Kenya: Child Newcomers in the Urban Jungle.*** 1992. 45 pp. ISBN 99-85401-09-0. Order Number ISUC 5.

Swift, Anthony. ***Brazil: The Fight for Childhood in the City.*** 1991. 41 pp. ISBN 88-85401-01-5. Order Number ISUC 2.

Innocenti Global Seminar Reports

Black, Maggie. ***Street and Working Children.*** 1993. 56 pp. ISBN 88-85401-13-9. Order Number GSR 4.

———. ***Monitoring the Rights of Children.*** 1994. 58 pp. ISBN 88-85401-19-8. Order Number GSR 5.

Himes, James R., Cassie Landers, and Joanne Leslie. ***Women, Work and Child Care.*** 1992. 78 pp. ISBN 88-85401-06-6. Order Number GSR 3.

Landers, Cassie. ***Early Child Development.*** 1990. 43 pp. ISBN 92-806-00-117. Order Number GSR 1.

Smith, Karen Houston. ***Participatory Development.*** 1991. 58 pp. ISBN 88-85401-00-7. Order Number GSR 2.

Innocenti Readings in Children's Rights

Ennew, Judith, ed. ***Learning or Labouring?: A Compilation of Key Texts on Child Work and Basic Education.*** 1995. 151 pp. ISBN 88-85401-20-1. Order Number RCR 1.

Innocenti Insights

Costarelli, Sandro, ed. ***Innocenti Insights: Children of Minorities: Gypsies.*** 1993. 78 pp. ISBN 88-85401-11-2. Order Number IN 1.

Innocenti Monographs

Models for Monitoring the Protection of Children's Rights. Meeting Report prepared by Maalfrid Grude Flekkoy. December 1990. 58 pp (mimeo). No ISBN given. Order Number M 2.

Lawson, Edward. ***Encyclopedia of Human Rights.*** Washington, DC: Taylor & Francis, 1991. 1,907 pp. ISBN 0-8002-8003-2.

This comprehensive one-volume encyclopedia includes material about human rights activities undertaken during the period 1945–1990 on the international, regional, and national levels. In addition to the main entries section, which is extensively cross-referenced, nine appendixes are included, containing a select bibliography, glossary, information about international human rights conventions and their status, and the structure of the UN human rights system. The index entry on children has 30 subtopics that are contained in the main entries section and one entry in the select bibliography, where listings are categorized under the headings of child labor, child soldiers, and children in adult prisons.

Macksoud, Mona. ***Helping Children Cope with the Stresses of War: A Manual for Parents and Teachers.*** New York, UNICEF, 1993. 139 pp. ISBN 92-806-2087-8.

This book provides specific recommendations for dealing with the stresses faced by children, reflecting the careful study of psychological and emotional strains children encounter during war. The book is organized for quick reference and is divided into two sections: what parents and teachers should know about children's responses to the stresses of war, and how parents and teachers can help them cope with these stresses. In the second section, specific recommendations are directed to parents or teachers, along with a chapter providing advice on when a child care specialist is needed. The second section employs hypothetical situations of children affected by wartime stress, followed by practical suggestions for dealing with each. A brief list of sources upon which the book was based is provided.

New York Times. **"What Grown-Ups Don't Understand. A Special Issue on Childhood in America."** *New York Times Magazine* (8 October 1995).

This special theme issue of the *New York Times Magazine* includes 22 articles about the lives of children, ranging from a statistical summary of the status of children in the United States to articles about how children view religious practices, ethical and moral dilemmas, child-parent relationships, and other concerns. The magazine articles are heavily illustrated with photographs of children in the contemporary United States.

Smyke, Patricia. ***Caught in the Cross Currents: What's Happened to Children and People Who Work for Children in the Ten Years since the International Year of the Child.*** New York: NGO Committee on UNICEF, 1989. 62 pp. ISBN 0-943965-06-3.

This paperbound pamphlet provides an interesting history of the developments in children's rights during the years in which the CRC was drafted. It is broken down into major areas such as health and education.

Trager, Oliver, ed. ***America's Children: New Generation, New Troubles.*** New York: Facts on File, 1991. 209 pp. ISBN 0-8160-2663-7.

This compendium of newspaper editorials includes selections from major newspapers on four topics concerning the condition of children in the contemporary United States: child abuse and crime, the American family, day care and health, and education. After a brief introduction, each section contains descriptions of key events, followed by the relevant newspaper editorials. The editor has made a comprehensive effort to provide diverse perspectives in the selection of the editorials, on both geographical and ideological grounds. A very limited select bibliography is provided, and the book is indexed by both editorial topics and newspaper titles.

UNICEF. ***Educating the Girl Child: An Investment in the Future.*** New York: UNICEF, 1991. 45 pp. ISBN 92-806-1003-1.

This pamphlet, which is updated periodically, presents issues associated with the health, education, and work of female children around the world.

Educational Materials

Amnesty International Human Rights for Children Committee. ***Human Rights for Children: A Curriculum for Teaching Human Rights to Children Ages 3–12.*** Alameda, CA: Hunter House, 1992. 68 pp. ISBN 0-89793-120-3.

Partially funded by Amnesty International USA, *Human Rights for Children* takes ten principles asserting the child's right to be protected and provided for from the 1959 UN Declaration on the Rights of the Child and develops activities to explain them to the young child, the primary child, and the upper-elementary child. The authors explain the meaning of each principle, offer active teaching strategies (such as drawing, measuring, discussing, visiting, and group awareness exercises), and suggest content area, materials, activities, and children's books. All of the lessons emphasize active student learning, are imaginative and interesting, and use a variety of easily obtainable materials. The focus is on the child's general development: identity, toleration for others, and family and community awareness; hence, the curriculum meets needs across the subject fields for presecondary social studies classes.

Canadian Human Rights Foundation. ***Stand Up for Children's Rights.*** Montreal, Quebec: Canadian Human Rights Foundation, 1993. 110 pp. ISBN 2-921337-10-X.

This book provides an introduction to the CRC in the form of five lessons for middle school. An active learning tool, it tackles the hard problems of racism, violence, injustice, refugees, and making the classroom a place for human rights. Handouts include selections from literature, poetry, and vocabulary. Lessons are realistic, thoughtful, and well planned. The book includes goals for each lesson and suggestions for things students can do to bring about children's rights.

Edmonds, Beverly C., and William R. Fernekes, eds. **"The Rights of the Child."** Theme issue of *Social Education* 56:4 (April/May 1992). Available from National Council for the Social Studies, 3501 Newark Street NW, Washington, DC 20016.

This is a special section of the NCSS magazine that introduces and gives a history of the UN Convention on the Rights of the Child to U.S. teachers and provides a rationale for its inclusion in the curriculum. Lesson plans, suggestions for teachers, and information on the state of teaching children's rights around the world are included. Emphasis is on teaching world and U.S. history, current issues, and international relations. The articles by government and nongovernmental organization representatives to the drafting of the document give an insider's look at the treaty's meaning and potential for ameliorating the condition of children, and lesson plans are pertinent. The international teaching section is the weakest, because the convention had just been adopted by the United Nations when the special section was written. Now UNICEF and nongovernmental organizations have been instrumental in including the convention in national and local curricula.

Fountain, Susan. ***It's Only Right!: A Practical Guide to Learning about the Convention on the Rights of the Child.*** New York: UNICEF, 1993. 77 pp. ISBN 92-806-3056-3.

The activities in this spiral-bound notebook of teaching ideas are worth the price of purchase. This is one of the few active learning curricula that introduce the CRC as a treaty to be understood by children and young people; the author accomplishes this by providing a set of "clustering cards" of the CRC's articles that can be xeroxed and distributed, then grouped according to type of right (e.g., protection, provision, participation, survival). Other activities include conflict-resolution cartoons and scenarios to complete. The emphasis is on empowering children by constructive activism (a "planning tree" is included for proposed action). A thorough teacher's section provides complete lesson plans and a well-devised rationale for teaching activism in this manner. The curriculum is aimed at ages 13 and above.

Hoffman, Dorothy, Cleo Simonett, and Mary Eileen Sorenson. ***A Child's Right: A Safe and Secure World.*** New York: United Nations Association of the United States of America and United Nations Association of Minnesota, 1991. 172 pp. ISBN 0-934654-94-8.

This curriculum guide is an introduction to the UN Convention on the Rights of the Child designed for the upper-elementary and middle grades, although many of the activities can be used with minor modifications at the secondary and postsecondary levels. Consisting of eight lessons emphasizing major principles in the CRC, including protection, provision, and participation rights, the curriculum guide provides comprehensive introductions, methodology descriptions, materials, and suggestions for closure. Important foundation documents for the study of children's rights, such as the Universal Declaration of Human Rights, the preamble to the UN Charter, and a full copy of the CRC text, are included. Contemporary issues in U.S. and other societies are employed within the lessons to establish relevancy and to serve as a basis for social action. Among these issues are censorship of learning materials, conflicts regarding hate speech, the plight of homeless children, problems of survival in the developing world, and attempts to eradicate illiteracy. A brief listing of resource centers for further investigation of children's rights is provided, along with an evaluation response form for users of the curriculum guide.

Nurkse, Dennis, and Kay Castelle. ***In the Spirit of Peace; A Global Introduction to Children's Rights.*** New York: Defense for Children International, 1990. 64 pp. ISBN 0-943965-14-4.

The CRC is examined through 23 principles (e.g., freedom from discrimination, refugee children, juvenile justice, rehabilitative care, protection of privacy). Each topic is a five- to ten-paragraph (or cartoon sequence) presentation of a children's rights violation and the background of the country in which it occurred; a map is often included. The authors provide discussion questions and activities for each story, as well as an unofficial summary of articles of the CRC and its full text. Based on the New York Board of Regents' guidelines, the booklet is illustrated by young people and is excellent for late middle school and high school world history, civics, and current events classes. The activities suggest investigation of the issues, examination of the community and the world, and ways to take action on behalf of children. The content is mature in nature, but presented in such a way that students will appreciate that they have some control over their environment; it celebrates those who stand up for children's rights and illustrates several examples from the United States.

O'Brien, Edward L., Eleanor Greene, and David McQuoid-Mason. ***Human Rights for All.*** A publication of the National Institute for Citizen Education in the Law (NICEL). Minneapolis/St. Paul, MN: West Publishing, 1996. 162 pp. ISBN 0-314-04943-6.

The Universal Declaration of Human Rights and the UN Convention on the Rights of the Child are the legal texts forming the basis of this excellent series of lessons, many of which emphasize the rights of children and young people. Human and children's rights are clearly defined in language that readers from ten years old and up can understand and appreciate. Chapters include: "What Are Human Rights?" "Political Rights in a Democracy," "National Security and Fair Procedures Following Arrest," and "When Human Rights Abuses Occur: What Can Be Done?" Each chapter contains definitions, explanations, and examples, along with conversations between people illuminating different perspectives on the problems. Comprehensive suggestions for student action are provided and linked to the major strategies employed to redress human rights within international human rights theory and practice.

Office on Global Education of Church World Service and the Center for Teaching International Relations. ***Children Hungering for Justice.*** Denver, CO: Center for Teaching International Relations, 1992. 32 pp. No ISBN given.

Three 20-page curricula are available on the topics of justice, street children, the right to food, and the role of the United Nations and the Convention on the Rights of the Child. The curriculum treats the same themes with increasingly mature activities and discussions for grades K–4, 5–8, and 9–12. Good background information and grade-appropriate lessons constructed for the class are provided for the teacher in each pamphlet. Charts, diagrams, and tables are helpful. Underwritten by the Church World Service, the presentations avoid ideology and let the teacher and student decide what is fair and just for the world's children. Teachers of geography, world and U.S. history, and current issues will appreciate these pamphlets, which can be purchased separately. The resource is highly selective of children's rights, but does a good job of making issues and possible solutions clear.

UNICEF. ***The Rights of the World's Children: A Development Education Kit.*** Geneva, Switzerland: UNICEF, 1989. 162 pp. ISBN 92-806-002-8.

Authored by a group of development education officers from seven national committees for UNICEF, this book is one of the early curricula based on the CRC. The emphasis is on the psychosocial development of the child, and the book focuses on teaching the middle school and possibly high school student about the rights in the convention as well as socially acceptable behavior. Teachers are given advice on how to present topics such as violence, child prostitution, and child abuse to their classes. It retells stories of individual children's lives, asks for discussion of artworks, etc., all in the context of the child's right to develop healthily.

UNICEF—UK and Save the Children. ***Teaching about the United Nations Convention on the Rights of the Child.*** London: UNICEF, 1993. [Obtain from UNICEF, UNICEF House, 3 United Nations Plaza, New York, NY 10017.]

> ***Teacher's Handbook*** (with the CRC text). 40 pp. ISBN 1-871440-03-3.
>
> Book 1: ***The Whole Child*** (the participation articles). 54 pp. ISBN 1-871449-02-5.
>
> Book 2: ***It's Our Right*** (the provision rights). 78 pp. ISBN 1-871440-04-1.
>
> Book 3: ***Keep Us Safe*** (the protection rights). 76 pp. ISBN 1-871440-95-X.

This is a thorough presentation of children's rights, geared for ages 8–13. The *Teacher's Handbook* offers a clear explanation of the CRC and its rights, the history of children's rights, and two concept maps explaining how the rights are related. Emphasizing active learning, each booklet offers a variety of stories, activities, worksheets, pictures, cartoon sequences, etc., to engage the child in learning about his/her own rights and appreciating the rights of all children. The content is multicultural and appeals to children with all levels of skills. The content is excellent for individual country studies as well as for current events, and for social studies principles such as Third World development. The provision and protection rights are rooted in real-world situations and offer children a variety of ways to take action in activities ranging from learning about a problem to writing letters and publicizing it. A small drawback is that the book is written for schools in the United Kingdom, but the lessons are fully applicable in the United States.

Journals and Periodicals

Child Survival Quarterly and World Immunization News. Task Force for Child Survival and Development, Carter Presidential Center, 1 Copenhill, Atlanta, GA 30307.

Childhood. New global quarterly journal. Contact Editorial Office, University of Trondheim, Norway, N-7055 Dragvoll, Norway.

First Call for Children. UNICEF—New York, bimonthly. ISSN: 1014-9023.

Newspaper format, containing an average of 16 pages; reports on UNICEF's activities around the world, nongovernmental organization events. Contains an extensive resource section of print and nonprint media, photographs, etc. An excellent way to remain on top of the news about children's rights in the world, accessible for high school students and adults.

Human Rights Quarterly. Published by the Johns Hopkins University Press. Subscriptions available from the Johns Hopkins University Press, Journals Publishing Division, 2715 North Charles Street, Baltimore, MD 21218-4319.

International Journal of the Rights of the Child. Published by Martinus Nijhoff.

The foremost multidisciplinary journal about children's rights for professionals and academics, featuring contributors from around the globe. Subscription information is available form Martinus Nijhoff Publishers, P.O. Box 163 3300 AD, Dordrecht, The Netherlands.

Teaching Tolerance. Published by the Southern Poverty Law Center. Subscriptions are free. Address: 400 Washington Avenue, Montgomery, AL 35601. FAX: (205) 264-3121.

This award-winning educational magazine highlights innovative materials, instructional strategies, and thematic stories emphasizing the importance of human rights, with special emphasis on respect for human dignity and tolerance for all cultural traditions.

Published twice annually, *Teaching Tolerance* can be received through written requests on institutional letterhead to the editorial address noted above.

Magazines and Journals for Young Adults

Refugee Children. Available from the United Nations High Commissioner for Refugees, c/o UNHCR ACTION, P.O. Box 2500 CH—1211, Geneva 2, Switzerland.

This 20-page magazine provides an overview of refugee problems facing children worldwide, interspersed with many photographs of refugee children, the problems they face, and their attempts to overcome daily obstacles in achieving fundamental human rights. A section entitled "Listen to what the children say . . ." contains first-person accounts by refugee children from diverse world societies. The magazine also includes action strategies, among them how to write to refugee children and support refugee assistance programs.

Tapori. Newsletter of the Fourth World Movement, 7600 Willow Hill Drive, Landover, MD 20785-4658.

The eight- to ten-page newsletter is written for young readers, and usually tells stories either by or about children who live in poverty. The stories recount the daily lives of children such as "Raphael, a child from Europe," "Jacinto, a child from Guatemala," and "Mario, a child from New York," and show their families and friends and the coping strategies they must use to live. The tone is realistic, yet gentle; the stories are factually told.

Nonprint Resources 9

This chapter contains resources in nonprint form encompassing the wide range of topics included under the heading of children's rights. In the category of databases and computer networks, the reader should note that the ever-changing nature of the Internet and other on-line networks precludes a totally current listing. The databases and computer networks listed here are those deemed most relevant and accessible at the time of publication. Other nonprint resources listed in this chapter have been chosen using one or more of these criteria: (1) their significance in illustrating the range and diversity of children's rights concerns worldwide, (2) their cogent analysis of one or more major issues related to the condition of children, either in the United States or internationally, and (3) their use and interpretation of accurate data about children's rights in an accessible, highly legible format.

Databases and Computer Networks

Gopher Sites

Gopher sites are designed with a uniform menu interface system that permits easy access to large amounts of information, as well as simple to complex searches. In contrast to the World Wide Web, Gopher sites do not require a graphical interface Web browser. They contain many information branches and are interconnected with many other Gopher sites worldwide, as well as with World Wide Web sites on the Internet.

Human Rights Gopher
gopher://gopher.igc.apc.org:5000/

Kidlink Gopher
gopher://gopher.kidlink.org:70/1

UNICEF Gopher
gopher://hqfaus01.unicef.org:70/11

World Wide Web Sites

The World Wide Web employs hypertext and hypermedia to link documents both within a given site and among sites on the Internet. The acronym "HTML" (hypertext markup language) is the format employed to place text documents, photographs, and other graphics on a World Wide Web site. Using the HTML format, links (often text highlighted in different colors, buttons, underlined text, or graphics of various types) are placed on Web sites that permit easy access to other components of a specific Web site or to different Web sites on the Internet. The "uniform resource locator" (URL address) is provided for each children's rights World Wide Web site listed in this section. Typing in the URL or saving it as a bookmark on one's computer once you have accessed the World Wide Web via a browser such as Netscape or Mosaic facilitates easy access to any of the children's rights Web sites shown here.

American Bar Association
http://www.abanet.org/

The American Bar Association's Web site is a comprehensive entry point to vast amounts of information about legal issues. Links to

ABA entities organized alphabetically (sections, divisions, forums, and other groups) are very useful in locating topical materials, including a large number of resources produced by the ABA Center on Children and the Law. Center publications and activities, ABA Child-Focused Policies, and Center News about current issues concerning children and the law are easily accessed within the Center's link on this site. Links to other legal-related sites, a public information link about ABA activities, and a legal technology link are also provided on the site's home page, along with e-mail, phone, and fax contact information.

American Civil Liberties Union
http://www.aclu/org/

The Web site of the ACLU contains wide-ranging information resources on the organization's activities concerning constitutional issues, with particular emphasis on the First Amendment of the U. S. Bill of Rights. The home page is very clear and well organized, with children's rights information easily accessed through a search engine or via subcategories listed on the home page, such as "students' rights." The subcategories contain ACLU briefing papers, the record of ACLU court litigation, student briefing papers on related issues, and additional materials from the ACLU archive. A feedback page facilitates e-mail communication to the ACLU, while the home page includes action strategies under the Act Now! button.

Amnesty International
http://www.amnesty.org/

Amnesty International's (AI) Web site includes current campaign information, the full text of the AI report *Human Rights Are Women's Right* (available in English, French, and Spanish), links to worldwide appeals related to human rights situations in three different countries (available in English and Spanish), the full text of Amnesty International Country Reports, a selection of documents outlining Amnesty International's mandate, addresses of AI sections worldwide, texts of AI news releases, a listing of AI publications, documents from AI about the establishment of a permanent International Criminal Court, information about the Amnesty Interactive CD-ROM, and a broad-based set of links to other human rights sites on the Internet. E-mail contact information is provided and all site information is updated daily.

Casa Alianza: Covenant House Latin America
http://www.magi.com/crica/casa/nza.html/

Casa Alianza is the Latin American branch of Covenant House, a children's welfare nongovernmental organization based in New York City. Under the direction of Bruce Harris, Casa Alianza acts on behalf of Latin American street children by providing refuge, education, and support for street children. Their Web site contains an overview on the plight of street children, suggestions for action strategies by individuals and groups worldwide, content summaries about the relationship of street children to human rights issues and concerning street children and AIDS, as well as links to other Web sites and non-Internet resources about street children. Additionally, the site contains a topical monthly forum regarding street children and development issues and a listing of resources for education about Casa Alianza's work and the condition of street children.

Child Abuse Prevention Network
http://child.cornell.edu/

Headquartered at Cornell University, this Web site is part of the Cornell University Family Life Development Center. This is a well-organized site for accessing wide-ranging resources on child abuse and its prevention. Links to related sites focusing on children's rights issues are included, such as the Children's House, the National Child Rights Alliance, Child Quest International, and others. Federal government child abuse resource links are provided, along with a series of listservs concerning child abuse research and technology applications in human services professions. Through this site, interested visitors can register to receive an electronic newsletter regarding new developments and activities of the Child Abuse Prevention Network.

Child Welfare League of America
http://www.handsnet.org/cwla/

The CWLA site provides general information about the organization's purpose and activities, how to become a member, publications available for purchase, emerging initiatives and upcoming events, and a list of links to CWLA member agencies. A listing of consultation services available from CWLA is included, along with a description of CWLA's role in public policy as an advocate of children in the United States.

Children First: A Global Forum
http://www.globalforum.org/

Containing the results of a Global Forum convened in Atlanta, Georgia, from 9–12 April 1996 that addressed child survival and development issues, this Web site includes topical updates composed during the Forum proceedings, press releases about the event, comments from global children regarding the topics included at the Forum, and a teacher's guide to facilitate classroom applications of Forum content and ideas. Links are provided to five of the sponsoring organizations: the World Health Organization, UNICEF, the World Bank, the United Nations Development Programme, and the Rockefeller Foundation.

Children Now
http://www.dnai.com/~children/children_now.html

Founded in 1988, Children Now employs policy development, mass communications, and community outreach programs to advocate the needs of children, with special emphasis on poor and at risk children and families. This Web site provides a descriptive overview of Children Now and its programs, membership information, a publications list, and "action alerts" to stimulate public involvement in policy initiatives and advocacy programs on behalf of children. Links to related Internet resources are provided on the site.

Children's Defense Fund
http://www.tmn.com/cdf/index.html

The Children's Defense Fund Web site, in addition to providing descriptions of the Fund's ongoing child advocacy programs, contains citizen action suggestions using e-mail, listings of new publications and resources, a complete publications list, and an in-depth set of facts and figures on the current state of children in the United States.

Children's House
http://childhouse.uio.no/

This Web site is an interactive resource center that generates and disseminates knowledge about children's issues. Fourteen different organizations moderate and oversee the varied aspects of the site. Among these organizations are UNESCO, Rädda Barnen,

Childwatch International, the Family Life Development Center at Cornell University, and others from Europe, Latin America, and Oceania. The site has a very comprehensive section on children's rights with extensive materials on the UN Convention on the Rights of the Child, educational resources about war and conflict, links to other educational materials about children's issues, and other UN and UNESCO children's rights publications. Training, conference and workshop postings, information resources on children's issues, research data, early childhood materials, and the activities of non-governmental organizations working on behalf of children also are included on the site. This site can also be accessed through the Rädda Barnen World Wide Web site.

Children's Rights of America
http://home.sprynet.com/sprynet/cra/homepage.htm

Included on this Web site is information regarding the purpose and programs of Children's Rights of America, how to detect and address signs of child abuse and neglect, descriptions of training seminars organized by this group, and topical pages with resources concerning child protection, missing children, and youth in crisis. E-mail communication is available on the site to Children's Rights of America headquarters, along with phone and postal mail contact information.

Covenant House
http://www.covenanthouse.org/

Based in New York City, Covenant House is a child welfare advocacy organization dedicated to protecting and safeguarding street children. This Web site contains a guided tour, a summary of the organization's 1994 annual report, descriptions of programs implemented on behalf of street children in New York, content summaries about the plight of runaway children, and related issues, along with extracts from the comments of donors to Covenant House and suggested action strategies to assist in Covenant House's work to help street children. Covenant House is the parent organization of Casa Alianza, its Latin American branch based in San Jose, Costa Rica.

End Child Prostitution in Asian Tourism
http://www.globalpassage.com/ECPAT/home.html

Containing background information about the movement to end child prostitution and sexual exploitation in the Asian tourist industry, this Web site describes programs developed by ECPAT and provides links to the text of newsletters published by the organization. A discussion of legislation against child sex tourism is available on the site. E-mail, phone, and fax contact information is listed as well.

First Page for Argentina
http://www.well.com/user/uki/argent.htm

Containing a wealth of information regarding the legacy of human rights violations in Argentina from the period of military rule (1976–1983), this Web site includes case studies of "desaparecidos" (disappeared individuals), some of whom were children. An electronic forum where individuals can post responses to listings in the archive of desaparecidos is a very powerful component on the site, with many postings provided by relatives and friends of the disappeared. Topical pages concerning the role of government officials, the clergy, and participants in the acts of terror against the Argentine population are provided, and much of the site is presented in both Spanish and English.

Food and Agricultural Organization of the United Nations
http://www.fao.org/

Containing broad-based information regarding agricultural development, nutrition, and the pursuit of food security, this Web site has well-designed links to a number of children's rights–related topics, such as nutrition, sustainable development, and global food and nutrition trends (the Global Watch link). The site can be searched easily, and a comprehensive publications list, events calendar, and set of news highlights complements the descriptions of FAO work in its various departments. The site can be read in English, French, and Spanish texts. An e-mail contact address is provided for feedback.

Global Childnet
http://www.gcnet.org/gcnet/

This Web site reports on the activities of Global Childnet, with descriptions of the organization's work in the areas of child health and development across the globe. The site contains an on-line electronic newspaper, the *Global Child Health News and Review.* Links to related on-line resources about child health and global development issues are provided.

Holt International Children's Services
http://www.thesphere.com/~holtbear/index.html

Emphasizing the topics of family reunification, in-country adoption, and international adoption, the Holt International Children's Services Web site provides descriptions of the organization's history, its programs, information and resources about adoption and family reunification, a listing of staff and upcoming events, and a page on human rights issues in China. E-mail, regular mail, and phone contact information is included.

Hope and Homes for Children
http://www.ducksoup.net/hope/index.html

Founded by Colonel Mark Cook, a former commander of the British contingent of the UN Protection Force in Croatia, this organization raises funds and constructs homes to house displaced children in the former Yugoslavia. The Web site contains a description of the organization's purpose, information and links to other resources about the conflict in the former Yugoslavia, and topical pages on efforts to rebuild the children's home in Sarajevo and the organization's newsletters. E-mail, telephone, fax, and regular mail contact information is provided.

Human Rights Interactive Network
http://www.webcom.com/hrin/welcome.html

This Web site is a comprehensive listing of links to human rights resources on the World Wide Web. Divided into nine categories, the site includes links to action strategies, urgent appeals regarding human rights issues and humanitarian catastrophes, on-line news services and electronic magazines, opportunities for work and travel, directories of groups and services worldwide dealing with international human rights and humanitarian assistance, consumer alerts concerning products related to human rights violations, and resources on human rights research and education, along with social educational services for youth. The site is available in a text-only version, and both English and Spanish versions are provided on demand. A search engine is included for keyword and boolean searches of available links. E-mail contact information is listed at the end of the site's home page.

Human Rights Web Page
http://www.traveller.com/~hrweb/

Providing an introduction to human rights concepts and issues, this Web site contains four main categories. What Are Human Rights? includes historical information about the development of human rights in the twentieth century, a conceptual introduction to human rights, and biographies of prisoners of conscience. Human Rights Legal and Political Documents includes UN and other documents about human rights, along with topical issue summaries, debates, and discussions about human rights issues. What Can I Do To Promote Human Rights? are action-oriented suggestions for site visitors, while Human Rights Resources provides a comprehensive listing of links to other human rights Internet sites and resources for learning more on the topic. E-mail contact information is listed at the conclusion of the home page.

Individual Rights in America: A Citizen's Guide to Internet Resources
http://asa.ugl.lib.umich.edu/chdocs/rights/Citizen.html

Emphasizing individual rights provided in the U. S. Constitution and Bill of Rights, as well as those embodied under select federal statutes and federal programs, this site offers much information about the legal basis of rights for many groups, including children. General legal resources pages about individual rights exist on this site, along with full-text documents (legal and nonlegal) and a directory of listservs dealing with individual rights and related topics. The section on the rights of youth and students provides links to the National Child Rights Alliance Home Page, and American Civil Liberties Union papers regarding the rights of students in public schools and the rights of minors to reproductive freedom.

Institute for Global Communications: Children's Rights
http://www.igc.apc.org/children/

Part of the IGC PeaceNet network, this Web site provides an alphabetical listing and set of links to children's rights organizations and projects, as well as information about the UN Convention on the Rights of the Child. Links to the IGC Children's Rights Networking page and the IGC Youth Resources page also are included.

Institute for Global Communications: Children's Rights Networking
http://www.igc.apc.org/children/crnetw.html

Containing a list with descriptions of selected organizations, individuals, and resources about children's rights, this Web site also catalogs a sampling of children's rights organizations who are on-line. The most important page on this site presents a set of links to electronic conferences on PeaceNet regarding children. Each conference link contains a brief description of the on-line conference topics.

Institute for Global Communications: Human Rights Resources
http://www.igc.apc.org/igc/hr/

This Web site includes five main subdivisions: action strategies concerning specific human rights issues and initiatives, human rights news and recent developments, human rights documents and clearinghouses, human rights organizations, and additional resources. Descriptions of links in each subdivision are comprehensive, and the site's contents are regularly updated. Links to other PeaceNet sites are listed after the additional resources section of the home page. The site is part of the Institute for Global Communications' (IGC) five interconnected networks: PeaceNet, EcoNet, ConflictNet, LaborNet, and WomensNet.

Institute for Global Communications: Youth Resources
http://www.igc.apc.org/igc/youth.html

This is a broadly defined set of links to organizations on the Internet that emphasize youth advocacy and involvement in public issues. Each link on the Web site is described, and a section of the home page provides a listing of newly added links, displayed before the alphabetical listing of resource links. Links to additional IGC resources on related topics such as Children's Rights and Communities and Families are included.

International Committee of the Red Cross (ICRC)
http://www.icrc.org/

The Web site of the International Committee of the Red Cross contains substantial resources on children's rights issues, with special emphasis on the protection of women and children, the effects of land mines in areas affected by war, international humanitarian law affecting children, and the operations of the ICRC in countries around the globe. A comprehensive publications list is available on the site, along with a section of photographs illustrating the current work of the ICRC, and background papers on the history and current operations of the ICRC. Many of the resource materials on the site can be downloaded and printed. An e-mail address for feedback is provided, along with links to other International Red Cross and Red Crescent Internet servers.

International Labour Organization
http://www.unicc.org/ilo/index.html

This Web site provides a well-organized home page with many links to the activities of the ILO, summaries of current labor issues such as child labor and human rights, a comprehensive listing of publications and information services, and links to other ILO sites around the world. The child labor link includes the full text of two important documents, the *ILO Programme on the Elimination of Child Labour* and *Child Labour*, a major policy document prepared by the ILO's governing body in November 1995. The human rights link contains the full text of all major human rights conventions dealing with international labor issues. E-mail, phone, and fax contact information is provided as well.

Korczak-City
http://www.ilk.de/Korczak.city/

Combining materials on the life, work, and legacy of children's rights advocate Janusz Korczak with contemporary on-line exhibits about children's issues worldwide, this Web site constitutes a "virtual city" that will exist simultaneously with actual exhibits on the same issues erected in public facilities in Warsaw, Poland. The site contains pages on Korczak's life and work, exhibitions of children's work and journalism, children's rights, and emerging issues related to children and the education of youth.

Legal Information Institute of Cornell Law School: Children's Rights Law Materials
http://www.law.cornell.edu/topics/children_rights.html

This Web site provides a listing of primary source material on children's rights law, primarily drawn from the U.S. Code; federal agency activities; U.S. Supreme Court decisions; and state laws. Links to other legal information sites regarding children's issues are included, along with an e-mail comment page for visitors.

The Multilaterals Project
http://www.tufts.edu/fletcher/multilaterals.html

A project of the Tufts University Fletcher School of Law and Diplomacy, this Web site makes available the texts of international multilateral conventions and other instruments. Subject heading pages lead users to comprehensive listings of full-text documents about particular issues, such as human rights, cultural protection, the rules of war, arms control, and others. Children's rights conventions and instruments are found on the human rights subject page. A search engine for keyword searches can be used to access all of the conventions and instruments on the site. Links to other sites with relevant resources are provided at the conclusion of each subject matter page. A link on the site's home page to the UN treaty database is provided, where users can access all multilateral treaties deposited with the UN secretary-general.

National Center for Children in Poverty
http://cait.cpmc.columbia.edu/dept/nccp/

Based at the Columbia University School of Public Health, this Web site contains pages with information about recent news releases and reports of the Center, child poverty news and issues, summaries of Center program activities, how to order publications and slides, and a directory of staff and advisory council members. Phone and fax contact information is provided.

National Coalition for the Homeless
http://www2.ari.net/home/nch/

This organization is a national advocacy network emphasizing strategies, information sharing, and public education dedicated to ending homelessness. The organization's Web site contains descriptions of National Coalition for the Homeless (NCH) programs and how to become a member, summaries of current legislative and policy issues, an on-line directory of homeless organizations in the United States, an updated calendar of events, firsthand accounts of what it means to be homeless, and related Internet resources on homelessness and poverty. E-mail, phone, and regular mail contact information is provided.

OneWorld Online
http://www.bbcnc.org.uk/online/oneworld/top.html

This global news and information Web site is organized into seven interconnected categories: News, Media, Guides, Education, Partners, Gallery, and Action. The Web site home page contains brief descriptions of each category's contents, with one story highlighted of the many available in that category. Children's rights contains its own pages within the Guides category, which are described as guided tours of key global issues. The children's rights Guide contains topical descriptions of four issues: children and war, children and school, children and sex, and children and the state, as well as brief summaries of the UN Convention on the Rights of the Child. Action strategies on global issues for visitor use are described in the Action category and are regularly updated.

Pangaea: Street Children
http://www.tc.umn.edu/nlhome/m027/bonzi/kids/kids.html

A very comprehensive introduction to the contemporary lives of street and working children around the globe, this Web site includes Amnesty International Urgent Action appeals regarding children, photographs and articles concerning street children, an alphabetical listing of organizations who address street children issues, and an annotated listing of journals/newsletters and videotapes about street and working children. An e-mail address for comments and discussions about the site's topics is included.

Rädda Barnen
http://childhouse.uio.no/www.rb.se/

This is the Web site of the Swedish branch of Save the Children, also known as Rädda Barnen. While primarily in Swedish, some English-language components are available on the site, including pages on children of war and a newsletter on child soldiers. The Children's House international children's issues resource Web site can also be accessed from the home page of this Web site. Phone and fax contact information is included for Rädda Barnen in Sweden.

Results: Generating the Political Will To End Hunger and Poverty
http://action.org/results/

This nonprofit, grass-roots citizen action group seeks to identify sustainable solutions to hunger and poverty in the United States and around the world, with particular emphasis on eradicating child hunger and poverty. The organization's Web site contains descriptions of programs and their impact, resource listings of related Internet Web sites, samples of media generated by organization volunteers, background summaries of topics such as child survival, action opportunities for visitors regarding legislation in the U.S. Congress, and topical pages with excerpts from books and interviews with major figures who deal with children's rights issues. E-mail, phone, and fax contact information is provided.

Save the Children
http://www.oneworld.org/scf/

Save the Children's Web site includes pages containing the organization's latest news and press releases referenced by date of publication, current issue summaries, descriptions of the organization's programs and work on behalf of children's rights (both historic and contemporary), and a listing of publications that can be searched under the topics of children and war/refugees and children's rights. Ordering information for all publications also is provided. E-mail, phone, and fax contact information is listed. This Web site can also be accessed through the OneWorld Online Web site.

UNICEF
http://www.unicef.org/

The UNICEF Web site contains extensive resources about children's rights worldwide. The home page includes summaries of major initiatives of UNICEF, with links to more detailed texts on those topics, such as *The State of the World's Children 1996* and *The Progress of Nations,* an annual ranking of nations according to their achievements in improving the status of children and women in areas such as health, nutrition, education, and family planning. UNICEF-specific links include Information, Functional Areas, Management Programs, and Areas of Interest, all of which have additional subcategories addressing specific issues regarding children's rights. The site also includes links to other UN agencies, other organizations dealing with children's issues, and lists of World Wide Web servers around the globe. The Voices of Youth Web site can be accessed from the UNICEF home page. An e-mail contact address is provided for feedback.

United Nations
http://www.un.org/

The United Nations Web site provides a general introduction to the multifaceted operations and programs of the UN, as well as links to all other UN organization Internet sites. Among the many resources available, the site contains the full text of recent major UN documents, summaries of global issues currently being debated and examined at the UN, a comprehensive listing of UN publications and resources for sale, news releases of the UN subdivided by major UN departments, selected photos of UN activities, and a listing of conferences administered and organized by the UN An extensive listing of UN departments and information resources is provided. For a full listing of all UN World Wide Web and Gopher servers on the Internet, use this address: http://www.unicc.org/, the home page of the United Nations International Computing Centre. An inquiry and feedback link is provided on the home page for visitors.

United Nations High Commissioner for Refugees
http://www.unicc.org/unhcr/welcome.html

Organized into four main sections, the UNHCR Web site includes a Contents category, which lists a table of contents of the very extensive UNHCR databases, also known as REFWORLD. The Overview category provides an introduction to UNHCR's worldwide activities, while the UNHCR category contains a short biography of the current United Nations High Commissioner for Refugees. The What's New category contains links for viewing new additions to the UNHCR Web pages.

University of Ottawa: Human Rights Research and Education Centre
http://aix1.uottawa.ca/~hrrec/hrc.html

This Web site represents the Canadian national centre at the University of Ottawa devoted to the study of equality rights, fundamental freedoms, and social and economic rights. The site is subdivided into Domestic Projects, International Projects, a Documentation Centre, Human Resources Development and Workplace

Discrimination Services, the *Human Rights Research and Education Bulletin,* the *National Journal of Constitutional Law,* and sections listing staff, programs, and the organization's annual report. Links to related Web servers in the field of human rights are provided, along with an e-mail contact address. Children's rights are included as a subtopic within the domestic projects pages.

Voices of Youth
http://www.unicef.org/voy/

Created on the occasion of UNICEF's fiftieth anniversary, this Web site contains electronic discussions organized into three forums, all dealing with issues affecting youth around the globe. The Meeting Place is a forum where current global issues are discussed, with special emphasis on how these issues impact children worldwide. Action strategies to address these issues in local communities are included. The Learning Place contains interactive global learning projects that connect schools and volunteer organizations around the globe. The Research Forum provides a location where teachers, trainers, policymakers, and development agency workers can discuss how to use electronic networks for global educational projects and exchange experiences in their localities with others worldwide. The Library is an archive of Voices of Youth discussions that can be browsed by visitors to the site. Feedback opportunities, a search engine for the contents of the site, and a help menu to assist in site navigation are available on the site's home page.

World Health Organization
http://www.who.ch/welcome.html

This Web site contains extensive information about the programs, offices, publications, and services of the World Health Organization (WHO). Information links on the site are updated regularly, such as the WHO Weekly Epidemiological Record, International Travel and Health information regarding vaccination requirements and health advice, and the Public Information releases concerning outbreaks of disease and trends in world health issues. A directory of NGOs in official relations with the WHO is provided, as are links to the WHO Gopher site and to a series of search engines and servers on the World Wide Web. E-mail communication with the WHO is possible using an inquiry link on the site.

CD-ROMs and Computer Software

Amnesty Interactive
Author: Amnesty International USA
Type: CD-ROM for Macintosh or Windows/PC
Cost: $10
Date: 1994
Source: The Voyager Company
1351 Pacific Coast Highway
Santa Monica, CA 90401
(310) 451-1383
FAX (802) 864-9846

This CD-ROM combines video, graphics, sound, and text in an excellent introduction to international human rights topics. Focusing on both the historic emergence of human rights concepts and ideas and the contemporary situation of human rights in the world, the CD-ROM contains an introductory sequence emphasizing the blend between universal human rights and cultural diversity. Five menu options (Stories, Places, Ideas, Rights, and Voices) provide easy access to information about human rights, with the Universal Declaration of Human Rights and the Amnesty International Annual Report serving as organizing structures for much of the information. Action strategies and selected major historic documents about human rights are included and can be printed as text documents.

Express Yourself
Type: Macintosh interactive computer software
Cost: $10 (includes shipping and handling)
Date: 1996
Source: American Civil Liberties Union
ACLU Publications
P.O. Box 186
Wye Mills, MD 21679
(800) 775-2258
FAX (410) 364-5215

This interactive HyperCard stack provides an introduction to historic and contemporary issues about the First Amendment of the U.S. Bill of Rights. Emphasizing cases involving young people, the software main menu contains five sections: Introduction, What's Up (topical issue summaries), Profiles (vignettes of landmark First Amendment cases and key figures in them), Challenge Game (a review game), and Speak Out (activities for social action). The "tools" menu contains print, notebook, and find functions. A thorough reference section about First Amendment issues and a concise glossary are provided.

Audiotapes, Films, Videocassettes, and Filmstrips

About the United Nations . . . Human Rights

Type: VHS videocassette plus teaching guide
Length: 16 min.
Cost: $29
Date: 1991
Source: United Nations Publications
Sales Section, Room DC 2-853
New York, NY 10017

The Convention on the Rights of the Child is summarized in this video, which explains the United Nations' efforts to aid children worldwide. Scenes focus first on problems: street children, child labor, child soldiers and torture and domestic abuse, child refugees and victims of famine, and then on UN programs that attempt to ameliorate their lives. Narrated convincingly by young actress Rita Wolf, the video comes with a 34-page teaching guide.

Anne Frank in Maine

Type: VHS videocassette
Length: 28 min. with discussion guide
Cost: $50
Date: 1979
Source: Anti-defamation League of B'nai Br'ith Materials Library
22-D Hollywood Avenue
Ho-Ho-Kus, NJ 07423
(800) 343-5540
FAX (201) 652-1973

Highlighting the experiences of a junior high class in Maine, this film depicts how study of the Holocaust, and particularly the *Di-*

ary of Anne Frank, influenced the attitudes of students and their parents concerning bigotry and prejudice. The effects on the participants of this instructional unit are emphasized, making the video an educational tool for both educators and students who are involved in study of these topics, or contemplating such work.

The Body Parts Business

Type: VHS videocassette
Length: 62 min.
Cost: $95
Date: 1994
Source: National Film Board of Canada
1251 Avenue of the Americas, 16th Floor
New York, NY 10020
(212) 596-1770
FAX (212) 596-1779

Children's rights activist Bruce Harris investigates the illicit sale of human body parts to supply the world's transplant community with organs from children and adults in developing countries. Employing case studies from Honduras, Argentina, and Russia, the film traces human rights violations involving murder and the subsequent sale of body parts on an international scale. Portraying a growing threat to the rights of children, the film presents a compelling case for international vigilance and concerted action to address this problem.

Chic Street Man: Guns Away

Type: Audiocassette
Length: 12 songs averaging 4 min. each
Cost: $12
Date: 1994
Source: Street Music
231 N.E. 94th Street
Seattle, WA 98115

Talented singer, actor, and composer Chic Street Man frequently performs at schools, singing his message of human rights, tolerance, and peace. This audiocassette includes blues and rap recitation (for which he provides a definition), and the cassette wrapper reproduces the lyrics. Particularly moving is "Celina," written to commemorate the 13-year-old daughter of a Honduran housekeeper killed by a death squad along with her mother and four priests in the early 1980s. Another song rhythmically exhorts youth to put away guns and live in peace; a number of original blues songs complete the tape.

Childhood: A Journey

Type: VHS videocassette with printed series guide
Length: 3 videocassettes, each 50 min. in length
Cost: $29.95 each; $59.95 for the 3-tape set
Date: 1993
Source: Christian Science Monitor Video
P.O. Box 1875
Boston, MA 02117
(800) 775-2775
FAX (617) 450-2017

This three-part documentary series examines the global status of children and issues related to children's rights in nine separate segments, three per videotape. "Care and Nurturing" emphasizes the topics of day care, child health, and intergenerational relationships between children and older people. "Sharing the Light" looks at education using a case study of learning in the Sudan, global children's television and its impact, and the benefits of involving children in the arts. "Preserving the Child" focuses on efforts to address the problems of street children, the effects of warfare on the growth of children in Northern Ireland, and the maintenance of traditional values among children in Navajo society. The breadth of coverage is impressive, as is the attempt to recognize cultural uniqueness within a framework of universal concern for children and their rights throughout the globe.

Children of Perestroika

Type: VHS videocassette
Length: 35 min.
Cost: $149 or rental
Date: ca. 1992
Source: Films for the Humanities & Sciences
P.O. Box 2053
Princeton, NJ 08543-2053
(800) 257-5126 (order); (609) 275-1400
FAX (609) 275-3767

The effects of *glasnost* and *perestroika* on the lives of children in the Siberian city of Kemerovo are shown in this video. Using a series of subtitled interviews in school and family situations with a voice-over narration, the video reveals how children are coming to terms with the appearance of Western culture in their lives, the need to reform stereotypes, and the dearth of opportunities for their futures.

Children of the Dream

Type: VHS videocassette with discussion guide
Length: 22 min.
Cost: $50
Date: 1995
Source: Anti-defamation League of B'nai Br'ith Materials Library
22-D Hollywood Avenue
Ho-Ho-Kus, NJ 07423
(800) 343-5540
FAX (201) 652-1973

This film presents a case study of an intercultural education project featuring students from urban U.S. schools and eight young people from Israel, born in Ethiopia and recently resettled to Israel. Detailing how the two groups dispelled stereotypes and misunderstandings, the film can be employed effectively to address problems of intercultural communication and prejudice.

Children of the Holocaust

Type: VHS videocassette
Length: 51 min.
Cost: $149 or rental
Date: 1994
Source: Films for the Humanities & Sciences
P.O. Box 2053
Princeton, NJ 08543-2053
(800) 257-5126 (order); (609) 275-1400
FAX (609) 275-3767

The right to life is asserted in this moving, sensitively made video. Four adults who were children during the Holocaust tell their stories and contrast their fates with millions of other children and adults who did not survive. Yorkshire (England) Television made this documentary and wrote a voice-over narration and subtitles for the interviews. Illustrated with family photographs and film footage from the Holocaust years, the video traces how each of the four survived either in concentration camps, on city streets, or hidden by non-Jewish families.

Children of War

Type: VHS videocassette
Length: 20 min.
Cost: $49.95
Date: 1993
Source: Turner Multimedia
105 Terry Drive, Suite 120
Newtown, PA 18940
(800) 742-1096
FAX (215) 579-8589

This video contains four brief CNN Newsroom segments on the impact of war on children in the Middle East, Bosnia, and Somalia. Hardships of daily life and coping efforts by the children and their families are highlighted.

The Children's World Summit

Type: VHS videocassette
Length: 45 min.
Cost: $49.95
Date: 1991
Source: Turner Multimedia
105 Terry Drive, Suite 120
Newtown, PA 18940
(800) 742-1096
FAX (215) 579-8589

Consisting of 11 brief reports on various aspects of children's rights worldwide, this video includes excerpts from the CNN World Report newscast. Linked by a series of narrative introductions, which also contain facts and statistics on the condition of children worldwide, the video focuses on the World Summit for Children held in New York City in 1990, and the subsequent call for worldwide ratification of the UN Convention on the Rights of the Child. The video segments address child health, children affected by war, the plight of female children, child illiteracy, progress made in reducing childhood mortality and illiteracy, child activism regarding the World Summit, and efforts made by international organizations and nongovernmental organizations to assist children in difficult circumstances. The report contains segments from countries in Europe, Africa, the Middle East, North America, Latin America, the Caribbean, and the Indian subcontinent, all produced between 1990 and 1991. Segments are concise and contain compelling video footage, along with interviews and reporter narratives concerning the topics, which make them useful for classroom instruction either by themselves or in thematic sets.

Democracy and Rights: One Citizen's Challenge

Type: VHS videocassette plus study guide
Length: 30 min.
Cost: $60
Date: 1989
Source: Close Up Publishing
Dept. C15
44 Canal Center Plaza
Alexandria, VA 22314-1592
(800) 765-3131
FAX (703) 706-0002

Featuring the retrospective impressions of Ernest Green, one of the "Little Rock Nine," this film highlights one of the major turning points of the U.S. civil rights movement: the integration of Little Rock Central High School in Arkansas. A high school student in 1957, Green recalls the events and activities of the time, mixing them with his comments about returning to the school in 1987, 30 years later. Historic film clips are employed to illustrate the very real dangers faced by the courageous students who stared down prejudice and bigotry with the assistance of federal troops some three years after the landmark *Brown v. Board of Education of Topeka, Kansas* decision declared unconstitutional the doctrine of "separate but equal" education.

Human Rights: Working for a Better World

Type: VHS videocassette
Length: 26 min.
Cost: Rental
Date: 1993
Source: Scholastic/NBC News Video
Scholastic Magazine
555 Broadway
New York, NY 10012-3999

Accompanied by the 3 December 1993 issues of *Junior Scholastic* and *Scholastic News* magazines, the video includes segments on the history of human rights, human rights in China, and children's rights and human rights heroes Nelson Mandela, the Dalai Lama, former President Jimmy Carter, and a number of young Americans, some of whom write letters for Amnesty International. Aimed at middle and high school audiences, nationally known NBC news reporters provide brief but excellent introductions to human rights, including an absorbing six-minute section on children's rights, and a bonus segment on the signing of the Arab-Israeli peace agreement.

If the Mango Tree Could Speak

Type: VHS videocassette (in Spanish with English subtitles) with study guide
Length: 58 min.
Cost: $250 or rental
Date: 1995
Source: New Day Film Library
22-D Hollywood Avenue
Ho-Ho-Kus, NJ 07423
(201) 652-6590
FAX (201) 652-1973

Ten boys and girls growing up in the midst of war in Guatemala and El Salvador are interviewed on topics such as war and peace, justice, ethnic identity, friendship, and marriage. The children are followed in the course of their daily lives; each has a segment lasting five to ten minutes. Their stories are disturbing, but their resilience in the face of harsh reality is inspirational. The video comes with a 32-page study guide developed by the Network of Educators on the Americas. Appropriate for middle and high school levels; suitable for community groups.

Kids in the Crossfire: Violence in America

Type: VHS videocassette
Length: 71 min.
Cost: $19.98
Date: 1993
Source: Social Studies School Service
10200 Jefferson Boulevard, Room 122
P.O. Box 802
Culver City, CA 90232-0802
(800) 421-4246
FAX (800) 944-5432

Structured as an open discussion with young people and selected adults such as U.S. Attorney General Janet Reno and actor Chuck Norris, ABC News commentator Peter Jennings examines the effects of violence on children's lives in the United States. Brief segments of the video provide focused examination of specific topics such as violence in schools, images of violence in the media and popular culture, and parents' responsibility concerning violence against children. Peer mediation and conflict resolution strategies are discussed as possible avenues to reduce violence in schools in the concluding segment of the program.

Korczak

Type: VHS videocassette (in Polish with enhanced English subtitles)
Length: 118 min.
Cost: $79.95
Date: 1993
Source: New Yorker Films
16 West 61st Street
New York, NY 10023
(212) 247-6110
FAX (212) 307-7855

Depicting the final years of Janusz Korczak's life from the 1930s to his death during the Holocaust, this film highlights the courage and commitment to children of one of the twentieth century's leading child rights advocates. Faithfully showing various elements of Korczak's educational philosophy, including the children's court and his emphasis on respect for every child's human dignity, the film is a powerful and moving account of Korczak's work and his spiritual triumph over the face of evil.

Listening to Children: A Moral Journey with Robert Coles

Type: VHS Videocassette
Length: 90 minutes
Cost: $19.95
Date: 1995
Source: PBS Video
1320 Braddock Place
Alexandria, VA 22314
(800) 424-7963
FAX (703) 739-5269

Combining six case studies of the moral lives of children in the contemporary United States with segments from a public forum with parents and teachers, this documentary illustrates how Robert Coles investigates the world created by children, using their own words and pictures as primary sources of evidence. Interweaving a structured narrative that places each case study in its own geographic, family, and cultural context, Coles demonstrates how children create their own moral lives by mediating the influences of parents, families, and schools and forging individual perspectives on right and wrong. The case studies have wide-ranging appeal, representing children in poverty and affluence, from diverse racial and ethnic backgrounds, and in single and dual parent households. The concluding parent and teacher forum permits Coles to establish linkages between the case study data and broad generalizations about the roles of family, the media, schools, and other institutions in shaping the moral lives of young people.

Lost and Found: The Story of Romania's Forgotten Children

Type: VHS videocassette
Length: 28 min.
Cost: $195
Date: 1992
Source: Documentary Educational Resources
101 Morse Street
Watertown, MA 02172
(617) 926-0491
FAX (617) 926-9519

This gripping documentary explores the results of Communist era policies that led to thousands of children being sent to state institutions where many are classified as "irrecoverables," or wards of the state. Neglect and deprivation are omnipresent for these children, who exist in conditions that have left three-fourths of them with severely retarded physical and mental development. The film provides hope for change based on international relief efforts to improve the living conditions for these institutional orphans, while simultaneously recognizing the enormous efforts that remain to help them regain their human dignity and learn how to live in mainstream society.

No Life for a Child: A Tape/Discussion Pack on the Convention on the Rights of the Child

Type: 6 audiotapes
Length: 15 min. each

Cost: On request
Date: None given
Source: UNICEF—UK
55 Lincoln's Inn Fields
London WC2A 3NB, England

The pack consists of six audiotapes of BBC-conducted interviews with children in the major world areas, a copy of the UN Convention on the Rights of the Child, and a booklet suggesting ways for secondary school teachers to use the materials in class. Topics are: children in armed conflict, child health, education, substance abuse, child labor, and children without families. The audiotapes focus on the children's lives, and the commentary gives information on the countries and conditions in which they are growing up. The British accents of the interviewer and the translators are clear and will probably not be distracting to U.S. students.

The Orphan Trains
Type: VHS Videocassette
Length: 60 min.
Cost: $19.95
Date: 1995
Source: PBS Video
1320 Braddock Place
Alexandria VA 22314
(800) 424-7963
FAX (703) 739-5269

This documentary tells the story of how the Children's Aid Society, inspired by the work of the minister Charles Loring Brace, worked to relocate thousands of homeless children from urban slums to Christian homes in the countryside. Between 1854 and 1929, over 150,000 children were relocated to farming communities throughout the United States to begin new lives with foster families. Integrating historical photos with interview excerpts from elderly survivors of the program, the film discusses the success and failures of the program, one of the first systematic "child-saving" efforts in United States history.

Out of the Silence: Fighting for Human Rights
Type: VHS videocassette
Length: 60 min.
Cost: $69

Date: 1991
Source: Chuck Olin Associates
11 East Hubbard
Chicago, IL 60611
(312) 822-9552
FAX (312) 822-9593

Besides providing an excellent introduction to the history of human rights and the contributions of nongovernmental organizations, this video consists of two case studies. The Czechoslovakian segment traces human rights from the origins of Charter 77 through the Velvet Revolution of 1989. The second segment highlights the effects of human rights violations on children and families in Guatemala and questions the recruitment of the so-called volunteer civilian patrols, and shows photographs of "disappeared" children and adults.

Peru: Children's Rights
Type: VHS videocassette
Length: 28 min.
Cost: $99
Date: None given
Source: Centre Communications
1800 30th Street, #207
Boulder, CO 80301
(800) 886-1166 (order); (303) 444-1166
FAX (303) 444-1168

The video is part of a series called "People Matter." It depicts the effects of Peru's civil war on children, revealing the physical and mental scars with which they are left. Their rights to protection and development are highlighted.

The Politics of Children: Hope for 100,000
Type: VHS videocassette
Length: 26 min.
Cost: $149 or rental
Date: 1994
Source: Films for the Humanities & Sciences
P.O. Box 2053
Princeton, NJ 08543-2053
(800) 257-5126 (order); (609) 275-1400
FAX (609) 275-3767

The video shows the effects of Romania's violent past on the lives of children who have been abandoned by their families because of poverty and other causes, and underlines the child's right to a family. This production of WSMV Television of Nashville, Tennessee, follows a local congressman who visits orphanages, street children, and sites where international volunteers try to improve the lives of children. The video shows harsh conditions in Romania and accepts intercountry adoption as one of the solutions for their current social and economic deprivation.

A Prayer for Children

Type: VHS videocassette
Length: 2 min., 48 sec.
Cost: $6
Date: None given
Source: Children's Defense Fund Publications
25 E Street NW
Washington, DC 20001
(202) 628-8787
FAX (202) 662-3510/662-3530

This montage of children in various situations is narrated by CDF president Marian Wright Edelman. The narration is a plea to address the ongoing concerns of all children and to "leave no child behind." Juxtaposed with images of children at play, in school, with parents, and in other pleasant surroundings are images of children threatened by violence, poverty, and neglect.

Rights and Wrongs: The World's Children

Type: VHS videocassette
Length: 26 min.
Cost: $49.95 for this segment; $199 for the entire 5-part series Rights and Wrongs
Date: 1993
Source: The Video Project
5332 College Avenue, Suite 101
Oakland, CA 94618
(800) 475-2638
FAX (510) 655-9115

Focusing on the contemporary condition of children worldwide, this segment of the five-part PBS series Rights and Wrongs examines international human rights through the perspective of young people. Case studies of violence (United States), homelessness and street children (Brazil), female children and their status (India), warfare's impact on children (Bosnia), and poverty (United States) are employed to showcase the severity of problems faced by children globally. Integrating the study of rights violations with the development and passage of the UN Convention on the Rights of the Child (CRC), this film effectively juxtaposes the emerging international consensus about guaranteeing children fundamental human rights with the ongoing problems faced by the world's children in achieving the goals set forth in the CRC.

The Rights of the Child

Type: VHS videocassette
Length: 23 min.
Cost: $15 or rental
Date: 1989
Source: UNICEF
Division of Information and Public Affairs
3 United Nations Plaza
New York, NY 10017

This early video on the Convention on the Rights of the Child, narrated by Richard Attenborough, emphasizes UNICEF's mandate to help children survive; to protect them from war, violence, and abuse; and to enable them to develop into healthy adults. Short episodes show situations of children around the world who must endure poverty, disease, abandonment, recruitment as child soldiers, and other violations of their rights. Toward the end of the documentary, hope is revived through rehabilitation programs, educational facilities, etc.

The Road to Brown

Type: VHS videocassette
Length: 58 min.
Cost: $69.95
Date: None given
Source: Social Studies School Service
10200 Jefferson Boulevard, Room 122
P.O. Box 802
Culver City, CA 90232-0802
(800) 421-4246
FAX (800) 944-5432

This videotape tells the story of how the legal assault on segregation was developed and engendered by the work of Charles Hamilton Houston, dean of Howard University Law School and the chief counsel of the National Association for the Advancement of Colored People (NAACP). Detailing the tragedy of segregation and its devastating effects on African-American life, the film shows how Houston and his colleagues mounted the legal offensive against segregation that set the stage for the landmark *Brown v. Board of Education of Topeka, Kansas* decision in 1954.

Separate but Equal

Type: VHS videocassette
Length: 194 min. on 2 videocassettes
Cost: $19.98
Date: 1991
Source: Social Studies School Service
10200 Jefferson Boulevard, Room 122
P.O. Box 802
Culver City, CA 90232-0802
(800) 421-4246
FAX (800) 944-5432

Featuring some of the most distinguished actors of the American screen, this dramatic version of the events culminating in the 1954 *Brown v. Board of Education of Topeka, Kansas* decision begins in 1950 with the legal challenge by African-American parents in Clarendon County, South Carolina, to segregated public education. Thurgood Marshall (Sidney Poitier), John W. Davis (Burt Lancaster), and Earl Warren (Richard Kiley) are the three key figures in the story, which comprehensively details the strategies implemented by opponents and advocates of the "separate but equal" doctrine, along with the frustrations and struggles encountered by each side, as well as by the members of the U.S. Supreme Court. The problems faced by children and parents who endured segregation are given particular emphasis in this poignant and authentic production.

Simple Justice

Type: VHS videocassette
Length: 137 min.
Cost: $99.95 (sold to educational institutions only)
Date: 1993

Source: PBS Video
1320 Braddock Place
Alexandria, VA 22314
(800) 424-7963
FAX (703) 739-5269

This dramatized account of the struggle to overturn legal segregation in public schooling closely adheres to Richard Kluger's book of the same name. Recounting the steps begun by Charles Hamilton Houston in the 1930s to train attorneys at Howard University in Washington, D.C., who would seek to dismantle the legal basis for segregation, the drama carefully details the gradual and systematic strategy that eventually triumphed under the leadership of Thurgood Marshall in the *Brown v. Board of Education of Topeka, Kansas* decision of 1954.

Soul II Soul: "Hate and Destruction"
Type: VHS videocassette with teaching guide
Length: 5 min.
Cost: $10
Date: 1993
Source: UN High Commission for Refugees Public Information
1775 K Street NW, Suite 30
Washington, DC 20006

This video was made by the British rock group Soul II Soul and filmmaker Eugene "Pebbles" Akiwumi; it comes with a three-page teaching guide. The message "We can stop the war of hate and destruction" is repeated in rap recitation as the group and others act out the situation of refugees met by a teenage hate group, suggesting not only the violence that can result, but a cause for the violence: the alienation of youth from an anonymous society. The video ends as young people reject the hatemongers and are reminded that anyone can become a refugee.

Students' Rights—Focus on the First Amendment: Confrontation in Government
Type: VHS videocassette
Length: 20 min.
Cost: $94

Date: 1988
Source: Social Studies School Service
10200 Jefferson Boulevard, Room 122
P.O. Box 802
Culver City, CA 90232-0802
(800) 421-4246
FAX (800) 944-5432

Employing videotape footage from the Cable News Network (CNN), this video addresses the conflicts concerning application of First Amendment protections to students in public schools. Differing viewpoints about recent Supreme Court decisions restricting students' freedom of speech in public school settings are presented and key issues are debated.

Women and Children with AIDS
Type: Audiocassette with study guide
Length: 27 min., 20 sec.
Cost: $10
Date: None given
Source: UNICEF
c/o United Nations Publications
Room C2-853, Dept. 007C
New York, NY 10017
(800) 253-9646
FAX (212) 963-3489

Designed to help women and children worldwide become more informed about Acquired Immune Deficiency Syndrome (AIDS), this audiocassette and study guide contains four exercises that form the core of a group workshop experience. Exercise A involves asking key questions about basic facts concerning AIDS, while exercise B reports on the situation of AIDS in Africa and again poses questions designed to provide discussion. Exercise C follows the same format as exercise B, but focuses on AIDS in the Caribbean. The concluding exercise D helps listeners develop community AIDS prevention projects. The study guide is coordinated with the audiocassette segments and provides a thorough introduction to the topics, helping discussion leaders effectively prepare to educate groups about AIDS using the taped case studies as the core material.

Poster Sets

Child Labor

Type: Set of 15 photo aids with study guide
Cost: $26.25
Date: None given
Source: Social Studies School Service
10200 Jefferson Boulevard, Room 122
P.O. Box 802
Culver City, CA 90232-0802
(800) 421-4246
FAX (800) 944-5432

This set of 15 documentary photographs is mounted on 11x14-inch heavy glossy stock, and depicts the dangerous conditions and unsafe workplaces in which millions of U.S. children worked during the early twentieth century. Both urban and rural settings are included in these compelling black-and-white photos. A brief study guide describing selected instructional strategies for use with historical photos is provided with the set.

Children under Fire

Type: Set of 12 posters
Cost: $7.50
Date: 1994
Source: Amnesty International USA
Midwest Office
53 West Jackson, Suite 1162
Chicago, IL 60604-3606
(312) 427-2060
FAX (312) 427-2589

This set of 12 striking 11x18-inch posters depicts violations of children's rights under the Amnesty International mandate. Because of the graphic nature of some of the photographs, adults should consider the appropriateness of the poster images when employing them in settings with young people. Published by Amnesty International United Kingdom, they are available from the Amnesty International USA Midwest Regional Office.

Glossary

The definitions given in this chapter are those commonly used by people working in the field of international human rights for children. They are not inclusive of all the definitions that might be given for these terms in international law or academia.

"Beijing Rules" The United Nations Standard Minimum Rules for the Administration of Juvenile Justice, drafted by the United Nations in 1985 to state high, uniform procedures and principles for juvenile justice systems.

best interests of the child The paramount legal principle that underlies U.S. law as well as the UN Convention on the Rights of the Child.

bonded labor Work for substandard pay in which the laborer is not free to leave an employer until an exorbitant sum, usually interest for a small loan, is given to that employer. Children have been sold into bonded labor by parents who can no longer afford to meet their basic daily needs.

capital punishment The imposition by the state of the death penalty for crimes.

child The UN Convention on the Rights of the Child defines a child to be any person below the age of 18 who has not achieved majority status in his or her legal system.

child prostitution The use by others of a child for sexual purposes, usually for monetary gain.

child soldier The CRC now considers a child soldier to be anyone age 15 or under who takes part in or is exposed to armed conflict as part of a military or paramilitary group. Many nations, along with the Committee on the Rights of the Child and interested NGOs, want to raise that age to 18 in an optional protocol that nations can sign.

Committee on the Rights of the Child The ten-member monitoring body of the UN Convention on the Rights of the Child. The committee meets three times a year in Geneva, Switzerland, and examines the reports of nations that have ratified the CRC. The committee may "invite" UN specialized agencies such as UNICEF and "other competent bodies" (which has been interpreted to mean nongovernmental organizations) to consult and/or offer help to nations having problems complying with the provisions of the CRC (Article 45). The committee issues "suggestions and recommendations" on its findings; these committee reports can be positive or less than positive about the sincerity of a nation's attempts to grant children's rights.

competent bodies The term used to describe intergovernmental and nongovernmental organizations that have been accorded an official status to act or consult upon specific issues by the United Nations and governments.

consensus The process by which UN bodies avoid putting countries in the position of having to affirmatively state whether they agree or disagree with a resolution that has been discussed. Any disagreement would be expressed in formal or informal discussion before a "consensus vote," which is not a "for or against vote." The UN Convention on the Rights of the Child was voted by consensus; in cases of disagreement as to wording, small drafting groups were formed to attempt to harmonize differences. The result was a treaty the drafters hoped would be acceptable to all nations.

convention An international treaty that is enforceable among the States Parties who ratify it.

"cruel, inhuman, or degrading treatment or punishment" The phrase used in the Universal Declaration of Human Rights and all subsequent relevant UN human rights treaties to expand protections of people from human rights violations, from the moment they are suspected of a crime or come in contact with a legal system until they are no longer suspect or in detention.

declaration An international document stating important principles that is drafted in the same way a treaty is written, but which is not open to signing or ratification. Nations voting for this document pledge to uphold the principles it contains; there is a respectable body of law and opinion holding that a declaration of the magnitude of the Universal Declaration of Human Rights is also binding on those nations that did not vote for it.

desegregation The process implemented to end legal separation of the races in the United States, ordered in education at the federal level by the U.S. Supreme Court ruling *Brown v. Board of Education of Topeka, Kansas* (1954).

especially difficult circumstances When applied to children, the term refers to those living in severe conditions such as poverty, prostitution, or abuse.

evolving capacities A term from Article 5 of the CRC, which recognizes that as children grow older they are entitled to exercise more of their rights as, concurrently, parents or guardians relinquish the exercise of those rights for them. There are no international standards for when a child assumes the exercise of one or more of his or her rights.

Geneva Conventions The 1949 agreements and 1977 protocols signed by nations to regulate the conduct of war and other armed conflicts. They are monitored by the International Committee of the Red Cross.

Head Start The program initiated in 1965 by U.S. legislative action to provide disadvantaged young children in preschool through the early grades with improved nutrition, health care, and educational assistance as a means of improving their performance in school and society in later life.

human rights The birthright of all human beings, as contained in the United Nations International Bill of Rights and its other human rights instruments.

humanitarian law The law developed before the nineteenth century, which is now expressed in the Hague Conventions and the Geneva Conventions and its Optional Protocols. It regulates conduct in situations of armed conflict, and seeks to protect civilians as well as govern the treatment of combatants.

Industrial Revolution The transformation of economy and society that resulted from the application of scientific technology at the time of the expansion of capitalism in Europe and other parts of the world, beginning in the eighteenth century and continuing into the twentieth century.

intergovernmental organization Separate, autonomous organizations related to the United Nations by special arrangement. Examples include the World Health Organization (WHO) and the United Nations Educational, Scientific, and Cultural Organization (UNESCO).

internally displaced people People who have had to leave their homes because of situations such as armed conflict or natural disaster, but who still remain in their own country.

International Bill of Rights The Universal Declaration of Human Rights (1948); the International Covenant on Civil and Political Rights (1966), the

International Covenant on Economic, Social, and Cultural Rights (1966), and the Optional Protocol to the Covenant on Civil and Political Rights (1966) constitute the central framework of the UN human rights system. The two covenants and the Optional Protocol provide an enforcement mechanism for the rights embodied in the Universal Declaration of Human Rights.

International Committee of the Red Cross/Red Crescent (ICRC) The nongovernmental organization that monitors the Geneva Conventions, with headquarters in Geneva, Switzerland; the ICRC is separate from national Red Cross/Red Crescent chapters. The committee monitors the treatment of prisoners of war and armed conflict, and supervises their release or exchange when requested. The ICRC also traces combatants and civilians missing in times of armed conflict and war.

international instrument Any declaration or treaty adopted in the UN system or among nations.

International Labour Organization (ILO) The intergovernmental organization established in 1919 as an autonomous institution with the League of Nations; it continues by agreement with the United Nations. Its function is to promote social justice, and to achieve this aim the ILO creates international codes of law and practice to raise international workplace standards concerning the conditions of labor, and has for much of the twentieth century taken a strong interest in the topic of child labor by developing a number of international instruments governing the activities of children in the workplace. It is composed of employers, workers, and governments.

juvenile justice system The separate treatment of minors by the legal system in the United States, established during the Progressive Era.

League of Nations The forerunner of the United Nations, established in 1919 by the Treaty of Versailles, which ended World War I.

legislative entitlements Benefits that are given by law and can be amended or repealed.

nongovernmental organizations (NGOs) Organizations that are not affiliated with the governments of the nations in which they are located. In the UN system, some international nongovernmental organizations are given accreditation by the Economic and Social Council (ECOSOC) and thus have the standing to consult with all of the bodies that ECOSOC constitutes and oversees. Amnesty International and Save the Children are nongovernmental organizations. NGOs often expose human rights violations as well as consult on ways to implement rights.

optional protocol An addition to an international instrument that is open for ratification to nations that have ratified the original document.

participation rights Rights that grant the active exercise of rights by the beneficiary.

power of publicity The power to embarrass a nation through the announcement (exposure) or publication of its violations of human rights. Nongovernmental organizations use it to effect change, and it is available to UN treaty-monitoring bodies such as the Committee on the Rights of the Child.

preamble The part of an international human rights instrument that states its guiding principles rather than specific obligations.

Progressives U.S. social reformers who responded to the dramatic growth of industrial capitalism by working for the betterment of the middle and lower socioeconomic classes, primarily during the period 1890–1919.

protection rights Rights that are legal safeguards against the violation of rights.

provision rights Rights that require positive action, and sometimes monetary allocations, for their implementation by governments.

ratify, ratification Putting the laws of a nation into conformity with an international treaty. In the United States, the ratification process consists of a signature by the president, submission to the Senate, which must "advise and consent," and then the final signature of the president. Once the treaty is ratified, the nation must put its laws into conformity with the provisions of the treaty if it has not already done so.

refugee A person who is outside his or her country of nationality because of a "well-founded fear of being persecuted for reasons of race, religion, or nationality, membership of a particular social group or political opinion. . . ." (UN Convention Relating to the Status of Refugees, adopted in 1950).

rehabilitation The process by which a victim is returned to home and/or community in the best possible physical, mental, spiritual, and moral health.

reservation During the process of ratifying a treaty, a government may make a unilateral statement purporting to exclude or modify the legal effect of a certain provision of the treaty when it is applied in or by that nation. This statement is registered with the monitoring body. States already party to a treaty may refuse to accept reservations that are incompatible with the treaty's purpose.

rights The inalienable birthright of all human beings.

sale and trafficking of children A crime that has been condemned in many international human rights instruments; the forms of sale and trafficking change with the times, but "the exchange of a child involving undue profit" is often given as a definition.

sex tourism The business of arranging travel to a foreign place so that the tourist can engage in sexual practices that are illegal in his/her country.

street children Children who have no other homes than city streets or who spend the majority of their time on the streets. Almost all street children have been forced out of their homes, have run away, or have been abandoned by their parents or families.

sweatshops Places where goods are manufactured or assembled by workers who receive substandard pay and who work in poor or unregulated conditions. In the United States and internationally, sweatshops are frequently associated with the garment trade.

target group A group with a similar aggregate of characteristics; a term used by social scientists, government, and nongovernmental organizations.

treaty An international agreement that establishes binding legal principles and provisions among the nations that ratify it; covenants and conventions are treaties.

umbrella articles Enforceable (operative) parts of a treaty that apply to all of the other articles of that legal instrument.

unaccompanied minors Children who have been separated from their parents or families during times of natural disaster, armed conflict, the flight of refugees, and other crises, and who are in need of protection.

UNESCO The United Nations Educational, Scientific, and Cultural Organization, founded in 1946, promotes collaboration among nations through education, science, culture, and communication. Headquartered in Paris, UNESCO emphasizes education for development, research, and training in developing countries; the study, preservation, and diffusion of the world's cultural heritage; and technical assistance and training for communications organizations and professionals.

UNICEF The United Nations International Children's Emergency Fund is the main specialized agency of the United Nations responsible for improving children's lives worldwide. Founded in 1946, its headquarters are located in New York City across the street from the United Nations complex.

United Nations Founded in 1945, the United Nations is the world's premier intergovernmental organization, addressing a broad cross section of global issues, problems, and concerns through its complex legal and organizational framework.

United Nations General Assembly The parent body of the United Nations, in which all member nations have one vote. UN treaties must be adopted by the General Assembly.

United Nations High Commissioner for Refugees (UNHCR) The UN office entrusted with international protection for refugees falling into its competence.

United Nations Rules for the Protection of Juveniles Deprived of Their Liberty Fundamental principles and rules for the treatment of young people for whatever reason they come in contact with a country's legal system, adopted by the UN General Assembly in 1990.

Universal Declaration of Human Rights (UDHR) Promulgated by the UN General Assembly in 1948, the UDHR is the foundation document for human rights in the UN system, and serves as the most significant statement of human rights principles for the world community.

Index

Beverly C. Edmonds, Ph.D., is executive director of Peace and Human Rights in Education, chair of Amnesty International USA's Children's Action Network Steering Committee, and a history teacher at the Branson School in Ross, California.

William R. Fernekes, Ed.D., is supervisor of social studies at Hunterdon Central Regional High School in Flemington, New Jersey. He has published extensively and served as a consultant for projects supported by Rutgers University, the National Council for the Social Studies, the National Endowment for the Humanities, West Virginia University, and the United States Holocaust Memorial Museum.